*Great Power Politics and the
Struggle over Austria, 1945–1955*

CORNELL STUDIES IN SECURITY AFFAIRS

Edited by Robert J. Art *and* Robert Jervis

Great Power Politics and the Struggle over Austria, 1945–1955

AUDREY KURTH CRONIN

Cornell University Press

ITHACA AND LONDON

First published 1986 by Cornell University Press.
Second printing, 1987.

International Standard Book Number 0-8014-1854-2
Library of Congress Catalog Card Number 85-24326
Printed in the United States of America
Librarians: Library of Congress cataloging information
appears on the last page of the book.

The paper in this book is acid-free and meets the guidelines for permanence
and durability of the Committee on Production Guidelines for
Book Longevity of the Council on Library Resources.

To my parents,
Rear Admiral Ronald J. Kurth
and E. Charlene Kurth,
with gratitude and love

Contents

Preface

This book is an analysis of one unusual and intriguing episode in postwar international relations, the agreement by Britain, France, the United States, and the Soviet Union at the height of the Cold War to terminate their ten-year military occupation of Austria and leave the country unified and neutral. The 1955 agreement, and especially the subsequent Soviet withdrawal, has mystified scholars for years. My purpose is to explore and explain the origins of this successful compromise between powerful states whose political and security interests appeared to be fundamentally incompatible. Examining the apparent motives of the great powers helps illuminate not only the events of the early 1950s in central Europe but also East-West and intra-alliance relations in Europe as they have since developed. In addition, I distill the crucial elements of the Austrian solution in the hope that these might lend insights, if not provide lessons, for other seemingly irresolvable great power disputes.

This project has progressed through many stages. Over the years of preparation, numerous people and institutions on both sides of the Atlantic have helped me.

IN THE UNITED STATES

For assistance in a myriad of ways, I am grateful to the following:
The Center for International Affairs, Harvard University, where I spent a year as a Ford postdoctoral fellow in European Society and Western Security and completed this book; the Ford Foundation, which provided my financial support; Samuel Huntington, director of the Center for International Affairs, for guidance and support; the

[9]

members of the Ford Program European Study Group and the Center for International Affairs National Security Study Group, whose contributions to my work seemed to me to be much greater than my seminar preparations on their behalf;

Robert J. Art and Vojtech Mastny, who each read the manuscript in its entirety and offered helpful criticisms; Michael Brown, who read the book more than once and provided careful, incisive comments; Roger Haydon, my editor at Cornell University Press, who made invaluable improvements to the manuscript; Lisa Lightman, who valiantly typed the endnotes.

In addition, I appreciate the help given me at earlier stages of my research by the following:

Joseph A. Presel, U.S. Department of State, who first pointed out that newly declassified U.S. government documents needed to be analyzed; Robert J. Donovan, who gave me useful advice about doing research on the Truman and Eisenhower administrations; William B. Bader, who kindly gave me research tips in the course of several conversations during a Ditchley Foundation conference in England;

The U.S. National Archives in Washington, D.C.: specifically, in the Diplomatic Documents Division, Sally Marks, and in the Modern Military Records Division, Edward Reese, Wilbert Mahoney, and especially John Taylor. All of these professionals spared no effort to help me find a great deal of interesting new information; the Library of Congress, whose truly dedicated staff assisted in finding even obscure sources that were unavailable anywhere else; the Harry S Truman Library in Independence, Missouri, especially Dennis Bilger; and the Dwight D. Eisenhower Library in Abilene, Kansas, especially James Leyerzaph.

IN ENGLAND

For invaluable assistance, I am grateful to the following:

The Marshall Aid Commemoration Commission, for giving me the opportunity to study in the United Kingdom as a Marshall Scholar and funding my endeavors in the International Relations Department of Oxford University, and the Warden, fellows, and staff of St. Antony's College, Oxford, for maintaining an intellectually stimulating and congenial environment;

The late Hedley Bull, Montague Burton Professor and head of the international relations program at Oxford, for convincing a skeptical

American of the importance of history in international relations; E. Adam Roberts, my supervisor at St. Antony's College, whose comments and cheerful encouragement compelled me to write the book; Jonathan Wright of Christ Church College, Oxford, who read the book in earlier forms and provided excellent suggestions for improving it; Peter Pulzer, Gladstone Professor of Politics at All Souls College, Oxford, who also provided helpful guidance;

Mark Kramer, Rhodes Scholar at Balliol College, Oxford, who read major portions of the manuscript and responded with incisive, useful criticism; Joel Peters, St. Antony's College, who also supplied sagacious comments;

The Royal Institute for International Affairs (Chatham House), London, for allowing me to use the press clippings library; the Public Records Office, Kew, for access to well-organized British government documents; the Bodleian Library, Oxford University, especially the staff of the Modern Manuscripts reading room; Rosamund Campbell, librarian of St. Antony's College, for making an extra effort to find the resources I needed and encouraging me at all stages of this project; and the Cyril Foster Fund, Oxford University, for funding a research trip to Vienna.

In Austria

I am grateful to the following for kindly agreeing to lengthy and sometimes repeated interviews:

Rudolph Kirchschläger, federal president of Austria; Bruno Kreisky, former chancellor of Austria; Gerald Stourzh, professor of modern history, University of Vienna; Andreas Khol, director of the Foreign Policy Academy, Vienna; Stephan Verosta, professor of international law (emeritus), University of Vienna; Manfried Rauchensteiner, historian at the Institute for Military History, Vienna. These gentlemen were exceptionally generous with their time and advice. Their comments and anecdotes made an invaluable contribution to the book;

Günter Bischof, graduate student in history whom I met at Harvard University, for helpful comments; Wolfgang Danspeckgruber, an Austrian strategist whom I also met at Harvard, whose useful (and often witty) observations on the manuscript were invaluable; and Joseph Leidenfrost, who has sent me materials from Vienna and kept me informed of the happenings in Austria related to my interests.

I am deeply indebted to members of my family: Doug Kurth, John and Linda Kurth, and especially Steven and Lois Kurth have cheerfully endured my impositions upon them during the time I was researching and writing this book.

My parents, Ronald and Charlene Kurth, have given me (among many other things) support, encouragement, and a desire to seek new challenges. And finally my husband, Patrick Cronin, a man of boundless creative energy, has read every word of this book at least three times and always provided insightful criticisms and devoted innumerable hours to helping me.

AUDREY KURTH CRONIN

Charlottesville, Virginia

Great Power Politics and the
Struggle over Austria, 1945–1955

For about 2,000 years now there has been a figure in mythology which symbolizes tragic futility. That was Sisyphus, who, according to the Greek story, was given the task of rolling a great stone up to the top of a hill. Each time when, after great struggle and sweating the stone was just at the brow of the hill, some evil force manifested itself and pushed the stone down. So poor Sisyphus had to start his task over again.

I suspect that for the next 2,000 years the story of Sisyphus will be forgotten, when generation after generation is told the story, the tragic story, of the Austrian State Treaty. Austria was promised its independence 11 years ago. When our forces moved into Austria 9 years ago they announced that they were there only to liberate. Now, year after year has gone by, when we have repeatedly been almost at the point of concluding an Austrian State Treaty, and always some evil force manifests itself and pushes the treaty back again. So we have to start again from the bottom of the hill.

John Foster Dulles,
at the Berlin Conference,
16 February 1954

Introduction

After occupying Austria for ten years following World War II, France, Britain, the United States, and the Soviet Union signed the Austrian State Treaty and agreed to withdraw their armies. The Republic of Austria, in sharp contrast to its northern neighbor, Germany, emerged from postwar occupation a unified, independent, and neutral country. Austria's neutral status in the center of Europe stands as an intriguing exception to the bilateral division of the continent after the war. The fact that Austria emerged from the quadripartite occupation neutral and in one piece has proven particularly significant, for the Soviet Union's relinquishment of the eastern portion of Austria in accordance with the wishes of the Austrians has certainly not been typical of Soviet postwar behavior. The four-power withdrawal following the signature of the Austrian State Treaty is the most recent alteration to the East-West line of confrontation in postwar Europe.

The events leading up to the Austrian State Treaty, signed in May 1955, provide a rare opportunity to understand East-West relations and postwar Europe. Soviet actions and motivations were more clearly exposed to Western scrutiny in Austria than in any other country, for Soviet occupation of the eastern zone was carefully monitored by a Western-oriented, Austrian national government. In the course of the eight years of negotiations for an Austrian treaty, moreover, Soviet behavior evolved from hard bargaining to blatant obstructionism. Then, in the space of a few weeks, Soviet leaders suddenly abandoned their obstructionist tactics and, indeed, showed such an eagerness to sign that they settled for terms less favorable than those they had earlier rejected. The withdrawal of troops shortly thereafter confirmed Soviet willingness to leave Austria an independent and neutral state and led to great jubilation within both Austria and the West.

[15]

The treaty, furthermore, inaugurated a brief détente between East and West, leading directly to the Geneva summit conference between leaders of the Soviet Union, the United States, France, and Great Britain and setting off a period of optimism later known as the "Spirit of Geneva," a temporary respite from the tension of the Cold War.

Although the Austrian treaty apparently played a crucial role as a catalyst for the first postwar détente in East-West relations, many important questions remain unanswered. Did the Western powers, as some writers have postulated, lose an opportunity to end the Cold War in 1955 when they failed to reciprocate a Soviet act of goodwill?[1] Was the Soviet decision to leave Austria primarily a conciliatory gesture? Or was it the result of a Kremlin calculation that the Russians could profit most, strategically and economically, by leaving? What lessons can be learned about Soviet negotiating behavior? Did the behavior of the Western powers directly influence the decision? Or was the decision to sign the treaty primarily a by-product of the struggle in the Kremlin to succeed Stalin? The reasons, economic, military, political, and personal, why the Soviet leadership suddenly decided to end the occupation of Austria help illuminate how Soviet authorities formulate foreign policy and, more importantly, whether Western policy influences Soviet decisions to the degree that most Western analysts presume. Today, as another generation of Soviet leaders struggles to come to power and East-West relations seem to be deteriorating, the agreement on the Austrian State Treaty, concluded under similar conditions, is particularly relevant.

To portray the Austrian issue as strictly an East-West problem is, however, to ignore a crucial aspect of the negotiations. The Western powers were not always in harmony with one another, and some of the most vehement debates over Austria's future occurred not at the international bargaining table but in the cloisters of the American bureaucracy. Without the benefit of secret British and American records, most previous accounts of the events leading to the treaty have focused upon obvious Soviet recalcitrance, which repeatedly derailed the negotiations.[2] Yet many questions remain about the role of the Western powers, and particularly the United States. Did the Western powers always negotiate earnestly and in good faith? What were the differences between British, French, and American policies? Were all of the Western powers really as deeply disappointed as the Austrians were when the Russians stymied progress on the treaty? Did each of the Western powers have reasons—military, economic, political—for secretly wishing to forestall the signing of a treaty of neutrality for Austria? If so, what were these reasons, and how did they change over the course of the lengthy negotiations? The evolution of Western policy toward Austria offers new insights into the development of postwar Western relations, the creation of the present configuration in Europe, and particularly the emergence of the United States as leader of the Western alliance.

Finally, examining the years of frustrating negotiations for a treaty yields an understanding of how the 1955 formula for Austrian neutrality came to be and whether that formula relates to the current security dilemma which some Europeans claim confronts them. Faced with an overwhelming conventional threat from the East, given no long-term security commitments by the West, and determined in any case to avoid partition between the two, the Austrians took the only course of action that promised to rid them of the occupation and declared their country a permanently neutral state. Since 1955 they have maintained strict military neutrality even as they have followed a policy of what is loosely termed positive neutrality, by joining international economic and political organizations that the neutral Swiss have traditionally avoided.

The complaints of many Europeans today echo some of the reasons behind the 1955 Austrian decision for military neutrality: a sense of inability to withstand Soviet conventional attack from Eastern Europe, a desire to assert and maintain an independent foreign policy vis-à-vis the Soviet Union, and an uncertainty about the strength of the American commitment to defend European territory. Indeed, many contemporary political pundits identify what they consider to be a growing tendency toward "neutralism" in Europe. In such circumstances it is useful to understand why, thirty years ago, the pro-Western Austrians opted for permanent neutrality as state policy and, more important, what international conditions enabled or encouraged them to pursue such an option. An understanding of the international conditions under which Austrian neutrality emerged will make it possible to speculate about whether the Austrian solution is unique or might be emulated in other territorial disputes among great powers. In particular, the partition of Germany at virtually the same time as Austria became unified and neutral highlights the important historical differences between those two countries, leading to more general conclusions about the conditions necessary for a country between two opposing power blocs to declare itself neutral.

Austria's Postwar Dilemma

Of all the issues arising from World War II, the future of Austria might have seemed among the easiest for the Allies to settle, for on few issues was there greater apparent agreement well before the end of the war. Certainly the Austrians themselves never expected the occupation of their country by Allied "liberators" to last for ten years.[3]

The earliest official reference to the need to liberate Austria from the Nazis was made by Prime Minister Winston Churchill in a speech on 9 November 1940. Stressing that Britain would never forget its obligations toward the enchained countries of Europe, Churchill emphasized that Austria was one of the countries for whom Britain had drawn the sword. During the following summer Churchill and President Franklin D. Roosevelt signed the Atlantic Charter, which stated the intention of the United States and the United Kingdom to respect the right of all peoples to choose the government under which they live. The charter implicitly included the Austrians among the people to whom an Allied victory would restore self-government.

More explicitly, in a 9 December 1941 radio message explaining why the United States had to enter the war, Roosevelt listed Austria among the countries to be liberated from Nazi rule. Joseph Stalin broached the restoration of the Austrian state later in the same month during his famous meeting in Moscow with British foreign secretary Sir Anthony Eden. With the sound of German artillery punctuating his sentences, the Soviet dictator expressed his determination to restore an independent Austria.

In October 1943, therefore, with the Red Army about to liberate Kiev and with Western troops advancing along the Italian peninsula, the Allied foreign ministers decided to issue a joint statement to formalize their intentions, enlist the support of the Austrian people, and simplify Allied postwar planning. Their Moscow declaration explained that the governments of the United States, Great Britain, and the Soviet Union did not recognize the 1938 annexation of Austria by Germany (the Anschluss) and solemnly promised to reestablish a free and independent Austria after the war. In addition, the declaration indicated Allied willingness to help Austria and neighboring states regain political and economic stability. A Soviet amendment reminding the Austrians that their participation in the war on the side of Hitlerite Germany could not be completely forgotten went almost unnoticed among the reassuring sentences of the communiqué.

Shortly after the declaration was published, the Free French government also subscribed officially to its tenets. Stalin, Churchill, and Roosevelt renewed the promises and obligations of the Moscow declaration at Yalta in February 1945. The future of Austria was also discussed at Potsdam, where in the closing hours of the conference the Soviet Union was granted, as reparations for war damage, the right to all external German assets in eastern Austria. The area of accord between the Allies on Austria was apparently so broad that these hastily arranged legal and economic provisions seemed unimportant. However, both the amendment to the Moscow declaration and the Potsdam reparations clause later supplied the basis for extensive war damage claims by the Soviet Union. They would haunt the eight years of negotiations for an Austrian treaty.

Legally, it could be argued, there was no need for a treaty with Austria. The small state was a victim of aggression, not a defeated enemy, and theoretically the four victorious powers need only have withdrawn their occupation forces and conducted bilateral negotiations with the Vienna government on any unsettled questions.[4] But in reality several problems remained to be settled among the powers themselves. In the years following the war Austria increasingly became an instrument rather than an object of great power policy; the country's fate was considered in the broader context of each government's conception of the future of Europe. As negotiations dragged fitfully on, the four powers used the term Austrian State Treaty, rather than "peace treaty," in their haggling. In the Cold War contest between East and West, however, Austria's wartime status was irrelevant.

Indeed, Austria's special status seemed at times detrimental to its future; had Austria been declared a belligerent power during the war, it might conceivably have achieved independence within a few months of the cessation of hostilities. Despite the efforts of U.S. secretary of state James F. Byrnes, however, Austria was not included on the agenda of the Paris Peace Conference in the summer of 1946. Soviet foreign minister Vyacheslav Molotov argued that the agenda was already overburdened and that it was more important first to conclude treaties with Bulgaria, Romania, Hungary, Finland, and Italy. As a result the Austrians, nursing a keen sense of injustice, watched the conclusion of peace treaties with Germany's former allies and waited impatiently for the evacuation of their own territory. Years later Karl Gruber, Austrian foreign minister, wrote that the loss of Romania, Hungary, and Czechoslovakia to the Cominform avenged this disregard of logic and justice at the Paris Peace Conference.[5]

But to pinpoint Austria's exclusion from the peace conference as the cause of the country's years of occupation by Allied troops is a gross oversimplification. For one thing, geographic position gave Austria tremendous strategic importance. Any Austrian settlement would have far-reaching influence on the future of southern Europe and was therefore of critical interest to the Soviet Union and the Western powers. Vienna was the Soviet Union's forward position in southern Europe and a military bridgehead in any conflict with the West. Furthermore, the Hungarian and Romanian treaties permitted the Soviet Union to keep troops in those countries in order to maintain lines of communication with Austria; the evacuation of Austria would eliminate the legal justification for Soviet occupation of much of Eastern Europe. The Austro-Yugoslav border gave Austria added importance, both as a source of potential Russian influence in Yugoslavia and later as a military staging area for probes against the "Titoists." For the Western Allies, on the other hand, Austria was a crucial link in European defense planning because of its location on the line of communications between Italy and West Germany. Without Austria, the West would have to detour all troops and supplies destined north or south around Austria and Switzerland, through France—clearly a logistical disadvantage. Moreover, Austria's lack of an army would permit Soviet troops to march unimpeded across the country's northern or eastern plain in launching an attack against the West.

Austria's economic value derived from its historical role as the center of north-south and east-west trade. For the Soviet Union, battered and starving in the aftermath of the German campaigns, eastern Austria's oil and industries were an important economic gain. For both sides, moreover, Austria was important politically. Evidence of two attempted communist takeovers during the years of occupation seems to indicate that the Soviet Union only reluctantly gave up the idea of converting the Austrians to Soviet communism. Hope of an eleventh-hour conversion was abandoned only when it appeared that longer-term Soviet revolutionary goals could not be served by harassing the stubbornly pro-Western Austrians. For the West, Austria became a protectorate whose "loss" to communism would have been a blow to Western unity and a serious loss of prestige, particularly for a fledgling superpower like the United States.

By virtue of historic and geographic position Austria was condemned to a prominent role in the postwar plans of both East and West. Wartime indications that the Allies would liberate Austria and then immediately relinquish their control over the country were misleading. France, Britain, the United States, and the Soviet Union may have readily agreed that the small country had not willingly been an enemy in the past, but none of the great powers wished to risk the possibility that Austria might, willingly or not, be an enemy in the future.

For ten years, therefore, Austria's future was accorded an awkward status in the international arena: not important enough to command the attention that the German problem received but at the same time too important to the broader interests of the great powers to be disregarded. The disagreement over Austria's future often had little to do with Austria itself and much more to do with the course of the Cold War. Retrospective awareness of the eventual divergence of the interests of the former wartime allies makes the intriguing question not why the occupation of Austria lasted as long as it did but rather why and how an apparently satisfactory compromise was ever reached.

Focus and Sources

This book emphasizes the actions of the four great powers between 1945 and 1955 in deciding the future of Austria.[6] It uses mainly American and British government documents to examine the problem of Austria in postwar international relations. It is not a study of domestic affairs within Austria, nor does it intend to provide a comprehensive history of the occupation in Austria after the war.[7] The role of the Austrians themselves in determining their own fate in the international arena will be described whenever possible and appropriate; for this purpose some of the key Austrian participants were interviewed and events in Austria that bore particular relevance to the policies of the great powers are examined. However, one fundamental premise is that the struggle over Austria was an integral part of a larger Cold War contest between East and West, and it is from that perspective that the subject is approached.

Newly declassified British documents are one major source of primary information, for during the early years of the negotiations Britain was the most influential of the Western powers in determining tripartite policy toward Austria. Recently declassified American documents are the other major source of primary material for the evolution of Western policy toward Austria, because in the later years of negotiations the Americans came increasingly to dominate the Western position. Most of these government documents are being analyzed for the first time, and they yield answers to questions about Western behavior which have never been satisfactorily explained. Together these British and American documents present a balanced perspective on Western policy toward Austria. More generally, they provide some insight into the gradual shift of international influence from the United Kingdom to the United States after the war.

French government documents would probably shed little more light on the evolution of Western policy. France was a "great power" more in form than in substance during the ten years after World War II; most often the French followed the lead of either the British or the Americans in the negotiations. In any case, the book is openly oriented toward the British and the American perspectives.

Unfortunately, Soviet historical documents remain closed to Western researchers. This regrettable fact skews any analysis of the situation, for Western policy is studied from within the bureaucracies while Soviet policy is observed largely from without. Nonetheless, a deliberate attempt has been made here to keep the account balanced. Soviet opinions and positions have been gleaned from the memoirs of contemporary statesmen (notably Nikita Khrushchev), newspaper and magazine accounts, and available secondary sources.

The Austrian State Treaty is frequently cited as an example of the triumph of painstaking diplomacy among the great powers, but it can more accurately be depicted as the result of unilateral actions by the negotiating countries, particularly the Soviet Union. Records of the negotiations as well as available policy documents of the participants reveal that the negotiations gradually became a sophisticated charade for the benefit of European and domestic audiences. The critical decisions were made elsewhere. Indeed, as Europe grew increasingly polarized, very little actual bargaining occurred between East and West; the Austrian negotiations became merely a forum for unilateral action. This description of the search for Austrian independence, therefore, will not simply reiterate the 379 meetings of foreign ministers and foreign ministers' deputies for Austria. Rather, it will be a uniquely encapsulated version of the course of the Cold War in the ten critical years following World War II and a critical elaboration of the larger lessons to be learned from the resolution of Austria's fate. Examining how the Austrians came to choose a third way between East and West sheds light upon great power arrangements that have persisted in Europe to this day.

[1]

The "Liberation" of Austria, 1945–1946

When the Red Army first reached the suburbs of Vienna, in early April 1945, the commander-in-chief of the Russian troops in Austria officially proclaimed his intention to liberate Austria from the Nazis, to respect the social order of the country, not to appropriate any Austrian territory, and to adhere to the principles of the Moscow declaration.[1] Naturally, the West felt reassured by this indication of what promised to be a cooperative Soviet attitude regarding Austria. Allied confidence soon faltered, however, when the Red Army unilaterally installed a provisional Austrian government in Vienna and then began systematically pillaging every scrap of useful materiel and industrial equipment from eastern Austria.

Even as the Russians stubbornly insisted that no requisitioning was taking place, private homes were seized for army quarters, vehicles were taken for Soviet use, and food supplies were diverted from a hungry population.[2] The occupation army was impressively thorough, collecting articles of furniture and removing even road and railroad signals for use in the Soviet Republics.[3] Whole factories were dismantled piece by piece and transported on rail cars to the USSR. In the first twelve months of the occupation approximately 64,000 major items of plant were sent eastward from Austria's metal, machine, and locomotive industries alone. The Austrian oil industry was also devastated, losing 80 percent of its oil-drilling equipment to the Russians.[4] Western complaints, lodged most persistently by the British government, had no effect on the Soviet mass looting of Austria.[5]

Much worse for the inhabitants was the behavior of Soviet troops as they entered Austria, which quickly—and some have claimed irrevocably[6]—turned the Austrian people bitterly against a Russian army they had first welcomed as liberators. Apparently in defiance of their superiors, Soviet troops raped and robbed the terrified civilians and indiscriminately looted and destroyed whatever property they could not transport eastward.[7] Whether or not supported by the Kremlin, or even by Soviet officers in Austria, the unbridled campaign of destruction stood in glaring contradiction to Marshal Tolbukhin's assurances given as the Red Army first entered the capital. At the end of one year of occupation the bitter joke circulating in Vienna was that Austria could probably survive a third world war, but it could never endure a second liberation.[8]

The American, French, and British armies entered Austria in late April and early May 1945. Although Western forces for the most part abstained from plunder and rape, the early weeks of their occupation were far from exemplary. Plans closely coordinated between the British and American commands had called for the British Eighth Army and the U.S. Fifth Army to occupy Austria from the south, moving up from the Italian peninsula. These Mediterranean forces were unexpectedly delayed, however, because the German army in Italy did not surrender until 8 May. In the meantime the British Third Army and the U.S. Seventh drove through Germany and occupied Austria from the north, while the newly formed French unit pushed in from the west. The French occupied only the western tip of Austria (Vorarlberg), and for the first eight weeks the United States held a large portion of what was eventually to be the French occupation zone. Unfortunately, British and American specialists in Austrian civil affairs were still trapped in northern Italy, and during the early weeks of the occupation the policy of the Western allies was in confusion; specialists trained for German jobs set up the British and American military governments, treated the Austrians as vanquished enemies, and made many blunders. It was not until the end of May that the appropriate military authorities arrived from Italy and began to sort out the anarchical situation in Austria.[9]

According to the general outline of plans developed in the European Advisory Commission before the Allies entered Austria, the country was to be divided into four zones of occupation with the city of Vienna, the seat of federal and administrative power, to be shared jointly among the four Allies. Because of controversy over the exact zoning of the city of Vienna, however, the commission's plan for Austria had not yet been finally agreed. This element of indecision contributed to the general confusion at the beginning of the occupation, for although there were no direct conflicts between the four armies, the commanding officers were unsure about the boundaries

[24]

of their territories, and the capital city was occupied solely by Soviet troops.

In the meantime the Western powers were, for obvious political reasons, anxious to establish a presence in Austria's capital. In early April the Soviet Union agreed to permit Western missions to enter Vienna. On 27 April, however, a Soviet-supported provisional government in Vienna proclaimed the establishment of the Second Austrian Republic. Two days later, on 29 April, the Soviet authorities announced their formal recognition of the provisional government for Austria and simultaneously refused to allow the French, British, and American missions to enter Vienna until specific agreement was reached in the advisory commission on occupation zones and control machinery for the city. The Soviet pronouncement surprised and disturbed the Western allies, particularly Churchill, who feared that Stalin was attempting to establish in Austria a hegemony similar to what he had already secured in Romania, by organizing the country and then presenting the Western Allies with a fait accompli.

On 30 April, therefore, Churchill sent an agitated telegram to Truman: "I am much concerned about the way things are going in Austria. The announcement of the formation of a Provisional Austrian Government together with the refusal of permission to our missions to fly into Vienna makes me fear that the Russians are deliberately exploiting their arrival first into Austria to 'organise' the country before we get there."[10] The prime minister emphasized the need to take a strong stand immediately, lest the Americans and British ". . . find it very difficult to exercise any influence in Austria during the period of her liberation from the Nazis,"[11] and asked Truman to join him in a message to Stalin insisting that the dictator instruct the local Soviet commander to allow Allied missions to proceed to Vienna. Churchill included a draft of his telegram to Stalin and asked the American president to endorse it. But Truman, who had been in office less than three weeks, declined to endorse the more seasoned leader's message and told Churchill that he had already that day sent a separate protest to Stalin. Truman's message for the Soviet leader expressed the same sentiments as Churchill's draft but the tone was somewhat more conciliatory, among other things referring to the "open mind" and "good faith" of the American government as well as the desire to "collaborate" over Austria with the Soviet authorities.[12]

As the critical early days of the occupation passed, it became apparent that Truman's perspective on the situation in Austria differed slightly from Churchill's. Agreeing that Western missions must be granted access to Vienna as soon as possible, Truman nonetheless feared that the Russians would use the presence of the Western powers to legitimate the misdeeds that they were committing unilaterally. Like Churchill, he also feared that Austria under Soviet "liberation" would go the way of Romania; but Truman seemed more worried that Moscow would exploit any significant U.S. presence in Vienna than concerned that the Russians would begin to organize Austria without Western participation. Churchill's original message was dispatched to the Kremlin on 1 May 1945.[13] On 3 May, Truman sent another, separate message to Stalin and later explained his views to Churchill:

[I] am inclined to think that it would be a mistake to have our respresentatives reside in Vienna to assume any functions or responsibilities there beyond surveying the zones, until full joint control of Austria can be instituted on a basis of full equality among the occupying powers. I fear that the Russians want before then to do things in Vienna that we would not approve, but that they want equally much to do them in our name rather than carry the onus alone. Until we can have equal control it seems desirable to maintain the position that what is done there is done unilaterally; otherwise we might slip into the uncomfortable position we occupy in the Allied Commissions in Rumania and Bulgaria.[14]

The heads of the Western missions were not permitted to enter Vienna until 3 June, nearly two months after Soviet troops first arrived, and Western forces did not occupy the city until late August. The general view among the French, British, and American armies was that the Russians were obstructing their entry into Vienna in order to finish the frenzied fleecing of eastern Austria, and this was probably true for the first weeks of the Russian occupation.[15] After the chiefs of mission were permitted inside Vienna, however, it seemed that the Soviet attitude, at least at the local level, had changed. In mid-June, U.S. military sources cabled, "It was evident to heads of mission that Russians are extremely eager to have Allies into Vienna at earliest possible date. Situation in city is deteriorating and Russian prestige is lowered every day we remain away."[16] The British head of mission also stated that the Russians "showed every desire to have the Allies with them in Vienna without delay."[17] Apparently, the local Soviet leaders worried about their inability to feed the civilian population. Once they became convinced that the other Allies would not be competitors for war booty[18] and that four-power control was a serious concept, they were eager for the arrival of the Western armies. But Stalin's attitude evidently had not changed, for the Allied heads of mission were ordered to vacate Vienna after only a week's inspection tour.[19]

The long postponement of Western entry into Vienna had two fundamental causes: Soviet obstructionism and American prudence. Washington's hesitancy to commit U.S. forces to Vienna was not, as some writers have postulated, the result of an American failure to grasp the importance of an independent Austria to the future stability of Europe.[20] Indeed, as early as May 1945 the president received a detailed report by the State Department describing Austria as the meeting point of Russian and Western influence, "a strategic center for which there is bound to be a political struggle."[21] Rather, Truman's unwillingness to become inextricably entrapped in a Soviet-controlled scenario militated against any early desire to rush into Vienna. The president's qualms were shared by the commander of U.S. forces in Austria, General Mark Clark, who was not eager to take on the responsibility of feeding the Viennese until the Russians agreed to release some of the food supplies that lay east of the city. Of the situation in the summer of 1945 Clark later wrote:

[The Russians] sought to utilize for their own purposes most of the supplies that normally would feed the city. Thus the Americans and British had to import food from home to supply the population. Since at that time we had not been able to move into Vienna, it seemed to me that we could refuse to take up quarters in the capital until the Russians accepted a reasonable settlement on the food question. This course of action would force the Russians to accept full responsibility for the food shortage in the capital, and we knew that they were eager to avoid the adverse political repercussions that would be sure to follow. I suggested this course to Washington, but in reply I was told not to accept such a rigid policy.[22]

Stalin's obstinacy outlived American hesitancy, however, and by the middle of the summer the American president had wholeheartedly joined Churchill in pressing the dictator to keep his word. Truman must have come to realize the overriding importance of a Western presence in the capital city, for Vienna was the heart of Austria and crucial to any centralized government of the country.

On 4 July 1945 the European Advisory Commission finally concluded an Agreement on Control Machinery in Austria and five days later outlined the zones of occupation and the sectors of Vienna assigned to each of the four powers. Stalin no longer had a legalistic excuse to keep the Western Allies out of Vienna, but he continued to stall.

THE POTSDAM CONFERENCE

With tensions growing between them, Stalin, Churchill, and Truman gathered at Potsdam in Germany for the last of the great wartime summit conferences. Midway through the conference the British electorate removed the veteran Churchill from his position as prime minister and replaced him with the inexperienced Clement Attlee, thus inevitably weakening Britain's voice. Indeed, it was symbolic of an emerging global power constellation that only Truman and Stalin, leaders of the two nascent superpowers, were present for the entire meeting. The Potsdam conference, held between 16 July and 2 August, was a final salute to the days of collaboration between the Allies and a portent of discord between East and West. In particular it was a fateful meeting for Austria, since decisions taken in haste at Potsdam bedeviled the Austrians and the Western powers across the ten years of occupation that followed.

The great powers took several actions during the Potsdam conference that directly concerned Austria; some were beneficial, some detrimental. The most elementary action was to place the Italian Peace Treaty before the Austrian treaty on the agenda of the conference, an administrative decision that, some have claimed, had unforeseen significance. For almost two years after the meeting the Russians refused to discuss a treaty for Austria until the peace treaties with Italy and other states were agreed.[23] Early in the conference President Truman proposed the establishment of a Council of Foreign Ministers to draw up terms of peace with enemy states and to work out the details of other territorial settlements in postwar Europe. This suggestion was subsequently accepted and its consequences for Austria proved to be positive. The effect of the proposal, coupled with the dissolution of the European Advisory Commission, was to relegate the practical problems of occupied Austria to the Allied Council in Vienna and simultaneously to elevate abstract questions of Austrian sovereignty to the newly formed Council of Foreign Ministers.[24] During the years of occupation, as a result, when Austria's future status seemed inextricably tangled in the momentous broader issues of the European settlement—and the German settlement in particular—the Allied Council continued to operate normally, unimpeded by the fitful negotiations at the higher level. Conditions in Austria were not as adversely affected by the ten years of struggle over the country's status as they otherwise might have been.

At the Potsdam Conference Churchill once again pressed the Soviet dictator to allow the British to take up their sector in Vienna. Stalin replied that agreement on the zones of the city had been reached just the day before—an assertion that was at least partially correct since it took several weeks for each of the powers to ratify the two accords and Truman had signed the two documents only the previous day. Western troops could begin moving into Vienna as soon as they wished, Stalin claimed. Satisfied, Churchill and Truman asked Stalin for a commitment to continue to supply food to the population of Vienna for a short time after the Western Allies entered, since the feeding grounds of the city lay to the east and it would take time to devise a more permanent arrangement. Stalin consulted with his subordinates and then agreed. Austrian payment for food that the Soviet Union provided to the starving Viennese would dog the treaty negotiations well into the next decade.

However, the most important decision taken at Potsdam was a last-minute, almost careless concession that the Western powers made to the Soviet Union on the question of reparations. Early in the conference the Soviet delegation on the economic committee had demanded that the Soviet Union be granted extensive reparations from Austria. The Western powers countered that Austria was unable to afford any reparations and also stressed that, under the terms of the 1943 Moscow declaration, Austria was a liberated country and thus not obliged to pay reparations. After extended debate the Soviet delegation agreed to drop its demand for Austrian reparations, and the British and American delegations congratulated themselves on their successful defense of the small country's interests. On the penultimate day of the conference, however, the question of the future ownership of German assets located in Austria arose. By "German assets" the British and Americans essentially meant "war booty"; but under the pressure of a deadline no one at this late stage in the conference took the time to define the term and include the definition in the protocol. When the question of ownership was referred to the heads of state, Stalin proposed that German assets in eastern Austria be assigned to the Soviet Union while German assets in each of the other three zones would become the property of the power occupying that zone. To the Western leaders it seemed as if Stalin were merely asking for official confirmation of the situation as it existed in Austria. With little hesitation, Truman agreed; and Attlee, with considerably more hesitation, soon joined him. As it turned out, this last-minute decision on undefined German assets eventually cost Austria at least twice as much as the $250 million worth of so-called Austrian reparations that the Soviet Union had so generously renounced.[25]

American, British, and French soldiers entered the city of Vienna shortly after the conclusion of the Potsdam conference, and the Austrian capital was legally placed under four-power control on 1 September 1945. The zonal agreement divided Vienna into sectors for each of the occupying powers and a central sector under joint control.[26] Each country appointed a high commissioner who was, in the early years, both the head of the occupation forces in that country's zone and the representative on the Allied Council, the body empowered to administer quadripartite military rule which held its first meeting on 11 September. The international sector was the old city of Vienna, the Innere Stadt. Throughout the Allied occupation the international sector was patrolled jointly by four military policemen—one British, one French, one Russian, and one American. Even at the height of the Cold War this lonely group of four men in a jeep, the symbol of a wartime alliance long since disintegrated, continued its rounds.

THE RENNER GOVERNMENT

While the Western Allies were still struggling for access to Vienna, the Russians had established a new Austrian government under Karl Renner, former Austrian state chancellor and president of the last elected Parliament. It seems that the Russians, who knew of Renner's reputation as a socialist thinker, intended from the start to use Renner as a puppet, and they gave him their full support.[27] Renner, bowing to Soviet pressure, and also recognizing that Austrian Communists had resisted the Nazis, formed a government consisting of an unprecedented proportion of Communists.[28] He also granted the Communists three cabinet posts, the portfolios for the interior and education and one of the vice-chancellorships. On 27 April 1945 the Renner provisional government published a declaration of independence for Austria.[29] With the Western Allies pleading for more time to consider whether or not the government was legitimate, the Soviet authorities decided to force the issue. On 29 April, at a ceremony sponsored by the Russians in the Vienna Rathaus, Karl Renner was officially installed as chancellor and the Renner government was formally presented to the Austrian people.

The Americans, as might be expected, had some misgivings about the Renner government, and the new British Labour government took an even less favorable view. The British objected to the makeup of the government, arguing that it was too Viennese (and so did not represent the Austrian provinces fully) and that the Communists were too strong.[30] U.S. officials, on the other hand, felt that the Renner government commanded as much confidence as any other nonelected group, and they were not too apprehensive about the number of Communists. The main American concern was the Soviet method of unilateral action.[31] Publicly, the Western powers refused for some months to recognize the Soviet-backed regime.

To the careful eye, however, it soon became apparent that Renner, a shrewd seventy-five-year-old veteran politician, did not intend to allow himself to be manipulated. For one thing, although he granted the Communists three key cabinet posts, he placed powerful deputies from other parties beneath them.[32] To the Ministry of Education (officially, the Ministry of Public Information, Instruction, Education and—ironically—Religious Matters, Renner appointed Ernst Fischer, a post-1939 convert to communism and an intellectual who was highly esteemed by persons of contrary political outlooks.[33] Franz Honner was named minister of the interior, and Johan Koplenig, secretary of the Austrian Communist party, became one of the vice-chancellors. Renner expanded the government at the first opportunity to include representatives from the Western occupation zones, thereby diluting communist influence and increasing the provincial voice. Privately, the chancellor assured American officials that the Russian authorities did not interfere with the functioning of his government nor exercise a veto over legislation.[34] Most important, Renner publicly urged democratic elections as soon as possible. The Red Army's forcible seizure of the oil fields near Vienna following the Renner government's refusal to enter into an oil agreement with the Soviet Union was final proof that the regime was not under Soviet control. Shortly thereafter, on 20 October, the Western Allies recognized the provisional Austrian government and gave it civil jurisdiction over the three remaining zones.

The early postwar existence of a national coalition government was critical in ensuring the future political and economic unity of Austria. In contrast to Germany, Austria had a civil administration operating even before the Allied Commission began its work; and in contrast to the control agreement for Germany, the agreement for Austria clearly anticipated the formation of a freely elected and self-governing regime.[35] Paradoxically, the Western powers' reluctance to recognize the provisional government actually benefited the new regime. The Russians were anxious for the Allies to legitimate the Soviet-sponsored government and wanted to prevent the emergence of a rival Austrian government in the Western provinces. (During August the Western powers had permitted a conference of Austrian political leaders from the Western zones to be held in Salzburg.)[36] To assure the predominance of the provisional government, the Soviet leaders allowed Renner to establish contact with the people in the Western zones and, although they had previously sealed the city completely from the West, the Russians even permitted the provisional government to hold a national conference in Vienna during September to which representatives from all regions were invited. Gradually, the new government gained administrative power and legitimacy. Early in the occupation, for example, the four powers solved the problem of inequitable distribution of food in Austria by agreeing to pool all food and to entrust its distribution to one Austrian government.[37] The national character of the government and its eventual recognition by all four occupying powers was undoubtedly a significant deterrent to any plans to partition Austria.

The November 1945 Elections

Shortly after the West recognized the Renner government, the Russians agreed to free elections under impartial control. Apparently the Kremlin believed that the Austrian Communists might come to power by using divisive tactics similar to those used successfully in other parts of southern Europe—specifically, by driving a wedge between the Socialists and the Christian Socials (now People's party), absorbing the Socialists into a worker's coalition party, and then infiltrating and undermining the Christian Socials from within.[38] The British, noting calls in the Soviet press for workers' unity and other evidence of Soviet activity, were particularly sensitive during the early years to apparent Soviet plans for developing a Socialist Unity party in Austria.[39]

But to the extent that such Soviet plans existed, they did not come to fruition. The results of the first election were a grave disappointment to the Kremlin. The Communists received only 5 percent of the vote, earned only four of the 165 seats in Parliament, and were forced to relinquish the powerful cabinet posts they had held in the provisional government. The one post the Communists did gain, the Ministry of Electrification, was insignificant and intended merely to placate them. The election was by all accounts a disaster for the Austrian Communists and also for their Soviet sponsors. At the time Stalin's representatives believed the defeat could be reversed; but years later a Soviet diplomat reportedly confided to Sven Allard, former Swedish ambassador to Austria, "Only now do we understand that we had already conclusively lost Austria by the election of November 1945."[40]

In the wake of the election Soviet and Western attitudes toward the Austrian government began to change markedly. Among the Western powers any misgivings about the Austrian government vanished and were replaced by enthusiastic support, often taking the form of an insistence that the new government had a right to administer internal affairs without Allied interference. Less than a year after the American recognition of the Renner government the U.S. War Department instructed its representatives in Vienna that "Maximum advantages should be derived for new control machinery agreement for Austria in terms of strengthening government and increasing national independence."[41]

The Soviet Union, on the other hand, rejected its former client and tried to whittle away at the authority of the Austrian government. After the election the Soviet Union began to restrict the movement of Austrian officials in the eastern zone and forbid political gatherings without a Soviet observer being present.[42] The Soviet authorities began a policy of creating ad hoc "denazification committees," composed of a majority of Communist party members and formed on short notice to pass judgment on Austrian officials in the eastern zone of whose activities Soviet leaders disapproved.[43] On the Allied Council the Soviet representative even attempted to force passage of a new constitution, challenging the validity of Austrian legislation in all four zones of occupation. After November 1945 relations between the four powers deteriorated, with the Soviet Union frequently opposing the other three powers in the council. It was shortly after the election that the Russians criticized as too weak the Allied policies on denazification and the disposition of German assets in Austria. These issues would reappear as a reason for Soviet intransigence in the lengthy treaty negotiations.

WESTERN TROOP REDUCTIONS

In part as a result of new confidence in the Austrian government, but also because of strong domestic pressures, the Western Allies felt that their first priority after the November election was to reduce the number of occupation troops in Austria. On 28 November the British Embassy in Washington sent an official note to the State Department suggesting that the four powers agree in principle that each would reduce its occupying forces to a level to be determined by the Allied Council.[44] State Department officials called a meeting with British representatives the next day. They agreed it was imperative for the Western powers to take advantage of the presently favorable position by seizing the initiative before the Soviet government did so, and thus they concurred that there should be a substantial reduction and equalization of forces of occupation. Given the discrepancies between zones, however, exact numerical equalization need not be insisted upon. Furthermore, authority should be transferred from the Allied military government to the Austrian government, and the zonal divisions should be eliminated altogether.[45]

The Americans, it seems, were becoming rather more enthusiastic about reductions than the British had intended them to be. A few weeks later, at an informal meeting in Moscow of the Soviet, American, and British foreign ministers, Secretary of State James Byrnes proposed the complete withdrawal of troops from Austria: official recognition of the newly elected Austrian government by the four powers, he suggested, would leave no grounds for maintaining troops in Austria. Both Molotov and Bevin replied that complete withdrawal would certainly *not* be a good idea, and only the British foreign minister was willing to state officially that any reductions at all were desirable.[46]

The British worried that the Austrian government would not survive a complete withdrawal of Western troops from Austria, but they might have been more open to persuasion by their American colleagues had the British not had the unique and serious problem of Yugoslav incursions into Austrian territory. The Americans had a tremendous strategic advantage in that their Austrian zone adjoined their German zone; even if all U.S. troops were withdrawn from Austria, they could quickly be replaced in the event of an emergency. The British enjoyed no such advantage. During the first months of occupation, moreover, Yugoslav partisans raided southern Carinthia and Styria weekly, and nearly a division of British soldiers (some 30,000 men) was required just to protect Austria's southern frontier.[47] Still, whatever the situation in Carinthia, the British Foreign Office knew that for domestic political reasons they could not reverse their public policy of urging troop withdrawals at the earliest possible moment. To satisfy the military requirement of protecting the frontier and also to respond to the political imperative of reducing the number of Soviet troops, senior officials in London agreed among themselves that a quadripartite reduction of between forty and fifty thousand troops was desirable.[48]

The seriousness of the border dispute was kept relatively quiet for many months, presumably in order to avoid publicly casting doubt on the territorial integrity of Austria. Before agreeing to major troop reductions the British Foreign Office considered issuing a communication stating that the United Kingdom recognized the 1937 borders of Austria and then trying to persuade the other three powers to concur. A clear statement of interest on the part of the Allies, it was hoped, would deter the would-be invaders south of Austria. But the Foreign Office was not confident that the State Department would agree to even an implicit territorial guarantee of this kind.[49]

When the British approached the Americans, however, Foreign Office officials were pleasantly surprised. After some discussion State Department representatives agreed that a four-power announcement guaranteeing the frontiers of Austria would be desirable and should accompany a decision to reduce Allied troops. The French also supported the proposition.[50] Unfortunately, the Russian response was much less favorable. The British Embassy in Moscow was curtly informed that the purpose of the Russian occupation of Austria was to ensure the disarmament of German forces in the country, and as this task was not yet complete, the reduction of Soviet troops was impossible. Moreover, the Soviet Foreign Ministry accused the British of deliberately maintaining some units of the German Army in the British zone of Austria, under the command of a White Russian colonel.[51] Stalin was apparently unwilling to allow the four powers to decide jointly whether Austria had been sufficiently disarmed, especially since he believed that at least one of the powers had hidden anti-Soviet motives; thus the determination of the necessary level of Soviet troops in Austria was a matter for the Soviet Union alone to decide.

The three Western powers repeatedly attempted to raise the matter of troop reductions on the Allied Council in Vienna, but the Soviet representative refused to discuss it.[52] Over the first months of the occupation, as a result, most troop reductions occurred unilaterally and without public acknowledgement. According to British intelligence sources, in November 1945 the Soviet Union had some 180,000 troops in Austria; the British, 75,000; the French, 40,000; and the United States, 70,000.[53] Five months later the Soviet Union had reduced its troops to approximately 140,000, but the demobilization of Western troops was far more drastic: in April 1946 the British had 28,000 soldiers in Austria, the French had 15,000, and the Americans only 13,000.[54] The number of Western troops had thus dropped significantly below the minimum envisaged by senior officials in the British government only a few months before, and the Red Army had actually increased its proportion of the total occupation force. The Soviet leaders continued to demobilize troops over subsequent months, with force strength reaching 125,000 men only one month later,[55] but the minimum number was always more than that of any one Western power, and indeed during the remainder of the occupation period it apparently did not dip below the combined total of Western forces. Certainly the Western suggestion of numerical quadripartite equality was never close to being realized.

The British feared that Soviet leaders would interpret the rapid Western demobilization from Austria as a sign of lack of will and would take advantage of the apparent opportunity to reassert communist hold over Austria. The hardening of Soviet policy in Austria during the early months of 1946 seemed to confirm that the Soviet authorities planned to turn the country forcibly into a communist salient in Western Europe. The U.K. Chiefs of Staff warned in ominous tones of the consequences that an extension of Soviet influence to the other zones of Austria would hold for Italy and particularly for France, "the preservation of which from Russian influence is essential to the security of Western Europe."[56] The military weakness of the French made their reliability questionable at best. The British were attempting to take a strong stand against the Russians, in the Allied Council and elsewhere, but felt that their own manpower difficulties and economic constraints seriously hampered their efforts. The Americans were most capable of supporting the Austrians against the Russians, British officials believed, but the Americans seemed primarily interested in returning home. "It is unfortunate that the American Commander-in-Chief is not a very reliable ally," one senior Foreign Office official wrote. "General Clark is apt to take a most irresponsible line and is mainly thinking of getting back to America as soon as possible."[57] The British ambassador in Washington expressed his frustration to State Department officials about American complacency toward the Communists in Austria, and the State Department agreed to instruct the U.S. representative to be tougher with the Soviet Union.[58] In the spring of 1946 few would have predicted that, as the years of Austria's occupation continued, the British and American roles with respect to the Soviet Union would be sharply reversed.

[36]

THE SECOND CONTROL AGREEMENT

The Agreement on Control Machinery in Austria, completed by the European Advisory Commission in July 1945, had been intended as an interim arrangement to be superseded, after a freely elected Austrian government was in place, by a more permanent agreement. Since the Austrians now had an elected government, the British representatives on the Allied Council in February 1946 submitted a draft for a new agreement. Debate over the second control agreement commenced in the Allied Commission for Austria during the spring of 1946.

Very quickly a division appeared between the Soviet Union and the three Western powers. The Western Allies were anxious to transfer as much autonomy as possible to the Austrian government. They therefore proposed that any legislative motion passed by Parliament would automatically become law after thirty-one days unless the four powers unanimously agreed to veto it. The Soviet Union opposed such an arrangement, preferring that the Allied Council exercise the right unanimously to approve Austrian proposals before they became law. On the subject of commercial agreements, however, the Americans stood alone in insisting that the principle of quadripartite approval be applied to bilateral agreements between the Austrian government and any one of the four powers.[59] The U.S. position seemed at odds with the policy objective of transferring as much power as possible to the Austrians; it was not supported by the British and the French, but it was most vehemently opposed by the Soviet representatives. (They were probably holding out hope of persuading the Austrians to sign a bilateral oil agreement similar to the advantageous bilateral contracts the Soviet Union had already concluded with other occupied countries.) Finally, in May 1946, after weeks of tough negotiating, a compromise was reached. The Americans agreed that the council would relinquish all control over bilateral Austrian agreements and the Russians agreed to passage of a slightly different version of the controversial Article 6: while constitutional laws required the consent of the Allied Council, all nonconstitutional laws would go into effect automatically unless the four occupying powers, within thirty-one days, unanimously agreed to veto them.[60] The second Allied Agreement on Control Machinery for Austria was signed by the representatives of the four powers on 28 June 1946.

Passage of Article 6 of the 1946 control agreement was the second major blunder that the Russians committed in the early years of occupation. It soon became apparent to the Western powers that the

Soviet authorities had not realized how much autonomy the Austrians would gain from having the power to pass their own legislation.[61] The requirement of council unanimity made it very difficult for the Russians to exercise a veto at all, since the Soviet Union was frequently the only power with objections. Between 1946 and 1953 the Soviet Union raised objections to over 550 nonconstitutional laws, with very little success. Moreover, even the provision blocking Allied interference in bilateral agreements proved to be a disaster for the Soviet Union. Not only was Russia ultimately unsuccessful in its bid for a voluntary oil agreement with Austria, but in 1948 the United States successfully used the regulation to implement the Marshall Plan in Austria without Soviet interference.[62] The clearest evidence that the Russians regretted their mistake in negotiating the second control agreement emerged several years later, in 1949, when the U.S. secretary of state proposed that the German control agreement be drafted on the Austrian model. The Soviet foreign minister flatly rejected the idea on the grounds that Article 6 of the Austrian agreement was inappropriate for Germany.[63]

The Russians allowed passage of Article 6 of the second control agreement for Austria for reasons that have never been clear. It cannot be argued that the Soviet negotiators did not understand the article, for they studied it carefully over the course of several weeks. Likewise, it is not likely that they misunderstood the term "constitutional," for it was in order to satisfy Soviet delegates that the word was added (the original wording covered all laws).[64] One American negotiator has since speculated that although the Russians knew that Article 6 would lessen their own hold on Austria, they realized that it would likewise reduce American leverage in the country.[65] If this was indeed the reason for Soviet agreement, then the negative motive of denying Austria to the West is an interesting portent of apparent Soviet motives years later, in the Austrian State Treaty negotiations. With hindsight, however, the only thing that can be said with certainty is that whatever the Soviet motive in agreeing to Article 6, the Austrian government benefited from the signing of the second control agreement, for just as a division was appearing between the Soviet zone of Germany and the three Western zones, the integrity of the Austrian state was strengthened.

Passage of the second control agreement was an extremely significant event for postwar Austria, since after June 1946 the country gradually gained de facto recognition as a sovereign state. In sharp contrast to neighboring Germany, Austria now effectively enjoyed freedom and legitimacy in all legislative actions except constitutional laws. The Austrian government had the power to enter at its own discretion into bilateral agreements with the four powers and within a few months gained the right to conclude trade agreements with any country except Germany.[66] Even regarding its constitution Austria made gains with the 1946 agreement. While amendments would still be a tricky business, the constitutional basis of the Austrian government was now secure: the Soviet Union could no longer hope successfully to press its earlier demand that the constitution be replaced, as it was most unlikely that the four powers would ever agree on a new one. In some ways, moreover, the growing rift between the great powers proved beneficial to the Austrian government, for when the four powers disagreed, the Austrian government often retained the power to act by default. In a strange twist of logic the so-called control agreement of 1946 actually helped increase the legislative freedom and international legitimacy of Austria after the war.[67]

EFFORTS TO OPEN FOUR-POWER NEGOTIATIONS

In the meantime the United States had been attempting at a higher diplomatic level to initiate four-power negotiations on an Austrian treaty. The Soviet Union, obviously reluctant to discuss Austria, kept its foreign minister busy thinking up creative excuses for postponing the start of negotiations. The Council of Foreign Ministers met in Paris from 25 April to 16 May, and again from 15 June to 12 July, in preparation for the Paris Peace Conference of twenty-one nations, which sat intermittently from July to mid-October 1946. At the April council meetings in Paris, American Secretary of State James F. Byrnes tried without success to convince Soviet Foreign Minister Molotov to include the Austrian State Treaty on the agenda. Molotov first argued that the Soviet delegation had not had the opportunity to study the draft the U.S. delegation had submitted. When Byrnes assured him that the U.S. draft, which was actually based on the Hungarian peace treaty, contained no surprises Molotov retorted that the agenda was too full, anyway: "May God help us to complete the work on the treaties which are now before us."[68] At the next session, in June, Molotov's objection was that the status of denazification and relocation of displaced persons in Austria was still unsatisfactory from the Soviet point of view; the evacuation of these people was a necessary prerequisite to Austria's independence, he claimed.[69] When Bevin raised the need to define German assets in Austria,

Molotov stolidly insisted that the issue was not on the agenda and could not be discussed.[70]

Even in the face of Soviet intransigence the Americans in 1946 optimistically—or perhaps naively—continued to believe that the Russians would sign the U.S. draft of the Austrian treaty. Indeed, had it not been for British pressure, the U.S. representatives to the Allied Commission in Vienna might not have signed the second control agreement, which was being negotiated as the Council of Foreign Ministers was meeting, on the grounds that signature in Vienna might jeopardize the treaty in Paris. On 22 June, in the midst of the Paris meetings of the Council of Foreign Ministers, Ernest Bevin wrote to Byrnes:

> [W]e cannot quite share the view that the signature of the control agreement would prejudice the chances of having useful discussions on the treaty, any more than the signature of the revised Armistice agreement with Italy, which you proposed and we accepted during the last session of the Conference, has interfered with the negotiation of the Peace Treaty with Italy.
>
> Austria is now on the agenda here and as you know we shall support you in pressing for the discussion of a treaty as the most urgent outstanding question relating to that country, but with the best will in the world, it will surely be impossible to do more than have a treaty referred for study to the Deputies or some other body, and as we know, their deliberations are only too likely to be prolonged.[71]

Shortly thereafter Secretary Byrnes issued new instructions to the U.S. representative in Vienna. The second control agreement was signed less than a week after the letter was written, and it is doubtful that the signing had any effect upon the negotiations over an Austrian treaty. Five months later, when the French, British, and American foreign ministers collectively urged the appointment of deputies to begin preliminary work on the draft treaty, Molotov finally agreed that work on the draft treaty might commence in the following year.

Possible explanations of Soviet stalling tactics during 1946 are many. Officially and in the press Soviet officials argued that Austria did not deserve to have either its own predicament or its claims against enemy states considered at the Paris Peace Conference. The Soviet rationale was that despite the incentive of the Moscow declaration, wherein the four powers had clearly invited Austria to contribute to its own liberation, the Austrians had done nothing to help the Allies. To the very end of the war the Austrians had fought on the side of Hitler's Germany, the Russians argued. Furthermore, as Deputy Foreign Minister Andrei Vyshinsky pointed out, the Paris Peace Conference was for enemy states; Austria was neither "an enemy of our enemies—nor [is] she an enemy herself."[72]

The Soviet reluctance of early 1946 to begin treaty negotiations may also have been prompted by the desire to continue extracting war booty from eastern Austria. On 6 July 1946 the Soviet commander-in-chief, Colonel General Kurasov, published throughout the eastern zone an order that included a very comprehensive list of items unilaterally claimed as the rightful property of the Soviet Union. The proclamation warned that "All persons who under any pretext whatsoever withold notification of where the above-named property is found, who attempt to conceal such fact or give misleading information, as well as all persons who through their acts in any way hinder the application of this order or damage the above-named property, are subject to punitive action."[73] In what was probably an attempt to exempt the proclamation from the terms of the new agreement, the order was backdated to 27 June 1946, the day before the second control agreement had been signed.[74] A few weeks later the Austrians attempted to nationalize all industries to prevent their confiscation, but in the face of Soviet refusal to allow the measure to be implemented in the Soviet zone—not to mention the realization that the government lacked the resources to compensate foreign interests anyway—the Austrians nullified the nationalization law.[75] At about the same time Soviet leaders began to put together a network of Soviet-run enterprises and retail shops in eastern Austria which later became known as USIA—the acronym came from "Upravleniye Sovietskovo Imuschestva v Avstrii" or Administration for Soviet Property in Austria. Throughout the remaining years of occupation products such as timber and paint from these enterprises were shipped to the Soviet Union and its satellites, financed by goods sold illegally (without payment of Austrian government customs or taxes) in the shops. In later years the USIA network became valuable to the Soviet Union as a source of goods and hard currency.

But Soviet motives for delaying an Austrian treaty were most likely related directly to Russian postwar activities in Eastern Europe. The years 1945 and 1946 saw the subjugation of Poland, Romania, and Bulgaria to Soviet control, and by the end of 1946 Stalin was in the midst of engineering a communist takeover of Hungary. At this crucial time Stalin had no desire to discuss the evacuation of Austria; negotiations would be an unwelcome distraction from more important matters and, besides, he had no desire to evacuate eastern Austria, a convenient buffer zone between Hungary and the West. Moreover, later events indicate that the Soviet authorities still believed in 1946 that the conversion of Austria to communism was possible: the first attempted communist putsch in Austria occurred in May 1947.

In 1945 and 1946, therefore, the Soviet Union had various reasons not to be anxious to take its place at the bargaining table. It is probably safe to assume that the Russians agreed to begin negotiating the Austrian treaty only when they felt that they could put it off no longer.

[2]

The Negotiations Begin, 1947–1948

At the end of 1946 none of the Western powers regarded the occupation of Austria as a long-term commitment. The rapid demobilization of Western forces from Austria was carried out under the assumption that the remaining troops would soon follow. The Western powers, and particularly the British, interpreted several apparently deliberate Soviet signals to mean that Stalin also intended to pull out of the country soon. On the Allied Council in Vienna the Soviet representative suddenly agreed to accept parity between the four powers in the division of occupation costs. The quadripartite level of reimbursement would be lower than what the Russian commander had been demanding unilaterally from the Austrians, and so the Soviet change of policy was interpreted to mean that the Russians expected the occupation to end shortly. More significantly, in December 1946 the Soviet Union announced that the reduced Soviet presence in Austria would permit the return of a considerable number of houses to their owners. As Soviet leaders had not previously acknowledged that they were withdrawing *any* forces from Austria, this public reference to troop reductions was encouraging in itself.[1] Hopeful speculation on the part of the Americans and the British was further enhanced by a remark made in Vienna by Soviet general Kurasov to U.S. general Clark: "I expect that there will be an Austrian Treaty. We have done enough for Austria and it is time we got out."[2] Even the formerly skeptical British foreign secretary Bevin considered these signs auspicious. Shortly before the first session of the deputy foreign ministers for Austria he reported to the cabinet that "[t]here was some reason to hope that the Soviet Government were now prepared to conclude a Treaty with Austria in the fairly near future."[3]

[43]

Although general differences between the Soviet Union and the Western powers had deepened over recent months, there was reason to hope that Austria might be exempted from the widening dispute.[4] Some Westerners thought that an Austrian treaty might perhaps even serve as a symbol of the lingering chance for future East-West cooperation.

FIRST MEETING OF THE FOREIGN MINISTERS' DEPUTIES

In a spirit of optimism, therefore, the first session of the foreign ministers' deputies opened in London on 14 January 1947. Whatever the hopes or intentions of the great powers and the Austrians, however, it soon became obvious that the conclusion of the treaty would be no easy task. Shortly after the opening formalities some important and contentious issues began to emerge.

In the initial hours of the conference, a dispute erupted over Austria's frontiers, with the Soviet deputy supporting Yugoslav claims to significant portions of Carinthia. The Austrian delegates, who had been invited to attend as observers, firmly denied the Yugoslav claims. Quickly the dispute became emotional, with members of the visiting Yugoslav delegation at one point attacking an Austrian spokesman ad hominem. In the interest of progress discussion of the issue was postponed, with the Soviet deputy still staunchly supporting and three Western deputies recommending rejection of Yugoslav claims.

After this initial flare-up over frontiers it became apparent that the question of external German assets in Austria was going to prove a more serious problem. The Russians held that they could rightfully claim as German assets all property in Austria that had belonged to the Germans in 1945 unless obtained by obvious and direct force. The claim, of course, meant that every factory, railroad, or public facility in eastern Austria was Soviet property, to be sold back to the Austrians in bilateral agreements at the discretion of the Soviet state. The Western powers rejected this broad interpretation of "German assets" on the grounds that such a price, to be extracted from a friendly country that could not even afford to feed its own population, was absurd, would prevent the reestablishment of the "free and independent Austria" promised in the Moscow declaration, and would give the Soviet Union tremendous political and economic leverage in postwar Austria. In addition, the Americans were keenly aware that Austrian recovery was likely to be financed by the United States; the

Soviet position would result in American taxpayers' money ending up in the coffers of the Communists.

The deputies reached one significant point of agreement, on what to call the four-power treaty with Austria. The Austrians were particularly anxious to avoid any inference that the country had willingly fought on the side of Hitler's Germany. During the years of the Anschluss, Austrian delegates argued, Austria had ceased to exist as a sovereign state, and thus the postwar settlement was not really a peace treaty but rather a legal instrument to reestablish Austria's statehood and independence. Eventually the representatives of the four powers agreed to name the document the Treaty for the Reestablishment of an Independent and Democratic Austria, or Austrian State Treaty *(Staatsvertrag)* for short. The title later became something of an irony, for as the years of negotiation and occupation passed, the treaty became less concerned with reestablishing Austria's "statehood"—a status that the country had arguably enjoyed on a de facto basis long before the document was signed—than with providing a suitable pretext under which the four powers could withdraw their troops in an honorable way.

Despite the deputy foreign ministers' inability to find solutions to contentious issues other than the title of the treaty, the session was considered a promising beginning. The assigned task had, after all, been completed: by the time the conference closed on 25 February, a preliminary draft of an Austrian state treaty had been prepared, with about half of its fifty-nine articles unanimously agreed.

The Moscow Conference of Foreign Ministers

When the Moscow Conference of Foreign Ministers opened in March 1947, therefore, there was still a certain amount of optimism in Europe, and particularly in Austria, concerning the likelihood of an imminent treaty. In his opening statement Soviet foreign minister Molotov bolstered these hopes by declaring that he believed the treaty could be completed in the course of the Moscow conference.[5] Indeed, discussion of Yugoslav territorial claims gave the Western delegates practical reason for encouragement. The Russian attitude toward Yugoslav demands seemed more lukewarm and ambiguous than it had been in London.[6] Despite a very emotional Yugoslav statement about the need to adjust the frontier with Austria, Molotov remained impassive and simply asked a few questions.[7] He certainly did not champion the Yugoslav cause. When the Yugoslav delegation

[45]

presented a claim for reparations from Austria, Molotov's response was to recommend that the claims "be considered in a favourable spirit." For their part, Britain and the United States argued that Yugoslavia's claims were out of order because the three great powers had renounced Austrian reparations at the Potsdam conference. France then irritated its Western allies by suggesting that the Yugoslav representative's claims for reparations be satisfied by reducing comparable Austrian claims for reparations from Yugoslavia. Although Molotov supported the French suggestion, he did not pursue it, thereby (uncharacteristically) passing up an excellent opportunity to exploit differences between the Western powers.[8]

The shift in the Soviet attitude toward the Yugoslavs, from staunch support to near-indifference, was not lost on the Western delegates. As the meeting continued, the Americans became so skeptical about Soviet backing for Yugoslav demands that one official status report to Washington read: "It is uncertain whether the Soviet action represents more than a gesture of support for a loyal ally, or whether the Soviet position will finally be abandoned in favor of agreement with the other delegations."[9]

On the question of German assets, by contrast, it was soon apparent that both Eastern and Western positions had hardened and that the chance for agreement was becoming remote. Molotov's relentless demands for German assets in Austria struck Western diplomats as unproductive, single-minded attempts to wear down their resolve. Much to the annoyance of the Western delegates, Molotov reiterated over and over again the statement that the Soviet Union renounced all claims to reparations from Austria. Since the Russians defined "Austrian reparations" and "German assets in Austria" as separate matters, Western delegates considered the renunciations meaningless and deceptive.[10] Later Molotov argued that at the Potsdam conference the United States and the Soviet Union had entered into an agreement that assets were to be a bilateral concern between the occupying power and the Austrians. The disposal of German assets in the eastern zone of Austria was thus none of the Western powers' business: "It was thereby decided that the United States Government would not interfere in matters concerning German assets in the rest of Austria. It follows that any kind of quadripartite arbitration is out of the question here," the Soviet foreign minister argued.[11]

If the uncompromising Russian stance was intended to bring forth concessions, it failed miserably. Indeed, it accomplished just the opposite: instead of encouraging compromise, it drove the three Western powers closer together in a determination to resist Russian demands. General Mark Clark, who went to Moscow with the U.S. delegation, complained in a letter to his wife: "I feel like I am going to kindergarten every day. . . . [The Russians] have not given in on a single point since we started. They delay the conferences, drag them out, hesitate on discussions, and are unable to delegate authority. This is all part of their pattern to confuse and wear down all of us and get us to give in."[12] The new U.S. secretary of state, George C. Marshall, was determined to sign no agreement that would turn Austria into an economic "puppet" of the Soviet Union. The British delegation also was firmly resolved not to sign a treaty that would require crippling political and economic concessions. Pierson Dixson, private secretary to Foreign Secretary Bevin, wrote at the time: "Never has the shameless rapacity of Soviet policy been so apparent. The division is complete: the Western Powers want Austria to live, Russia wants her to moulder under Soviet domination. Unless the Soviets do a real volte-face, give up their charming double policy of loot and domination, there is not a chance of agreement or of four-power treaty."[13]

As the attitudes of the Soviet Union and the Western powers became increasingly polarized, the battered Austrian delegates tried desperately to keep the Moscow conference from failing over economic issues. The Russians, who had failed before the conference opened to woo the Austrians into a bilateral settlement of the German assets issue, were unsympathetic, and in the negotiations they no longer carefully maintained a friendly attitude toward the Austrians. Turning to the West, the Austrians begged the three powers not to defend Austrian interests so vigorously; the Austrian foreign minister, in view of the tremendous political importance in Austria of an early treaty, asked the Western powers at least to consider the Soviet proposals.[14] At this point the Soviet occupiers were no longer transporting Austrian equipment en masse to the Soviet Union but instead were operating Austrian factories in the eastern zone under USIA. This development must have heightened the Austrian fears that the Russians were planning to stay, and it increased the pressure on the Austrian government to encourage an immediate settlement. Austrian representatives needed at least the appearance of progress in the negotiations, to encourage their constituents at home.

American secretary of state Marshall replied that the Austrians must be patient; he understood their concerns, and in the future he would do what he could to allay their economic hardships. But for now Marshall felt very strongly that the United States had to convince the Soviet Union that its unjust demands would not be tolerated. It had to avoid treading the path of appeasement.[15]

[47]

The meetings of the Moscow Conference of Foreign Ministers must be understood in the more general context of East-West relations in 1947. In March, American concern over possible Soviet designs in Greece prompted President Truman to deliver, before a joint session of Congress, a speech calling for American support for "free peoples who are resisting attempted subjugation by armed minorities or by outside pressures." His purpose was to rally U.S. domestic support for economic aid to Greece, but in a matter of months the so-called Truman Doctrine effected a major shift in U.S. foreign policy from earnest negotiation with the Russians, a legacy of Roosevelt's wartime diplomacy, to positive anticommunism. The American public found brutal Soviet takeovers in Eastern Europe to be perfect examples of the subjugation of free peoples, and such actions could be resisted elsewhere only by Western strength and vigilance. The speech was delivered just two days after the opening of the Conference of Foreign Ministers, in seeming disregard of possible consequences for the negotiations. Clearly, the American position with regard to the Soviet Union had hardened even before the talks began.

Soviet behavior at the talks could not have been better calculated to calcify opinions in the West. "Many were the hours we listened to the same old records, the same technique, the same fruitless arguments about minor matters, the same distortions and the same blaring propaganda," complained one American delegate.[16] But Soviet leaders were driven, at least in part, by personal insecurity and genuine need. In 1946 the Soviet Union had experienced the worst drought of the century; the last comparable drought, in 1891, had been partly responsible for the decline of tsardom.[17] Twenty million Soviet people had died in the war against Germany, and Austrian soldiers had fought with the Nazis. From a Soviet perspective it must have been especially galling that Austria, whose citizens—willingly or not—had so recently participated in a campaign of slaughter and destruction in the Soviet Union, enjoyed living conditions that were probably better than in many parts of the Soviet Union. To make matters worse, the Western powers seemed to be quibbling over resources that the Soviet Union desperately needed, and Stalin began to conclude that the Western powers did not want the Soviet Union to recover. The Soviet people felt justified in demanding massive payment for the losses they had suffered, for most of which they could never truly be compensated; moreover, Stalin used promises of huge reparations to placate a starving populace and to stem domestic unrest.

Thus neither side was willing to make significant concessions in the negotiations over Austria, and as a result the split between East and

[48]

West grew wider. The general context of East-West relations condemned the Moscow Conference of Foreign Ministers to failure before it began.

THE AUSTRIAN TREATY COMMISSION

The Austrians were bitterly disappointed by the conference, but their hopes were not completely dashed. Near the end of the Moscow meetings U.S. secretary of state Marshall proposed that, as the ministers could not reach agreement on the Austrian treaty because of Soviet obstinacy, the problem should be submitted to the General Assembly of the United Nations.[18] Soviet foreign minister Molotov replied, once again, that Soviet claims for German assets were in accordance with agreements reached at Potsdam. These claims could certainly be settled between the great powers, just as similar Soviet claims had been settled and incorporated in the peace treaties for Romania, Hungary, Bulgaria, and Finland. He insisted that there was no need for reference to the United Nations; instead, Molotov proposed that the unresolved articles be referred to a treaty commission, which would meet in closed sessions in Vienna. Encouraged by the proposal, the other foreign ministers agreed.[19]

The Austrian Treaty Commission met in Vienna eighty-four times over the next five months and studied more than seventy different proposals. Throughout the entire period the Soviet delegates stuck tenaciously to their initial demands regarding German assets in Austria (Article 35 of the draft treaty), and the British and American delegates refused to make the major concessions required to reach agreement.[20] The French delegates took pains to appear impartial in this East-West standoff, but on all points of substance they supported the Anglo-American position.[21] Many of the meetings were taken up by a careful, paragraph-by-paragraph review of the draft treaty and the positions of each power on each issue. The exercise was useful because it clarified the points of disagreement, but no significant compromises were made.

As the relationship between the Soviet and the Western delegates to the treaty commission grew more strained, so the Anglo-American partnership seemed to be strengthened. According to the head of the British delegation, by the end of the five months of commission meetings, "[O]ur relations with the United States Delegation could not have been closer, better or more fruitful. . . . The technical branches of the two Delegations were virtually integrated into a single unit. . . ."[22] This Anglo-American partnership seemed to be the only fruit of the venture: despite the frequency and intensity of the meetings, the Austrian Treaty Commission seemed to be unable to make progress.

THE 1947 COMMUNIST UPRISING

As so often in the Austrian treaty negotiations, however, the exchanges across the bargaining table were one thin thread in the fabric of the international situation. Reasons for the treaty commission's lack of progress, despite its numerous meetings, were again related to events separate from the negotiations. Indeed, in the month that the commission began its meetings, a most important event influencing the negotiations occurred literally outside the negotiating room in Vienna. In May 1947 communist-sponsored food riots led to an attempted communist putsch and strengthened the Western powers' suspicions that the Soviet Union intended to turn Austria into a communist satellite.

There had certainly been earlier signs of apparent Soviet intentions to incorporate Austria in the eastern bloc. When the Red Army first marched into Vienna, propaganda broadcasts encouraged Austrian nationalism and urged the formation of anti-Nazi coalitions composed of socialists, Communists, liberals, and conservatives. The same propaganda was used in East European countries, where the resulting "national fronts," grouping activists from all parts of the political spectrum under a nationalist banner, were instrumental in the formation of "people's democracies."[23] Stalin's sponsorship of what he envisioned as a puppet government is another indication of his plans. President Karl Renner's unexpected "betrayal" of his patron was not so precipitous as to prevent the Russians from ensuring that the minister of the interior packed the police force with Communists, later a key factor in the 1947 uprising. With clever planning, agricultural resources also provided political leverage for the Russians. When Austria was suffering from severe food shortages, the Soviet authorities secretly hoarded some of the food in their sector and then supplied it at their discretion to factory workers in Soviet-run industries. Naturally, this policy increased Soviet popularity among workers in the eastern zone and increased unrest in the other three zones.[24] Likewise, it was probably no accident that the Soviet sector of Vienna contained most of the working-class areas, the most likely source of support for a communist takeover. Russian attempts to set up Soviet-Austrian companies on a "fifty-fifty" basis failed because the Austrian government backed by the Western powers refused to enter into the agreements; but the same tactic was successfully used to gain control of the economies of Hungary and Romania.[25] Indeed, postwar events in Hungary echoed loudly through Austria and added to the anxiety of the Austrians. Numerous signs pointed to Russian hopes of turning Austria into an eastern bloc country.

The first attempted communist takeover of Austria occurred in the spring of 1947, just after the end of the Moscow Conference of Foreign Ministers and before the first meeting of the Austrian Treaty Commission. The winter of 1946–1947 had been extremely harsh; shortages of food, electricity, and heating fuel had compounded the general misery.[26] UN food shipments ceased in May; Marshall aid did not reach Austria until a year later, though in the interim Austria received two installments of U.S. congressional relief aid. Taking advantage of economic hardships and capitalizing on bitter disappointment over the failure of the Moscow conference, on 5 May 1947 the Austrian Communist party staged a food riot. About five thousand demonstrators beseiged the Chancellory, and the Austrian federal chancellor, Leopold Figl, was forced to receive a delegation led by the Communist vice president of the Austrian Trade Union Federation.[27]

Both the demonstrators and the Austrian government leaders knew that the police force was infiltrated by Communists; they also knew that the Allied Council had so severely limited Austrian weaponry and ammunition that the police were ineffective in any case.[28] Austrian leaders also noted with apprehension the presence of Russian officers who were cheered by the crowd as they walked by—and in particular the assistant to the Soviet military commander, who seemed to be keeping a close watch on the proceedings.[29] For several anxious hours it was unclear whether the demonstrators might overthrow the government, although the refusal of the socialist trade union leaders to call a general strike would, it was hoped, undermine the strength of the Communists and prevent them from successfully executing a putsch.

With emotions heightening, the crowd around the Chancellory surged forward and threatened to take the chancellor's office by force. In desperation the Austrian government appealed to the Allied Council for help. The Soviet Union was apparently unwilling to risk military confrontation with the Western powers, for the enhanced threat of intervention by the Western powers seems to have compelled the Soviet Union to take action to abort the putsch. According to an unpublicized account that Austrian leaders gave the British, shortly after the Austrians requested assistance a uniformed Russian appeared at the Chancellory and spoke to the leaders of the demonstration.[30] By the time the Allied Council met to consider the plea for help, the crowd was dispersing. The putsch had clearly failed.

It has never been proved that the Soviet government had a direct hand in inciting the rioters, but Soviet leaders certainly encouraged and supported them. It is also dificult to determine from the available historical evidence just how serious a threat the uprising posed to the Austrian government. What did matter for the purposes of the Austrian treaty negotiations was that the Western powers believed that the Soviet Union was behind the 1947 uprising. The events of 1947, moreover, were merely a portent of much more serious communist activities a few years later. By increasing tensions between the Western powers and the Soviet Union, this and subsequent incidents played a part in prolonging the negotiations and the four-power occupation of Austria.

EVENTS IN HUNGARY

A week after the riots, when the Austrian Treaty Commission began to meet in Vienna, the Americans and the British were determined to prevent the Soviet Union from gaining the economic leverage needed to turn an independent Austria into a communist client. The commission had been meeting for only three weeks when events in neighboring Hungary redoubled their determination.

Hungarian premier Ferenc Nagy had been watching developments in Austria with great concern and had realized, after the Moscow conference failed to resolve either the Austrian or the German problem, that "new Soviet pressures would follow which might perhaps sap our remaining strength."[31] At the end of May 1947, under pressure from Soviet-supported Hungarian Communists, Nagy was forced to resign and flee to Switzerland. Communist influence in Hungary grew steadily over the next five months. By the time the treaty commission adjourned in Vienna, the Communists had a strong hold on the Hungarian government and their main organizational rival, the Smallholders party, was nearly in ruins.

The historical links between Austria and Hungary were probably on the minds of the Allies throughout the treaty commission's negotiations, causing the Western powers to be still more reluctant to grant to the Soviet Union concessions that might put Austria in a situation similar to that of Hungary. But in the economic proposals that the Soviet Union presented during the commission meetings were even more blatant, contemporary links between Hungary and Austria. For example, an official in the British Foreign Office observed:

> The Russians have been careful to admit that the assets they acquire should operate under Austrian law subject to guarantees against expropriation and a provision for the export of profits. This sounds quite innocuous but, in the course of discussion, it has become apparent that what the Soviet really mean is nothing less than the export of gross profits and the produce of the factories into the bargain. This is indeed what is happening in Hungary. Moreover, the Russians have refused to discuss a time-limit for their demands. . . .[32]

From the Soviet perspective, the Russians had little desire to test the strength of the Hungarian Communists by withdrawing Red Army troops from Austria unless they acquired a larger degree of economic control through a treaty. In addition to the crucial fact that withdrawal might allow Western influence—and possibly even Western troops—to reach the borders of Hungary, the Soviet Union would lose its legal justification to maintain troops in Hungary, which was to protect its lines of communication with Austria. These considerations were unlikely to encourage the Soviet Union to modify its negotiating position.

THE MARSHALL PLAN

Meanwhile the United States began its own economic initiatives in Europe. In June 1947 General Marshall announced the massive program of American aid that came to be named for him. Austria was included as a recipient of U.S. aid. But Marshall Aid would not begin immediately, and so the United States and Austria on 25 June 1947 signed a separate aid agreement for deliveries of food, medical supplies, fuel, and other necessities.[33] The following month the United States announced that it would stop accepting reimbursement for occupation costs and indeed would refund all occupation payments made by the Austrians between April 1945 and June 1947. These two decisions, taken so quickly after the May riots in Vienna, were intended to help stabilize the economic situation in Austria.

The Soviets responded with a protest in the Allied Council that

U.S. aid was, among other things, impinging upon Austrian sovereignty. Nevertheless, the Austrian government took the courageous step of accepting the American invitation to participate in the Marshall Plan and to attend the July 1947 discussions in Paris, at which the actual European Recovery Program would be drafted. The Soviet Union and its satellites had already pulled out of the discussions, so the Austrians made their announcement in the full knowledge that it would be seen as a direct snub to the Soviet Union.[34]

In this turbulent atmosphere the agenda of the Austrian Treaty Commission was reduced to a meticulous examination of points of disagreement in the economic clauses. The commission was unable to resolve any of them. No significant conclusions had been reached when the commission officially ended its meetings on 11 October 1947.

By the autumn of 1947, in sum, public attention in Europe and the United States was beginning to focus on the differences emerging between the Soviet Union and the Western Allies. The economic difficulties in the Austrian treaty negotiations were one small facet of the growing East-West rift.

DISAGREEMENTS AMONG THE WESTERN POWERS

Quite apart from the publicized East-West disagreements, however, contradictions and controversies among the Western Allies were quietly occupying a great deal of the time and attention of diplomats, particularly in Washington and London.

One very contentious point was that legally Britain was still in a state of war with Austria. As British diplomats explained over and over to their American colleagues, in 1938 His Majesty's Government had recognized both de facto and de jure the German-Austrian Anschluss. In British eyes, therefore, Austria had been an integral part of Germany during the war and as such was fully involved in the German defeat, with all its consequences.[35] Unlike the Americans and the French, the British felt that the Moscow declaration of 1943 had been issued as a statement of intent; it did not affect the enemy status of Austria. Likewise the recognition of the Austrian government following the November 1945 elections had not terminated the state of war between the United Kingdom and Austria.[36] As far as Britain was concerned, the only way to end the state of war with Austria was to conclude a peace treaty.[37]

Of course, the British position of being "technically at war with

Austria" did not accord with the American and French positions. The Americans had never explicitly recognized the Anschluss, and recognition of the postwar Austrian government had sufficed to sever any connection between Germany and Austria as well as to give Austria a friendly status. The French subscribed to the American interpretation so the British stood alone. The U.S. State Department, acknowledging the British right to interpret their foreign policy as they wished, nonetheless made clear its dissatisfaction with the Foreign Office position. As far as the Americans were concerned, Britain's rigid legal interpretation posed a serious political threat to the Western negotiating position and a possible future detriment to Austria's economic position. Labeling Austria a belligerent lent weight to the case for Austrian war guilt—the Soviet Union could use it as a pretext for extracting more resources from the country.[38] In addition, naming Austria an enemy country was an unnecessary and unwelcome political blow to the Austrian government.[39] If legal principles were strictly observed, then Stalin could rightly claim that the Soviet Union alone among the great powers actually denounced the Anschluss. The Americans feared that the exposure of these legal technicalities could only be damaging to Austria and to Western interests.

It was for these political reasons, and under pressure from the Americans, that the British had gone along with the other powers in renaming the Austrian peace treaty a state treaty. But in the early months of 1947 the British government stuck to the position that a state of war with Austria still existed; debate continued between the State Department and the Foreign Office, as well as within the Foreign Office itself. Some British officials seemed to feel that a moral principle was involved by which Austria was at least technically an enemy. Only a treaty could provide final absolution and full restoration to a peaceful status. The requirement of legal consistency weighed less heavily on the Americans, leading British experts to believe that there was no legal case for following the American lead. Other British officials argued for more flexibility because the case of Austria was not historically unique. Early in the debate an official in the German Department of the Foreign Office wrote:

I do not know whether any help can be got from the not dissimilar cases of Abyssinia and Albania. But I have never quite understood wherein their position differed so essentially from that of Austria that, although before the war we recognised the incorporation of both in a country that was subsequently to become our enemy, nevertheless no difficulty seemed to result from their automatic reemergence as non-enemy and technically friendly states. Similarly, I understand that the treaties signed with Czechoslovakia and Poland after the 1914–1918 war were not "peace" treaties in the strict sense. None of this, of course, alters the fact that Austria is at present indubitably enemy territory and that we and the other three powers are in occupation of it by right of conquest. But it does seem to afford some precedent for taking, if it is deemed expedient, a step which would have the effect of putting an end to Austria's enemy status and transferring her to a relatively more favourable position. And I believe it would be expedient. . . .[40]

In the end political imperatives overcame legal consistencies. On 16 September 1947, without a treaty of any kind, the United Kingdom issued a statement officially renouncing the state of war with Austria.

Another disagreement among the Western allies originated in the 1947 American decision to stop accepting reimbursement for occupation costs from Austria. This decision removed a significant financial burden from Austria, and it also yielded the Austrian government a lump sum of $30 million in returned payments.[41] The British and the French were, of course, perfectly happy with American generosity toward Austria. A problem arose, however, when the Austrians, playing upon the sympathies of Western governments as well as upon international public opinion, began to pressure the other occupying powers to follow the American example.

Austrian appeals did not seem to bother the Russians. For the first few years after the American waiver the Soviet Union stuck to the argument that Austria was responsible for its participation in the war on the side of Germany; it was therefore obligated to pay for the occupation that was cleansing the country of fascism.[42] But the British and the French were more vulnerable to the appeals, especially when the U.S. government began to support the Austrian request.

The British and the French governments were squeezed between strong domestic pressures to cut back on foreign spending so that poor economic circumstances at home could be improved and negative international publicity for forcing the Austrian government to pay for an occupation it claimed it did not desire. In response to public and private petitions the British were time and again forced to state their regrets that the United Kingdom could not afford to meet the costs of the occupation of Austria in sterling.[43] The Austrians were receiving military protection from the presence of the Western powers, the British argued, and once the treaty came into effect, the Austrian defense budget might be just as large as the occupation payments. Meanwhile, the United Kingdom would try to economize, but the only alternative to Austrian payments was the early with-drawal of British troops from Austria.[44] The French offered similar arguments, adding that France had already reduced the number of its troops to a minimum, and unless the Austrians wanted the French to withdraw before the other occupying powers did, it was in Austria's vital interest to pay for the cost of the occupation.[45]

But as the years of negotiation and occupation passed, the Austrian government became ever more persistent in its requests for relief from occupation costs, and the Americans also pressured the other Western allies more steadily.[46] As a result, after 1947 every meeting of the Allied Council to agree on the quadripartite level of occupation costs to be levied during the year provoked a minor crisis among the three Western powers.

Crucial to the evolving relationship between the three Western powers was the precarious position of France. Despite its relative geographical proximity to Austria, France seemed unable to devote its primary attention to the Austrian problem. The French government moved from one domestic crisis to another throughout the years of negotiations for an Austrian treaty. The Fourth Republic was characterized by political and economic instability—periodic strikes, ministerial resignations, changes of government, and constitutional crises. The French delegates to the Austrian treaty negotiations had no firm base on which to rest an Austrian policy; apart from a few initiatives, French policy tended to be reactive. Often trying to maintain the appearance of an objective intermediary between the other two Western powers and the Soviet Union, France nonetheless tended to follow the lead of the United States and the United Kingdom when it came to votes on substantive issues.

Perhaps more important, French defense policy became increasingly oriented after the war to staving off the imminent collapse of the French colonial system. As a result, France had few remaining resources to devote to missions of less relative importance, such as the occupation of the French zone of Austria. As early as June 1947 the governor of the French zone complained of the situation to his British colleague:

"Monsieur Voizard said that he was hampered . . . by the difficulty of keeping his staff and by the reduction in the number of the French forces. He did not think that in the Zone and Vienna there were many more than 6000 French troops in all. As for his own staff the Ministry of War found it difficult to spare serving officers and they were constantly posting those whom he had elsewhere to meet the demands of North Africa, Madagascar, Indo-China, etc."[47]

Conflicts in French colonial areas, particularly in Indo-China, intensified. As each year of the occupation of Austria passed, so the interests, foreign policy, and resources of France were yet further diverted from the problem of Austria.

THE LONDON CONFERENCE OF FOREIGN MINISTERS

The foreign ministers' deputies for Austria convened in London in November 1947 and continued to meet during the fifth session of the Council of Foreign Ministers. The main stumbling block in the London meeting was, as always, fundamental disagreement over the meaning of "German assets." Progress was impossible as long as the representatives could not decide exactly what they were negotiating. In the early days of the London foreign ministers' meeting, for example, Molotov made the ostensibly generous offer to accept 10 percent less than the amount he had originally demanded. Bevin wryly retorted that it would be rather difficult for the council to calculate 10 percent of an unknown quantity.[48]

To solve the dilemma, the French raised a suggestion that they had unsuccessfully brought before the Austrian Treaty Commission a few months earlier. The foreign ministers, instead of arguing over the definition of the term, should try to enumerate what specific Austrian resources the Russians would require. German assets would be divided into two groups: first, oil resources and shipping, of which the Soviet Union would receive a set percentage of production, and second, other German assets in eastern Austria, for which the Soviet government would receive a lump-sum payment from the Austrian government. The French suggestion also specified the business interests and percentage of production involved.[49]

The French proposal appealed to the British and the American foreign ministers, but Molotov refused to consider it a basis for negotiation. U.S. secretary of state Marshall became exasperated by the Soviet position and asked Molotov just how he proposed to reconcile the differences between the Soviet and American positions. Molotov once more repeated his familiar refrain about the legality under the Potsdam agreement of Soviet claims to German assets in Austria.

Recognizing that the foreign ministers' conference had reached an impasse with regard to an Austrian treaty and was in even sharper discord over the future of Germany, Secretary of State Marshall moved to adjourn the council on 15 December 1947. British foreign minister Bevin supported the motion but asked his colleagues whether the Austrian treaty might be sent again to the deputies; his request was approved without opposition.[50] Thus the conference adjourned without evidence of progress toward a treaty.

The Western Allies were understandably frustrated by Soviet intransigence at the London conference, but regardless of the impression they conveyed publicly, the Americans and the British were not at all surprised by the Soviet position. Before the conference even opened, British Foreign Office officials had coached Secretary of State Bevin on the best tactics and timing he could use to refer the treaty to the deputies when the foreign ministers reached a deadlock.[51] In the event, that is exactly what he did. In consultations before the conference American and British diplomats considered the possibility of proposing troop withdrawals without a treaty, provided that a quadripartite guarantee of Austria's borders could be agreed first.[52] The Western delegates may have been hoping for an Austrian treaty at the London conference, but they were not really expecting one.

Most interesting, the Austrians did not necessarily want a treaty in late 1947—at least not at an exorbitant Soviet price. The Austrian leaders wanted the public appearance of progress toward a treaty, but when it came to the actual signing of a burdensome agreement they were far less enthusiastic. Indeed, a month before the opening of the London conference the Austrian president quietly communicated to the Western powers his unwillingness to accept an unsatisfactory treaty. In a meeting with the British political representative in Vienna, President Renner stated calmly but firmly that if the four powers signed a treaty granting the Russians what they demanded, the Austrian government would not abide by it. After the meeting the British political representative in Vienna, W. H. B. Mack, reported Renner's position to Ernest Bevin:

> The Austrian Government could not agree to such a treaty and would prefer the occupation to continue indefinitely. The cost of the occupation to Austria would be far less than the assets which the Russians were claiming. I asked Dr. Renner why he supposed that the three Western Powers would agree to continue to maintain troops in Austria if the Austrian Government rejected a treaty which they had approved and recommended to the Austrian Government for acceptance. Dr. Renner replied that Austria was of such importance that the Western Powers could not afford to walk out and leave the Russians in sole possession of the field.

The British representative further informed the foreign secretary that he believed that these views were not exceptional in Austria but were held by the majority in the Socialist and People's parties.[53] The views of the Austrian leaders in 1947, contrary to popular belief and contemporary accounts, may have added to the Western powers' incentives to hold out for a treaty more favorable to Austria rather than to the pressure to sign a treaty at any cost.

As for the Soviet Union, it had few incentives to sign an Austrian treaty at the end of 1947, and events developing outside the negotiations provided ample reason to delay. As the London conference opened, France was just emerging from a series of general strikes led by the French Communists and (it was believed by the Western delegates as well as the Austrians) instigated by the Cominform.[54] During the conference the French government underwent a constitutional crisis brought on by the November election of a national assembly consisting of nearly equal numbers of Communists and members of the Mouvement Républicain Populaire. Meanwhile, in the United States the Congress was debating an Interim Aid Bill that could provide an additional $600 million in emergency aid for Austria, Italy, China, and France. In Soviet eyes the economic and political status of Europe was still unclear. The traditional centers of influence in Europe had been devastated by the war and imminent American economic influence was vying with potential Soviet political influence to determine the postwar configuration of the continent. In particular, the international position of both Austria and Germany was in the balance. As has been the case more than once in Soviet foreign policy, uncertainty begat paralysis in the Soviet negotiating position: Stalin and Molotov were resolved not to risk giving up what might later prove useful in the contest over Europe unless the economic advantages of signing a treaty for Austria were overwhelming.

Halfway through the London conference Bevin confided to Marshall that he believed the Russians wanted to break off discussions in order to avoid signing any treaty on Austria; therefore, Bevin believed, the Western powers should deprive the Soviet Union of the opportunity to do so.[55] When Molotov subsequently proved completely inflexible in the negotiations, it was Marshall who actually proposed the adjournment and Bevin seconded it. The negotiations ended, but the wider contest continued: on 15 December, the day the London conference adjourned, Congress passed the Interim Aid Bill.

The London conference made no real progress toward an Austrian treaty, but it did produce one unanticipated sign of hope for future progress. As so often in the course of the negotiations, the Soviet

Union did not want to exclude the possibility of an economic agreement over Austria. At the closing session of the London conference Molotov, to the surprise of the other foreign ministers, suddenly reversed his earlier position. He announced that the Soviet Union would be willing to discuss the general objective of the French proposal and would present its own counterproposal as well.[56] Adjournment having already been proposed, the foreign ministers did not open debate on this unexpected proposition but turned the matter over to their deputies.

THE 1948 LONDON DEPUTIES' SESSIONS

With the French and Soviet proposals as a basis for compromise, the deputies convened in London on 20 February 1948. Their meetings lasted for three months, with some encouraging signs of progress. For the first time the Soviet Union showed a willingness to bargain over the specific economic assets it would require of Austria. By May 1948 both the Soviet Union and the Western powers had made concessions on specific items, and the gap between the opposing positions on German assets had been narrowed significantly. Just when it appeared that there might be grounds for a treaty, however, the Soviet delegation raised the question of Yugoslavia's claims for reparations and territory, and the 1948 London deputies' session adjourned in failure.

The Western powers found Soviet mention of Yugoslav reparation claims ludicrous. It was difficult enough to agree to Soviet claims to "German external assets" existing in Austria for regardless of who made them, claims to reparations from Austria itself had been specifically prohibited by the Potsdam agreement. More to the point, Austria had technically never been at war with Yugoslavia, so there was no legal basis for claiming war damages. As for territorial demands, the Western powers had long ago made it clear that they would not sign a treaty that altered Austria's 1937 borders. The Western powers had hoped that bilateral agreements between the two countries could accommodate Yugoslavia's concern over minorities in Austria's southeastern territory after the four powers had withdrawn from Austria.[57] The Soviet Union's stubborn support for the Yugoslav position seemed, in light of the clarity and firmness of the Western position, deliberately calculated to put off agreement on a treaty.

The firm Soviet backing of the Yugoslavs surprised the Western powers. In the London deputies meetings of February and March

1948 the Russians had shown some reservations about Yugoslav claims. Austrian foreign minister Karl Gruber reported: "[The Yugoslav delegate's] remarks were so violent that a Russian diplomat openly stared at him and tapped his forehead. This tiny gesture made us [the Austrians] feel for the first time that things were not going so smoothly between Russia and [Y]ugoslavia as we had hitherto assumed."[58] The Americans had been skeptical of Soviet support for Yugoslavia for at least a year, ever since the Moscow conference in March 1947. Even as the delegates met during 1947 and 1948, sparks were flying between Moscow and Belgrade. Why, the Western delegates wondered, were the Russians suddenly so moved by the merit of Yugoslav claims? Perhaps the enthusiastic show of loyalty was a last-ditch effort to avoid a split with the Yugoslavs, but it is not likely. Later, as discussed below, it was revealed that Stalin had privately informed the Yugoslavs during the 1947 Moscow conference that he intended to drop their claims, and indeed when he did eventually decide that it was in the Soviet interest to conclude a treaty, Yugoslavia was abruptly abandoned.

In fact, the reason for the Soviet change of attitude had very little to do with Yugoslavia. In April 1948, just before the talks between the deputies broke down, Austria became a member of the Organization for European Economic Cooperation (OEEC), a permanent body created to facilitate the distribution of Marshall Aid funds. Some analysts have argued that Russia needed the state treaty in 1948 in order to forestall Austria's participation in the Marshall Plan.[59] In fact, precisely the opposite is true: the treaty's reparations payments would have further impoverished Austria and increased its need for Western aid. Indeed, the massive influx of European Recovery Program money which began just after the Austrian treaty talks adjourned, most likely convinced the Soviet leaders that the participation of an independent, united Austria in the Marshall Plan would guarantee Austria's complete integration into the Western economic system and would in all likelihood prompt its political and military integration as well.

Stalin found Austria's situation particularly sensitive: it was the only country partially occupied by the Soviet Union to be participating in the Marshall Plan.[60] As such, it was located in what was for the Soviets an extremely disadvantageous place. Five days after the London deputies session began, the Soviet Union helped to stage a communist coup in neighboring Czechoslovakia; over the months the deputies were meeting, a drastic purge was ridding the country of its Western democratic government and converting Czechoslovakia into a people's democracy. Austria, a Western state receiving Western money, was a bad influence on the new Soviet satellites across the border, Hungary and Czechoslovakia, not to mention the influence of unruly Yugoslavia to the south.

Besides, in 1948 Stalin still entertained some hope of converting Austria into a communist state, and he certainly did not want to hand Austria over to the West. During the first year of Marshall Aid, Austria received more money per capita than any other country.[61] In the face of so many American dollars only the Russian presence in eastern Austria could prevent the country from joining the Western camp and threatening the freshly consolidated Soviet "protective zone." Stalin therefore used the Yugoslav issue deliberately to delay an Austrian treaty.

There is no question that the ostensible cause of the breakdown of the London deputies' talks was the Soviet position with regard to Yugoslavia's territorial claims. That was the explanation which the newspapers publicized and the Western public quite justifiably believed. However, some evidence exists to suggest that the Soviet Union had not intended to force the actual breakdown of the talks, only to use the Yugoslav issue to delay negotiations indefinitely. The Soviet Union apparently did not expect the strength of the Western reaction and the breaking off of the talks. The British deputy, James Marjoribanks, was the one who actually precipitated the adjournment, by pressing the Soviet representative as to whether the Soviet Union envisioned the cession of any Austrian territory to the Yugoslavs. When the Soviet delegate said "yes," the three Western powers declared that they could not negotiate over Austria's frontiers, and the meeting adjourned sine die.[62]

Stalin had good reasons in 1948, as already mentioned, to put off the signing of the Austrian treaty. More interesting, perhaps, is the evidence behind the transcript of the negotiations that the Western powers had second thoughts about signing a treaty as well.

Misgivings of the Western Powers and the Austrians

The United States, leader of the Western powers, always maintained its outward support for all efforts to get a treaty. However, significant portions of the American bureaucracy opposed the treaty and tried to stall the talks. In 1948 and 1949, particularly, a few voices of relief could be heard amidst the general chorus of Western disappointment whenever the treaty negotiations broke down.

[63]

The loudest voice was that of Lt. Gen. Geoffrey Keyes, commander of U.S. forces in Austria. In February 1948, while the London discussions were in progress and agreement on a treaty seemed possible, the general met with the American delegation. He expressed serious doubts about the wisdom of signing a treaty that would require Western withdrawal when the Austrian economy was still in a shambles and when no Austrian Army existed to resist possible Soviet aggression. His worries were undoubtedly heightened by the abrupt communist takeover that month in Czechoslovakia, a shock to the West and an ominous precedent for Austria. In a top-secret message to Washington the U.S. delegation to London requested clear instructions regarding the desirability, from a strategic viewpoint, of concluding an Austrian treaty.[63] The secretary of state, Dean Acheson, forwarded the request to the secretary of defense, Louis Johnson, and the Joint Chiefs of Staff commissioned a study to determine the military implications of a treaty.

Completed in March 1948, the report to the Joint Chiefs by the Joint Strategic Survey Committee came out while the London negotiations were still proceeding. Noting that the current draft treaty called for the evacuation of Austria within ninety days, the study pointed out that an indigenous army could never be organized, trained, and equipped in such a short time. An unprotected Austria would be highly vulnerable to Soviet attack. Moreover, "once these forces were withdrawn, even if hostilities did not develop, it would require a major effort to reoccupy this area, an effort which the Western Powers would not have the immediate capability to undertake successfully. Therefore, to withdraw from Austria without provision being made for her continued security would obviously create a military vacuum which the U.S.S.R. could readily fill."[64] If it were absolutely necessary for other than strategic reasons to sign the treaty, the Western powers must at least extend the period of withdrawal and obtain Soviet agreement for the Austrians to begin organizing an army.

The misgivings of the Defense Department must have had some influence upon the American negotiators in London. In the winter of 1948 it was not in U.S. strategic interests, as articulated by the military, immediately to conclude a treaty. The direct cause of the breakdown of the London deputies' conference was, without doubt, Soviet obstinacy with regard to Yugoslav claims; there is room for speculation, however, about whether the Western powers helped provoke Soviet intransigence.[65] Austrian foreign minister Gruber claimed that the British delegate, Marjoribanks, told him in advance that he had instructions to break up the conference if the Soviet government did not give a favorable answer on the frontier question.[66] Such an explanation does indeed fit with subsequent Western policy. Following the report to the Joint Chiefs of Staff, the United States began the clandestine assembly of the equipment necessary for a gendarmerie regiment in Austria.[67] By December 1948 an active program in the Western zone was forming police batallions and units of a future Austrian army. And while all this activity was going on, the negotiations were suspended.[68]

More interesting yet is evidence that even the Austrians, who appeared the disappointed victims of the great-power game and argued publicly that all they wanted was a treaty, may have secretly applauded the breakdown of the London negotiations. In his memoirs, first published in Vienna in October 1953, Austrian foreign minister Gruber wrote of the "terrible dilemma" that the British delegate's alleged plans to close the negotiations posed for the Austrians. They were confronted with two possibilities, "either to assume responsibility for the violation of our frontiers or to risk the postponement of the conference."[69] But British Foreign Office documents indicate that Gruber at the time may not have been nearly as unhappy about the British policy as he would have had his countrymen believe.

> I asked Dr. Gruber whether he had any criticism of the way in which Mr. Marjoribanks had broken off the treaty negotiations. He said on the contrary that the timing had been quite admirable and that it had been fully concerted with himself and with the Austrian experts. His only complaint was that not nearly enough publicity had been given to the reasons for the rupture and we had missed an admirable chance of putting the Russians "on the spot." He said that, in his opinion, the sudden breakdown of negotiations had been a very painful surprise to the Soviets, whose plan, he thought, was to keep the negotiations ticking over for as long as possible (meanwhile exploiting their position as an Occupying Power particularly in the economic sphere) but on no account to have a treaty this year. . . .[70]

Nor was this an isolated statement. Several weeks after the London negotiations broke down, Gruber was reportedly telling the British representatives in Vienna "that there was no hurry about a treaty but that there must be activity of some kind or people would despair." He stressed the communist threat in the elections to be held the following year and warned that "[e]ven a small Communist gain would be fatal."[71] The Austrian foreign minister seemed to imply that in 1948 protection from the communist threat was a higher priority than completion of a treaty; and the behavior of the Western powers in the negotiations certainly reflected such a view.

Although they expressed their disappointment publicly, Austrian leaders did indeed have reason to be relieved in 1948 when the treaty negotiations broke down. A treaty with enormous reparations payments for the Soviet Union or territorial concessions for Yugoslavia would have threatened the survival of the Austrian government after the withdrawal of the occupying powers. In 1948 the Western powers understood this vulnerability; it seems that the Soviet Union recognized it also. When a satisfactory treaty protecting Austria's sovereignty appeared impossible to attain, the Western powers, with the full support of the Austrian foreign minister, deliberately broke off the negotiations. Nonetheless, it must be emphasized that although the British proved themselves the more skillful tacticians in the negotiations, it was the Soviet support for Yugoslav territorial claims which prevented a satisfactory treaty and was thus ultimately responsible for the breakdown of the talks.

From a Soviet perspective, the breakdown of the negotiations had forestalled Austria's complete integration into the Western economic system, but the magnetic pull of Marshall Aid funds for Austria continued. More alarming was the influence of Western economic power in Germany, where it had begun to creep across the occupation lines. In June 1948, only a few weeks after the Austrian negotiations in London ended in failure, the Soviet Union instituted a blockade of the city of Berlin. The Russians could not compete with the attraction of American wealth, and thus they used their best resource—military power—to turn Eastern Europe into a fortress.

Subsequent events proved that Stalin had not yet given up hope of easing Austria into that fortress. But with the failure of the communist putsch of May 1947, the best policy seemed to be continued occupation of Austria, taking advantage of the revenues earned in eastern Austria from factories under Soviet management, negotiations when necessary to placate Austrian and international public opinion, and avoidance of a treaty settlement except on terms so advantageous to the Soviet Union as to be more attractive than the status quo.

Thus the process continued. Negotiations stalled, stopped, and started again, always apparently because of Russian intransigence but usually because of incidents outside the negotiating room and outside Austria. International attention waned, leaving the frustrated negotiators with a sense of isolation and unimportance. At one point in the London negotiations of 1948 the representatives had even been

[66]

forced out of their meeting place, Lancaster House, to make room for what was considered a much more important conference—the inaugural session of the newly founded Brussels Union. At times the Austrians felt that even the Americans were not taking the discussions quite seriously enough. In 1948, when the Austrian foreign minister expressed relief that a career diplomat had been appointed to head the American delegation, he was jokingly told: "Our first Deputy was a general, then we had a banker. After that we looked for a bishop but as we couldn't find one, we had to fall back on a diplomat."[72]

After the London deputies' conference of 1948 failed, the problem of Austria was completely submerged in a tidal wave of East-West events. Negotiations were suspended for the remainder of the year, while the breakdown of four-power control in Germany and the imposition of the Berlin blockade, as well as the public expulsion of Yugoslavia from the Cominform, increased the harshness of the Cold War and dimmed the prospects for an Austrian treaty.

[3]

The Paris Initiative, 1949

The Western powers came to believe before 1949 that even if they made concessions, the Soviet Union would not agree to a reasonable treaty. In 1947 the only treaty the Soviet Union wished to sign levied such uncompromising, draconian economic penalties on Austria that the Western powers did not consider it reasonable. In 1948, when on the basis of the French proposal both sides made compromises and for a while a treaty seemed possible, the Soviet Union seized upon Yugoslav border claims to disrupt talks. Quite apart from the Western powers' reservations concerning the treaty, it seemed that whenever progress was being made and a compromise treaty taking shape, the Soviet Union would use some extraneous argument to break down the negotiations.

During the first two years of the negotiations it seemed obvious to the Western powers that Stalin did not want a treaty unless it made of Austria another Soviet vassal state. The events surrounding the negotiations—the coups in Eastern Europe, the foibles of four-power control in Germany, the problems of Soviet-Yugoslav relations—focused Stalin's attention on the consolidation of his European empire, encouraging him to grasp tightly to every inch of European territory gained in the war. Indeed, at times it seemed as if the Soviet Union did not really have an Austrian policy, in the positive sense that Western diplomats used the word, but only a negative idea of what it did not want to concede.[1]

The Western powers themselves showed signs of ambivalence about signing a treaty before 1949. They feared that the unarmed, destitute state would be easy prey to a communist coup—whether organized from within Austria or orchestrated from the Kremlin. The Western powers needed time to help Austria regain its economic footing and become a less vulnerable target for the Soviet threat.

Officially, everyone in the West wanted a treaty; secretly, some feared that they might actually get one.

Even the Austrian government had qualms about a treaty. As each of its neighbors to the east succumbed to a communist takeover, the Austrian government quite naturally imagined a similar fate. It did not relish the prospect of facing Soviet pressures without tangible Western support.

These conditions left little realistic chance for an Austrian treaty during the first two years of negotiations. During 1949 a change in Soviet foreign policy appeared to change matters. The first promise of a treaty for Austria, albeit on terms that favored the Soviet Union, came between June and November 1949. This fleeting opportunity and the Western response to it reveal a great deal about the motivations of the Soviet Union and the relations between the Western powers. With the exception of 1955, when the treaty was actually signed, 1949 was the most important year of negotiations for an Austrian state treaty.

When the year began, the talks were still suspended; no date for resumption had been set. Throughout the latter half of 1948 the great powers had been preoccupied with the Berlin blockade and the international atmosphere had not been conducive to talks on Austria. More specifically, the negotiations had been stultified by Soviet support of Yugoslav territorial claims. In January 1949, however, clear evidence of a split between Tito and Stalin led to speculation in the West that the Soviet Union might drop the Yugoslav cause. As the year opened, moreover, the Kremlin launched a "peace offensive" in the Soviet press, urging worldwide conciliation in glowing terms.

Western diplomats, although skeptical of Soviet motives, felt that Austria might offer the Soviet Union a chance to prove its peaceful intent.[2] When the Austrians suggested that talks might restart in early 1949, therefore, the Western powers agreed. With the concurrence of the Soviet Union, talks between deputy foreign ministers were scheduled for London in February 1949.

Western policy toward Austria had evolved over the eight months the talks were suspended. In particular, the U.S. Department of State had produced a report, "The Austrian Treaty in the Council of Foreign Ministers," which discussed in straightforward terms U.S. policy toward an Austrian state treaty. While emphasizing that "[o]ur primary objective in an Austrian treaty should be [a] viable, independent state free from alien domination," the report concluded that for the sake of a stable and economically viable Austria, an early treaty should be sought. Labeled NSC 38, it was submitted to the National

Security Council on 8 December 1948. NSC 38, according to the cover letter, was intended to clarify and explain U.S. policy in the hope "... that the report will be useful to our military and diplomatic representatives both abroad and in Washington."[3]

The American delegate to the London talks, Samuel Reber, certainly found NSC 38 useful and even encouraging. In a meeting just before the talks began Reber, according to his British colleagues, reported:

> The U.S. Government had now come definitely to the view which they understood had been ours all along, but as to which they themselves had been undecided, that an Austrian treaty was desirable. It was therefore his clear instruction to work for one. Mr. Reber thought that there still might be some differences of emphasis as between U.K. and U.S. views on the danger on the one hand of indefinitely prolonging the occupation of Austria and on the other hand the risk of an Allied withdrawal. But the U.S. Government had now cleared up their mind on the principal question.[4]

Thus in January 1949 members of the State Department were optimistic about the prospects for a quick treaty and confident of a clear American policy to seek one.

MEETINGS OF THE DEPUTIES RESUME

The deputy foreign ministers' talks opened on 9 February 1949, with thirty-five articles agreed and eighteen outstanding.[5] Because of progress made the previous year toward a settlement of the question of German assets (Article 35), the focus shifted from Soviet economic claims to Yugoslav claims.[6] To the disappointment of the Western powers, however, the Soviet Union did not alter its position; the discussions floundered whenever the sanctity of Austria's prewar frontiers (Article 5) or the renunciation of reparations from Austria (Article 34) were examined.[7]

Still, the talks continued for fifty-three meetings, with the three Western powers holding out hope that the Soviet delegate would receive new instructions from the Kremlin. At one point the Yugoslav delegation modified its demand from a border change to an autonomous area for the Carinthian Slovenes. The Western delegates considered the shift a favorable sign; nonetheless, the Soviet position of unconditional support remained unchanged. By April the British deputy, James Marjoribanks, was writing that his Soviet counterpart, Georgi Zarubin, seemed embarrassed that he had no new instructions.[8]

Finally, the three Western delegates decided to move for an adjournment. The discussions were suspended from 6 to 10 May, to allow the Soviet delegate one last chance to receive new instructions from Moscow. When nothing happened on 10 May, the talks were formally adjourned until the Council of Foreign Ministers met in late June. After the adjournment American deputy Reber informed the State Department that he was convinced that the Soviet delegate was once again using the Yugoslav claims to prevent conclusion of a treaty.[9]

DEVELOPMENTS IN WESTERN DEFENSE

There was indeed a very important reason why the Soviet Union might have considered spring 1949 an inopportune time for an Austrian treaty. On 4 April, in Washington, the foreign ministers of twelve Western nations signed the North Atlantic Treaty. The pact was designed to provide mutual assistance against aggression; as such, it strengthened the Western position in the treaty negotiations. It ensured that Soviet military action against not only the actual territories of the signatory nations but also "the occupation forces of any party in Europe" would be treated as an action against all of them.[10] The likelihood that Stalin would try to force political change in Austria and thereby risk a confrontation with the Western powers was significantly reduced.[11]

At about the same time plans were moving forward in the West to equip a special Austrian gendarmerie force. Each of the Western powers had already started to train and equip Austrian police within its zone and to make preliminary arrangements for an Austrian army.[12] In early February 1949 the American government decided to make available from stocks in Germany the military equipment necessary for a gendarmerie regiment.[13] This special force was to deal with threats to the Austrian government, preclude the need for direct Western involvement, and eventually form the nucleus of a national army. In February the commander of U.S. forces in Austria, General Keyes, was directed by Washington to discuss the possible issue of American equipment first with the Western Allies, then with the Austrians.[14]

The British and the French quickly gave preliminary approval to the plan, and the Austrians also seemed favorably disposed, so the

United States began to stockpile equipment in Austria.[15] Gendarmerie headquarters was to be in the U.S. zone, with one batallion in the French zone and one in the British zone.[16] But in late March the French suddenly expressed misgivings, arguing that the Soviet Union might use evidence of a military buildup as an excuse to take countermeasures in the Soviet zone. To minimize this possibility, the three Western powers agreed to collect no heavy equipment for the gendarmerie force. The Austrians decided that they would man the force only with current members of the gendarmerie, not with new recruits.[17] By June most of the equipment had been assembled in Austria but, pending final approval by the three Western governments and a definite request from the Austrian government, it had not yet been issued.[18]

Evidently Soviet leaders knew that military equipment was being collected in western Austria for the gendarmerie. It cannot have been a tremendous surprise to them. On 8 May 1947, directly after the attempted coup, Austrian chancellor Figl had written to the Allied Council stressing the urgent need for improved police forces.[19] Quadripartite agreement on action proved impossible to reach. In March 1949 reports of a military buildup in Austria began appearing in the Soviet press.[20] In April the Soviets even accused the Western powers of delaying the treaty talks to allow the United States time to turn the western zones of Austria into a U.S. military base.[21] Any remaining doubts that the Soviet Union knew about the program were removed on 26 April, when the Soviet representative to the Military Directorate of the Allied Council urged the prohibition of militarized training in Austrian gendarmerie schools. Still, there was no real East-West confrontation; the Western powers did not respond to the charges and (to their surprise) the Soviet delegate did not insist that the charges be referred to the full Allied Council.[22]

The Western powers had obviously supplied the Soviet Union with incentives to stall during the deputy ministers' meetings in the spring of 1949. But events occurring inside the Soviet Union also help to explain the delay of new instructions for the Soviet delegate.

CHANGES IN THE SOVIET POLITBURO

In the weeks before the Paris Conference of Foreign Ministers opened, Stalin apparently decided that it was time for a change in Soviet foreign policy. The failure of the Berlin blockade was an embarrassment, and Tito's now widely known heresy was intolerable. In

March 1949, therefore, he shook up the Politburo. Veteran foreign minister Molotov was among those who fell from grace—he remained a member of the Politburo and Council of Ministers, but he lost his position as foreign minister and his wife was exiled. He would not regain the foreign minister's post until after Stalin's death.[23]

Tired of struggling with "old lead bottom" Molotov, the Western powers considered this Politburo shuffle a positive sign. They hoped that Soviet policy toward Austria might change at the Paris conference and that revised Soviet negotiating instructions, which all four deputies to the treaty negotiations had anticipated for months, might be carried out personally by the new Soviet foreign minister, Andrei Vyshinsky.[24]

AN AUSTRIAN PROPOSAL

In the meantime Austrian foreign minister Gruber was becoming impatient. Between the May suspension of the deputies' talks and the June discussion of Austria at the Paris Conference of Foreign Ministers, Gruber began publicly intimating that the West should change tactics. He met British foreign secretary Bevin on 7 June 1949 to advance an idea that he had been unofficially suggesting to Western delegates for some time.[25]

Karl Gruber, convinced that the Soviet Union would not agree to a treaty soon, wanted the Western powers to take action without a treaty. After publicly blaming the Soviet Union for the delay, the three Western powers should propose that the Austrian government be allowed to create its own security force and then insist that all four powers withdraw eight months after that force had been established. The draft treaty was not a particularly happy economic prospect in Austrian eyes anyway—except as it might rid the country of Soviet occupation—and so Gruber envisioned his proposal as a means to get a quick Soviet withdrawal without great penalty. Treaty negotiations could then continue. As in 1948, therefore, the Austrian foreign minister was arguing that the top priority was not the treaty itself but rather the establishment of an Austrian army and the evacuation of the occupied powers. According to this reasoning, a country with an elected government need not and should not endure military occupation.

Ernest Bevin asked whether the proposal might not lead to East-West partition, but the Austrian diplomat seemed convinced that the national government with a national armed force could maintain the integrity of the country. Bevin also mentioned the German assets problem, but Gruber responded that the terms of settlement were not as important as the advantages that would be gained from immediate evacuation. Bevin's subordinates sympathized with Gruber's motives, but they worried that the Soviet Union would not withdraw from Austria until its economic claims had been assured and until a general European settlement had been reached. Still, there was a surprising amount of feeling within the Foreign Office that if dead-lock on the treaty continued, the Austrian proposal might be worth advancing. Shortly thereafter, however, new developments in the foreign ministers' conference superseded Gruber's suggestions.

The Paris Conference of Foreign Ministers

The Paris Conference of Foreign Ministers met from 23 May to 20 June, but the Austrian question was not discussed until 12 June 1949. Aware of the vitriolic relations between Belgrade and Moscow, the Western powers decided to test Soviet loyalty to the Yugoslavs. Largely on American initiative, they offered a compromise on the first day of the Austrian discussions: if the Soviet Union would stop sup-porting the Yugoslav claims, the Western powers would agree to substantial satisfaction of Soviet economic demands.[26] Foreign Minis-ter Vyshinsky abruptly abandoned Yugoslav claims and agreed that Austrian property inside Yugoslavia would satisfy Yugoslav repara-tions claims. In return the Western powers agreed to a lump-sum payment by Austria of $150 million for German assets, accepted the Soviet claim to 60 percent of the oil exploration areas of Austria, and granted the Soviet Union all the former property of the Danube Ship-ping Company in eastern Austria.[27] The issue that had stymied the foreign ministers' deputies for months was thus resolved within a few hours.

At the Paris conference the Soviet Union abruptly forsook the Yugoslavs in return for economic gains. Soviet leaders publicly claim-ed that the British and the Yugoslavs had been secretly negotiating over Yugoslav claims, clandestinely undermining the Soviet posi-tion—an allegation that officials in the British Foreign Office privately admitted was true.[28] Stalin's respresentatives argued that they had been sincere in their support for the Yugoslav cause but had been betrayed by Tito's deceitfulness.

The Yugoslavs had another, more interesting interpretation of the events of the previous two years which a member of the Yugoslav delegation to the treaty talks disclosed to the British Foreign Office. During the Moscow Conference of Foreign Ministers the Yugoslav delegation was summoned to the Kremlim and informed that the Soviet Union intended to reject Yugoslav claims in order to reach an agreement on the treaty. To avoid the appearance of a breach between the two countries, the Soviets asked the Yugoslavs to retract their claims and give the Soviet Union a modified Yugoslav position within forty-eight hours.

With this ultimatum, the Yugoslav delegation hurriedly consulted Belgrade and was instructed to reduce demands essentially to the compromise position that the four powers reached at the Paris conference in 1949. Hastening to meet the forty-eight-hour time limit, the Yugoslav delegate attempted to deliver his government's message in person to Molotov or Vyshinsky or Gousev, the Soviet deputy for the Moscow conference. He was curtly informed that this was impossible, and eventually the Yugoslav emissary was forced to deliver the proposal to a low-level minion in the Soviet Foreign Ministry. As he turned over the proposal, however, the irritated Yugoslav shrewdly insisted that the Soviet official give him a written receipt, acknowledging both that he had received the document and that it was a Soviet request which had prompted its delivery.

The Yugoslav government heard no more about the message until two years later, at the Paris conference. There Vyshinsky reduced the claims to the fallback position that the Yugoslavs had long ago conceded. In return the Soviet Union received hefty economic compensation from the Western powers on behalf of Austria. Later, when the Soviet government publicly asserted that Yugoslav demands had been dropped because of the Yugoslav government's treacherous secret dealings, the Yugoslav Foreign Ministry produced the receipt as proof that the claims had been reduced two years before, at explicit Soviet demand. The Yugoslav press reportedly publicized the document, but nothing came of it. According to the Yugoslav interpretation of events, therefore, the Soviet Union had been biding its time for two years to reap maximum economic benefits from a change of policy that the Soviet government had already compelled the Belgrade regime to make.[29]

At the end of the Paris conference the foreign ministers issued a communiqué describing the compromise on Yugoslav claims and German assets. They directed their deputies to reach agreement on the treaty as a whole by 1 September 1949. Certainly there were promising signs from Austria that the Soviets intended to sign a treaty by that date. In June the Soviet high commissioner, General

Tikhomirov, stopped the Soviet bank in Vienna from issuing further credits, thereby implying that he expected the occupation to end soon. Likewise, Soviet-run factories in Austria stopped accepting orders that would require more than a few months to fulfill.[30] Meanwhile the deputy foreign ministers, to comply with their instructions, decided to begin meeting on 1 July 1949 in London. Hopes in Austria were high that the Soviet Union was planning to sign a treaty during the London deputies' session.

U.S. POLICY CONSENSUS DISSOLVES

In the meantime, however, developments within the United States were taking a very different course. The Department of State's December 1948 policy report on the treaty negotiations, NSC 38, and subsequent policy bulletins had not been well received at the Department of Defense. Defense had considerable reservations about the wisdom of a quick settlement on State's terms. For months the question of what U.S. policy should be wandered the corridors of the American bureaucracy, with Pentagon policy makers taking increasing exception to the optimistic program of Foggy Bottom diplomats.

The Paris meeting of the foreign ministers prompted Secretary of Defense Louis Johnson to submit an opposing report on Austria to the National Security Council. Completed during the Paris negotiations, NSC 38/1 took exception to NSC 38 and faithfully echoed the conclusions of the Joint Chiefs of Staff report of March 1948. Dated 16 June 1949, NSC 38/1 was published in the midst of Secretary of State Dean Acheson's negotiations over Austria (12–20 June). Clearly the Defense Department was concerned that Acheson was making compromises that might not be compatible with U.S. security interests. "[T]his appears to be a situation in which the integration of foreign and military policies is required[,] for our military security interests as well as the conduct of political relations with the Austrian Government are involved," Defense Secretary Johnson wrote. He urged that the State Department be requested to submit its views on future U.S. policy with respect to Austria, taking greater account of the military aspects of the situation there.[31]

The heart of Johnson's argument was contained in his 14 June letter to Acheson, a copy of which was attached to NSC 38/1:

[I]t is apparent that, if a treaty is arranged at the current meeting of the Council of Foreign Ministers, it will be impossible for Austria to have

reasonably adequate security forces prior to the withdrawal of all occupation forces within ninety days after the treaty comes into effect,
which is called for in the present treaty draft. It is recognized that political and economic considerations may dictate the conclusion of a treaty
for Austria now. However, from the strategic point of view, withdrawal
of occupation troops before Austria can organize, train, and equip reasonably adequate secruity forces would create a military vacuum in central Europe in which the communists, following their common practice,
may be expected to seize power and dominate the country, thus creating
a Soviet salient in the East-West line. . . .

Regardless of the method employed, the National Military Establishment considers that the peace treaty for Austria should become effective
only after the United States is assured that Austrian armed forces are
reasonably adequate to perform all tasks envisaged in the treaty.[32]

Informed of the Defense Department's firm stance, an irritated secretary of state tried both to allay the anxiety of the military and to
shore up his own negotiating position. He emphasized in his message from Paris that the final details of a treaty would probably take a
long time to work out. The earliest a treaty could actually be signed
would be September or October, after which ratification by all the
governments involved would take another six months. And then the
treaty itself contained a ninety-day grace period before withdrawal
was to be completed. Surely this schedule would give enough time to
create adequate Austrian security forces. Even if it did not, Acheson
argued, ratification could be delayed in order to prevent the creation
of a military vacuum.[33] Acheson obviously did not want his negotiating position cut from beneath him in the middle of the foreign ministers' meeting.

Back in Washington, Acheson tried to have NSC 38/1 stricken from
the agenda of the National Security Council. He insisted that there
was no significant difference in the views of the Defense and State
departments. The problem, he argued, was simply a matter of imple-
menting an agreed program. If the deputy foreign ministers successfully completed a treaty, then the military would be consulted about
the adequacy of Austrian security forces before the treaty came into
effect. An actual treaty might warrant National Security Council concern with Austria, but short of that nothing had really changed. The
State Department, Acheson argued, should continue trying to
achieve a treaty, and NSC 38/1 should be removed from the agenda of
the National Security Council.[34]

But Acheson could not close Pandora's box. Once the secretary of
defense raised doubts about U.S. policy and placed them before the

National Security Council, the bureaucractic process dictated that State lose its monopoly on plans for an Austrian treaty. Acheson's letter to the NSC secretary was duly labeled NSC 38/2 and coupled with NSC 38/1 under "Items for Consideration" on the agenda of the forty-third meeting of the National Security Council, to be held on 7 July 1949.[35]

The Department of Defense was concerned about Austrian security after the Western powers withdrew. Equipment for a gendarmerie regiment had been sitting unused in the Western zone for months. The Austrian government, although initially wanting help from the Western powers, had hesitated to request that the equipment be issued to Austrians; it had also hesitated to provide a program for the organization and training of the regiment.[36] The delay probably stemmed from concern about Soviet reaction. Indeed, the French were nervous enough about the proposal; it was likely that the Russians would be even more disturbed.

By the time the official Austrian request finally arrived and was formally approved by the British and French governments, it was mid-June. Actual training of the regiment did not begin until July.[37] For the U.S. Defense Department the readying of a single Austrian gendarmerie regiment was a long-drawn-out struggle, the way littered with political and financial pitfalls. It is not surprising that military experts considered State Department plans, which called for a complete Austrian army—with or without Soviet agreement—to be formed in the months between the signing of a treaty and its coming into effect, completely unrealistic.

At the National Security Council meeting on 7 July 1949, military representatives argued that one newly trained Austrian gendarmerie regiment was insufficient to maintain internal order and offset the danger of a communist coup. Senior defense experts believed that the Soviet zone commander would create, before the Soviet force was withdrawn, organizations capable of executing a successful coup.[38] It was therefore only prudent to make national security arrangements sufficient for the whole of Austria, to offset any attempted putsch after Western troops left the country.

The obvious solution was to train a full Austrian army, but there were a number of problems with the proposal. First, by the summer of 1949 the Allied Council had reached no agreement about an Austrian security force. If the Western powers went ahead only in the Western zones with preparations for an army, the Soviet Union would undoubtedly react with its own major military preparations in the eastern zone. The result would be an escalation of tensions between the four powers and partition of the country.[39]

Second, if a treaty were signed within the next few months, then even allowing time for its ratification there would be insufficient time to complete the logistical arrangements for the army. According to General McNarney of the U.S. Air Force, in July 1949 the United States had no definite plans for training an Austrian army.[40]

Finally, because of previous delays in the treaty negotiations, no money was available in the summer of 1949 for equipping an Austrian army. Defense Secretary Johnson wrote in NSC 38/1:

> The Foreign Military Assistance Program initially contained an item for 100 million dollars for aid to Austria in order to equip an Austrian armed force of approximately 53,000 (including one gendarmerie regiment of approximately 1,500). When it appeared unlikely that any treaty for Austria would be concluded during the Fiscal Year 1950, this amount was reduced by the Bureau of the Budget to approximately $11,620,000, an amount sufficient for equipment of the gendarmerie regiment only. Thus, additional funds would be necessary if a treaty for Austria were to be concluded this year and if the materiel for the balance of the 53,000 Austrian armed forces were required. Further, even after the additional funds were available, it is doubtful if the bulk of the additional equipment could be furnished within one year.[41]

At no point did military representatives on the National Security Council suggest that the security aspects of signing an agreement be considered paramount. But the Defense Department strongly believed that State, in its single-minded quest for an Austrian treaty, was taking too little account of vital financial and strategic problems related to withdrawal from Austria.

Members of the National Security Council studied the positions of both State and Defense regarding future Austrian policy. They reached no decisions. The dispute was referred to the NSC staff for the preparation of a study.[42] Only one week after the deputy foreign ministers had begun negotiating in London, U.S. policy toward an Austrian treaty was thrown into a state of limbo.

THE DEPUTIES MEET AGAIN IN LONDON

As instructed by the foreign ministers, the deputies for Austria had convened in London on 1 July 1949. They set about reaching agreement on a treaty based on the terms of the Paris communiqué. Several articles were quickly agreed, and it looked briefly as though the deputies might be able to reach agreement by the 1 September deadline.[43] However, negotiations soon bogged down over what precise assets the Soviet Union was to receive.

The Soviet deputy insisted that the Paris communiqué be followed word-for-word, whereas the Western powers, and particularly the United States, maintained that the communiqué was intended as a guideline, not an edict. The difference in interpretation led, for example, to a disagreement over the oil exploration rights to be ceded to the USSR. The terms of the Paris communiqué entitled the Soviet Union to 60 percent of oil exploration lands in eastern Austria. To the Soviet Union, this provision meant that the section of eastern Austria which had virtually all of the untapped sources of oil but which coincidentally was approximately 60 percent by area of the eastern zone, was the USSR's to exploit after the withdrawal. The United States protested: this arrangement might match the *letter* of the communiqué, but it did not suit the *purpose* of the settlement. It would leave the Russians in control of virtually all of Austria's future production.[44]

The momentum toward agreement, as so many times before, was lost in East-West bickering over economic issues. In a personal letter to a Washington colleague a disillusioned American delegate, Coburn Kidd, wrote:

> On the first day Mr. Mallet, the British Deputy, said that he felt we must all be optimistic this time, and I suppose he continues to be optimistic, like Job, with gritted teeth. If you ask me, however, I should say that you need have no hope, anticipation, or apprehension that you will awaken one morning to find the Treaty on your doorstep. I am aware that any such judgment is colored by temperament, and that for aught I know the Russians may be nine months along and ready to give birth to an agreement. There are certain signs. But I am a sceptical midwife. . . .[45]

In its description of British determination and American skepticism during the negotiations, Kidd's letter foreshadows a divergence that occurred in American and British approaches to the treaty over the subsequent three months.

BRITISH AND AMERICAN PERSPECTIVES DIVERGE

In August 1949, with the American bureaucracy still battling over the desirability of a treaty, the British began to believe that, as distasteful as the move would be, the Western powers should grant the Russians all their demands for German assets (Article 35) in order to get a treaty. Private conversations with Soviet deputy Zarubin led British Deputy Mallet to conclude that agreement on Soviet demands under Article 35 would produce Russian agreement to all other unsettled articles. On the same day as his meeting with Zarubin, Mallet wrote to the British legation in Vienna: would Austria be able to fulfill the obligations of a treaty incorporating the Soviet version of Article 35, and would the Austrians want such a treaty? Likewise, Mallet wrote to Bevin's personal secretary, warning him that if the British mission in Austria answered his queries in the affirmative, "I shall have to ask the Secretary of State to decide the question . . . and to point out that, if his decision is to seek a settlement now, we shall probably have to put considerable pressure on the Americans before they will agree. . . ."[46]

One week later Sir Bertrand Jerram, British political representative in Vienna, informed Mallet that in his opinion the Austrian economy would be no worse off with a treaty on Soviet terms than it was under Soviet occupation—with the important caveat that Austria's dependence on foreign aid would be increased and prolonged.[47] The position of the British military was also clear. The Chiefs of Staff had firmly stated eighteen months before that, assuming the Foreign Office had obtained a comprehensive settlement and no treaty was signed before a stable Austrian government was in control, it was definitely in British interests to withdraw troops from Austria.[48] An adequate treaty and the assessment of Austrian government resistance to communist infiltration was left to the Foreign Office.[49]

Mallet, confident of backing from the local Foreign Office representative and the military, met with Foreign Secretary Bevin to ask him to decide British policy and, still more important under the circumstances, whether the United Kingdom would be able to convince the Americans to go along with that policy. Bevin said that he personally favored signing the treaty, on Russian terms, by 1 September. If the Americans still wanted to hold off signing the treaty, however, he would follow their lead as long as the onus of such a decision were placed entirely on them.[50]

A few days later Mallet met with French deputy Marcel Berthelot and American deputy Reber. He informed them that the foreign secretary wanted an early treaty for three reasons: first, it would allow him to cut down on British expenditures; second, the effect of a treaty on the general political environment would be favorable; and finally, the Austrians themselves wanted a treaty and would suffer politically and economically if the deputy foreign ministers' meetings again end-ed in failure. Reber and Berthelot promised to convey these views to their respective governments.[51]

As American secretary of state Acheson's support for a treaty was dissolving beneath him, therefore, British foreign secretary Bevin was deciding that the Western powers should double their efforts to pursue the treaty. Yugoslav claims were out of the way, and for the first time the Russians seemed genuinely willing to sign a treaty if the Western powers would pay their price. Bevin's determination to get a treaty was strengthened by a meeting with Austrian foreign minister Gruber, who informed him that Austrian experts were working out detailed plans for payment of the German assets debt. Gruber asked the foreign secretary to influence the Americans to yield somewhat to Soviet demands so that a treaty might be signed.[52]

With the 1 September deadline approaching, Bevin put before the U.S. ambassador the case for concessions to the Soviets and rapid signature of the treaty. As far as financial aspects were concerned, Gruber had assured him that the Austrians would be able to pay. In any case the Americans must look at the wider political significance of the treaty. Early conclusion of an Austrian treaty would encourage Marshal Tito by removing Soviet troops from his northern border, would enable the Western powers to bring Austria into the Council of Europe and other international organizations, and would have a good effect on western Germany, Bevin argued. These advantages warranted paying the small price to the Russians.[53]

Lacking new instructions from Washington, Ambassador Douglas was forced to repeat the position that the United States had held since the deputies' meetings began. Granting the Soviet Union's demands would give the USSR dangerous economic influence over Austria, and the Senate would never ratify such an agreement. Austrian claims that they would pay for the treaty were implausible, and as soon as the Austrians found themselves in trouble, they would call upon the United States to rescue them. It was easy for the British to argue that the economic aspects of the treaty were not of primary concern when the British would not be financing such an agreement.[54]

Undeterred, Bevin decided to bypass formal diplomatic channels with a personal appeal to Acheson. On the same day that he met with the U.S. ambassador, Bevin dispatched a telegram to the State Department, concluding, "I spoke to the United States Ambassador on these general lines this morning, but I should be grateful if you would convey a personal message from me to Mr. Acheson in the above sense as the Deputies have to terminate their discussions by September 1st and there is very little time."[55]

Whatever Acheson's personal reaction, however, he was powerless to effect any major change in U.S. policy. The future course of U.S. action with respect to Austria was still tied up in the National Security Council, and Acheson could do nothing until there was some agreement over the desirability of the draft treaty. The State Department still hoped that the Soviet delegates would stop insisting on extracting their pound of flesh from Austria. Any lessening of Soviet demands might help the State Department achieve consensus for a treaty in U.S. foreign policy circles.

But the State Department's hopes were disappointed. The deadline for the conclusion of the treaty came, and there were still nine articles outstanding. On 1 September the United States proposed that the four powers recess the talks, to reconvene in New York on 22 September. The French and the British deputies agreed; the Soviet deputy would not commit himself to attend a New York session, but he promised to refer the proposal to Moscow.[56]

During the recess the buzz of consultations in and between Vienna, London, and Washington intensified. In Vienna the Austrian vice-chancellor confided to the British high commissioner that the Austrians could force the Americans to agree to a treaty by publicizing Austria's frustration over U.S. inflexibility in the talks; however, his government would not do so because it could not afford to jeopardize American aid and goodwill.[57] In another meeting Austrian foreign minister Gruber claimed that the American refusal to make concessions was encouraging the growth of Pan-German ideas in Austria.[58] Austrian reservations about the treaty vanished. All senior Austrian officials were nervous about the effect of a stalemate on the results of Austrian elections planned for the following month.

In London, Foreign Office officials were absolutely convinced that the Russians wanted a treaty and that it was only American stubbornness over the issue of German assets which was preventing agreement. Formal and informal meetings with Soviet representatives seemed to confirm this view:

> [T]he Soviet Ambassador asked the Minister of State to lunch yesterday. He spent almost all his time complaining that we did not wish an Austrian Treaty. The Minister of State formed the impression that the Soviet were genuinely anxious to have a treaty now but that Zarubin was greatly afraid to stir beyond the Soviet interpretation of the Paris direc-

tives to deputies. The Minister naturally made no offers to the Ambassador since it is our view that the three Western powers must be completely agreed.[59]

During September, Bevin and his subordinates became increasingly exasperated by the Americans. The French, on the verge of another governmental crisis, apparently supported the British. But the Americans seemed to be moving even further away from the conciliatory approach to the Soviet Union which the Foreign Office favored. When the three powers tried to agree on a joint message to encourage the Soviet Union's return to the bargaining table in New York, the United States seemed more interested in responding to recent inflammatory Soviet press statements than ensuring progress in the negotiations.[60] "The [American draft of the] request to the Soviet Government to agree to the New York proposal is no longer put in a clear and objective manner, but is lost in a welter of recrimination," one British official complained. "And the statement of position is so accusatory and unyielding as to achieve the opposite of what we and the French (at any rate) intended by it."[61]

In Washington the State Department remained embroiled with the Senate and the Pentagon over what American policy should be. Members of Congress were quietly but firmly expressing their reluctance to support any treaty that would require major payments to the Russians.[62] Whatever the abstract arguments for a treaty, any withdrawal without Senate ratification of an agreement and continued U.S. aid to Austria would greatly imperil Austria's independence. Acheson could not move without support from Congress, and with daily reports of communist victories in China the Congress was not particularly well disposed toward Communists of any kind. Economic difficulties in Western Europe seemed to be promoting an increasingly belligerent attitude on the part of the Soviet leadership. News during September that the Soviet Union had detonated its first atomic device removed any remaining traces of congressional willingness to make concessions to the Russians for any purpose. Indeed, a growing body of American opinion in Congress and elsewhere opposed the withdrawal of U.S. troops from Austria at a time of such enhanced danger.[63] The British kept arguing the wider implications of an Austrian settlement, emphasizing the importance of getting the Soviet Union to withdraw from Austria and satisfying Austrian domestic opinion. But most congressmen felt that they were focusing on the widest possible perspective of American foreign policy when they argued that it was simply ludicrous further to imperil Austria with a draconian agreement by which only the Soviet Union would bene-fit—at American expense.

Meanwhile the Pentagon was receiving the persistent messages of the U.S. commander in Vienna, General Keyes. He did not believe that the treaty in its current form would benefit Austria, because Austrian security was woefully inadequate and the Austrian econo-my was too weak to take on the burden of payments to the USSR. General Keyes's viewpoint strengthened Defense Secretary Johnson's determination to resist a dangerous agreement. To the frustration of State, Johnson refused to support any treaty that the State Depart-ment signed until Congress provided $88 million to buy small arms and ammunition for Austria. Furthermore, Johnson would agree to no changes in the occupation force negotiated by the State Depart-ment in lieu of a treaty unless he had personally approved them in advance.[64]

Clearly, Acheson was losing the bureaucratic battle for control of U.S. policy toward Austria. By now, as one of his subordinates re-ported, the secretary of state was "slightly burned up about the whole procedure and ha[d] expressed himself in no uncertain terms concerning the military attitude."[65]

But the situation was to become still more difficult. Acheson was forced to defend a confused and almost nonexistent American policy to the British and the French. The American argument that a treaty containing so many concessions to the Russians would never get through the Senate seemed illogical to them; Bevin believed that the Soviet occupation constituted a worse drain on the Austrian econo-my, which the Americans were presently subsidizing, than the treaty terms would be.[66] The occupation itself was too expensive, and the French and British governments were unsure about whether they could continue to maintain troops in Austria. More important, Bevin believed the greatest danger was the partition of Austria. In a tripar-tite foreign ministers' meeting held in Washington, Bevin told Acheson that to avoid partition he would accept any treaty that got rid of the Russians; the Western powers might hold out for better terms, he said, but the odds were that they would be forced to give in anyway in the end.[67]

THE DEPUTIES MEET IN NEW YORK

The four deputy foreign ministers began to meet in New York on 22 September 1949, as planned. While their deputies were in session, the four foreign ministers also met informally (on 26 and 28 September and 5 October), to try to break the deadlock over the few remaining disagreements. Acheson tried, in each of the meetings, to persuade Vyshinsky to modify his economic demands. But the Soviet foreign minister would not make the slightest compromise.[68]

Between these meetings the three Western ministers consulted. The French premier was forced to resign in early October because of an economic crisis in France, so for almost the entire month French foreign minister Schuman and his deputy, Berthelot, had no government. As a result, French policy with regard to Austria was, in effect, to follow the British lead.[69] Acheson still lacked a consensus in the American bureaucracy, so his position was completely inflexible. Only Bevin had the freedom to maneuver politically, and in the tripartite meetings he continued to act as protagonist for a treaty on Soviet terms.

The British foreign secretary developed some new arguments for his reluctant American colleague. To his fears that Austria would be partitioned Bevin added the speculation that a united Austria might become disgusted with Western behavior and make its own peace with the Soviet Union.[70] Or, if such a notion were too distasteful to the anticommunist Austrians, the government might once again look north, to Germany.[71] Either possibility would be disastrous for Western interests and, indeed, for world peace. When these geopolitical and historical arguments failed to move Acheson, Bevin tried a more personal, political approach. How could Bevin explain a breakdown in negotiations now to his party and to the Cabinet, both of which strongly favored a treaty? A powerful group in Parliament, moreover, would force him to explain why the Western powers were delaying a treaty. Most important, however, he believed that his own public support rested upon his resolute pursuit of a treaty. Within the next few weeks the devaluation of the pound would probably cause industrial problems in Britain, and the Soviet Union would undoubtedly try to exploit such discontent. Thus "it would do no harm if an agreement were reached with the Soviet on the Austrian Treaty and the situation calmed down somewhat for a fortnight or so. They were agreed as to the diagnosis of the evil. There could be no harm in applying a conciliatory bedside manner for a short period!"[72]

The whole case for Western concessions rested, of course, upon the conviction that the Soviet Union wanted an Austrian treaty now and that it was a unique opportunity for the Western powers. Bevin certainly believed it was, and following a meeting with Vyshinsky the British foreign secretary felt even more certain. On 1 October 1949

[86]

Bevin wrote in a personal letter to Acheson: "I came to the conclusion that the Russians desire a Treaty. I cannot ascertain the reason, but it appears to me quite clear that Stalin has instructed that, within reason, an effort should be made to clear up this matter. . . ."[73] Subsequent signs of Soviet intentions were still more favorable: Vyshinsky eventually told the other three foreign ministers that if the Western powers agreed to the Soviet version of Article 35, the remaining articles would present no difficulties.[74]

But Acheson still could not take responsibility for making concessions to the Soviet Union. He finally admitted to his Western colleagues that whatever his personal feelings, he would not agree to conclude a treaty on Soviet terms unless he had the approval of the National Security Council, the Senate Foreign Relations Committee, and the president.[75]

By mid-October 1949, therefore, the greatest obstacle to an Austrian treaty incorporating Soviet economic demands appeared to be the American bureaucracy. Wearied by French and British pressure and impressed by evidence of Soviet intentions, Acheson returned to Washington determined to forge a consensus one way or another in U.S. policy.

BUREAUCRATIC BATTLE OVER U.S. POLICY

The National Security Council met on 20 October 1949 and again considered American policy with respect to Austria. Acheson argued that failure to achieve a treaty would precipitate the permanent division of Austria and enhance the danger that the Austrians would tend toward either pan-Germanism or communism.[76] Above all, the breakdown of negotiations after so much progress had been made and so many hopes raised would shatter Austrian confidence in the United States. The world would blame the Americans.

The Department of Defense reemphasized that the United States would be foolish to sign a treaty without adequate provision for the security and defense of Austria. Four years' progress toward Austrian recovery and stability would all be lost. The National Security Council could request money to finance an Austrian army, and last-minute arrangements might even be made for the army's training—these things might make a treaty more feasible. A longer time period for the withdrawal of U.S. forces would also make the treaty more attractive for the military. Defense representatives, realizing that State had primary responsibility for the economic and political aspects of the treaty, stressed that they did not actively *oppose* the State Department's position. But they absolutely could not *concur* in the recommendations of the Department of State, the most important reason being that the local military representative adamantly opposed the treaty as it now stood.[77] To the annoyance of State Department officials, the under secretary of the army referred over and over to a message received from General Keyes on the day before the meeting of the National Security Council.

> If we assume that all concessions are acceptable and that the four powers and Austria sign ratify and deposit the treaty it is felt here that Austria cannot withstand Soviet domination any more than her neighbors Czechoslovakia and Hungary were able to ward off communist inroads. Austria cannot pay the cost of the present treaty. Soviet penetration in the economic field is assisted by the concessions agreed in Article 35. Those can and will lead to political crisis and assist in political penetration. The lack of provision for an adequate security force in being at the time of ratification of the treaty will lessen Austrian will to resist the imminent inclusion of Austria in the Soviet sphere of influence. From my local point of view I feel that if the treaty as presently proposed and further modified by the concessions suggested in your [telegram] is concluded it can only be interpreted as a Soviet victory. A victory won by typical methods of stubbornness and intransigency; won by advancing exorbitant demands and gaining their ends through minor and relatively unimportant concessions.[78]

The meeting of the National Security Council ended inconclusively.

Harry Truman's fabled desk sign, "The Buck Stops Here," was accurate; Johnson and Acheson decided to ask the president to decide. Describing the upcoming meeting in a personal letter, one State Department member observed, "This puts the President in a rather difficult spot and if he were not an amiable man I believe he would get very mad with his Secretary of State and Secretary of Defense for bad staff work, and ask them to go back to the NSC to work out an agreed recommendation."[79] But when Johnson and Acheson met with the president on 26 October 1949, Truman made the final decision: "The President stated that he had given the problem careful consideration and felt without question that the Treaty should be concluded in order to obtain the withdrawal of Soviet military forces from Austria and to gain the general political advantages which will be derived from this action. He considered that steps can and should be taken by the Department of State and the Department of National Defense prior to the withdrawal of the occupation forces to establish

an adequate Austrian security force."[80] After four months of inter-
departmental wrangling the United States finally had a clear policy.

MAJOR CONCESSIONS BY THE WESTERN POWERS

The president's decision was a turning point in Western policy
toward Austria, for it enabled the three Western powers to make
what the Soviet delegates had indicated were prerequisite economic
concessions. Two days after Truman's decision the U.S. deputy,
speaking on behalf of the Western powers, presented a compromise
proposal to the Soviet delegation in New York: the Western version of
five remaining unsettled articles for virtually all of the Russian demands under Article 35. But the Soviet deputy flatly refused to consider a package approach. First the four powers must reach agreement on Article 35, he insisted, and then the other disputed articles
could be considered.[81]

In Washington, a few weeks later, President Truman signed NSC
38/4, a document officially stating that "the President has determined
that it should be United States policy to agree at an early date to a
draft Austrian treaty on the best terms available."[82] On the same day,
18 November 1949, events took a dramatic turn at the deputies' meeting in New York. With the French reserving the right to make future
conditions, the three Western deputies gave way completely to Soviet
demands for German assets in Austria. The Western powers entirely
conceded Soviet terms under Article 35 in the belief that the signs
since June of Soviet plans to leave Austria were accurate and that
Vyshinsky's and Zarubin's assurances were reliable. The capitulation
was potentially so controversial in the West that the French, British,
and American representatives kept it a secret: "The three Western
Deputies agreed to avoid announcing our surrender on Article 35
until progress had been made on the other articles. We agreed to say
merely that progress had been made in the discussion about Article
35 in connexion with other articles."[83] The Western powers had finally, reluctantly, taken the step that the British had advocated for
months.

SOVIET POLICY CHANGES

By mid-November 1949, however, the Soviet Union had obviously
decided it did not want a treaty. To the dismay and indignation of the

Western powers, the Soviet deputy accepted their concessions and offered nothing in return. Three days later Zarubin announced that he could not negotiate the remaining articles of the treaty until bilateral talks regarding payment for postwar relief supplies were completed between the USSR and Austria. The Austrians were willing to pay for these supplies, mostly dried peas taken from German Wehrmacht stores in Vienna and distributed to the starving population immediately after the liberation.[84] But in bilateral exchanges the Soviet Union apparently refused to settle on a price. In Vienna the Soviet foreign minister invited the Austrians to submit their proposals for payment in writing. The Austrians did so; there was no Soviet response. Undaunted, the Austrians dispatched one letter after another proposing terms of payment, but Moscow offered no reply. Asked repeatedly about the letters, the Russian deputy high commissioner in Vienna gave the Austrians a standard response: "We are studying the matter."[85]

The "dried pea debt" negotiations were allegedly held in Vienna, but little was heard of them.[86] As the months went by, the Soviet Union either spoke in ambiguous terms of "difficulties" in the negotiations or else refused all comment about their progress.[87] It was clear to the Western powers that the Soviet Union was not interested in concluding the bilateral talks.[88] The four-power negotiations were effectively made hostage to Soviet behavior in an arena where the Soviet Union exercised complete control.

The deputies met intermittently over the subsequent months, but they made no further progress toward an Austrian treaty. The dried pea debt was the first in a long series of excuses that the Soviet Union used to obstruct the negotiations. The momentum of the Paris agreements was lost completely; after November 1949 the Soviet Union showed no desire to sign an Austrian treaty, even on attractive financial terms. Indeed, 1949 was the last year of genuine four-power negotiation for a treaty.

Bureaucratic inefficiency and domestic disagreement in the United States had delayed the evolution of a common Western negotiating position by putting off the economic concessions that the British felt were inevitable. For a short period of five months the Soviet Union seemed to be offering an unprecedented opportunity for a treaty. By the time the U.S. State Department had received a mandate to pursue that opportunity, it was too late; the opportunity was gone. But how genuine had the fleeting opportunity been? Had the Russians wanted a treaty in the spring of 1949, or did they simply trick the Western powers into believing they did?

Every indication is that the Soviet Union's apparent willingness to sign a treaty immediately after the Paris conference was genuine. Soviet actions in Austria certainly implied that the occupation would soon be withdrawn. Moreover, the Soviet delegates would not have bargained so hard over economic issues had they not intended to sign a treaty. The Soviet Union could have used extraneous issues long before November 1949 to prevent agreement. Indeed, the concessions that the West eventually made under Article 35 would have resulted in a treaty that granted the Soviet Union economic advantages comparable to those from occupation but without the presence of Western troops.

Had the treaty been signed in 1949, Stalin would probably have had increased economic leverage over the Austrian government. In the autumn of 1949 the Austrian Parliament was not sure that it could make even the first payment of the debt it would owe the Soviet government under the treaty.[89] Inability to pay that debt could have had serious consequences. As Acheson pointed out to Bevin, the first payment was due two months after the treaty's signature, and four-power troop withdrawals were slated for three months after signature. Stalin could have used Austria's failure to make payments as a reason to keep Soviet troops in Austria, had he wished to do so.[90] If the Western powers then decided to keep troops in Austria to offset Soviet troops, the situation would have been similar to the status quo ante, with the important difference that the USSR would have achieved legal justification for its exorbitant economic demands. In any case the Soviet Union would have been in a very strong economic position once the treaty was signed.

Greater economic control over Austria would have been an attractive asset to Stalin's plans in Europe. By mid-1949 Stalin was just completing economic consolidation in Eastern Europe; greater economic leverage over Austria could only help in that consolidation. Britain and especially France were experiencing major economic difficulties following the war, and their economic instability could only help the international communist cause. An Austrian treaty would be one way to decrease the stabilizing influence of the United States in Europe by ensuring American withdrawal from Austria. Furthermore, the Soviet Union was quite aware that U.S. dollars used to aid Austria could be funneled into the USSR through payments for German assets. For these reasons the Soviet delegates seemed very willing to sign a treaty and squeezed every possible economic concession from the Western powers.

But the negotiating tactic changed in the autumn of 1949. There is

[91]

no reason to believe that Foreign Minister Vyshinsky overstepped his authority when he gave assurances in October that the remaining articles of the treaty would present no difficulties if the Western powers would agree to Soviet economic terms. Vyshinsky was a shrewd politician, best known for his role as prosecutor general of the USSR in the great purge trials of the 1930s.[91] After Vyshinsky returned home to the Soviet Union he remained in Stalin's favor and continued as foreign minister until the leader's death. Clearly Vyshinsky enjoyed Stalin's confidence (to the extent that such a thing was possible). When Vyshinsky and his deputy, Zarubin, changed their negotiating tactics from hard bargaining to obvious obstructionism, it can only have been with Stalin's blessing.

Indeed, there is only one explanation for the change in Soviet negotiating behavior in 1949: Stalin changed his mind. By the time it had become apparent that the Western powers were going to sign the treaty, Stalin was no longer interested. By November the rationale for signing an agreement was no longer convincing, and the economic assets that had been so enticing in previous months were no longer of primary importance. In the autumn of 1949 four things prompted a major change in Soviet foreign policy, and the decision not to sign a treaty and not to withdraw from Austria was only a minor part of that change.

The Soviet Union's sudden decision to obstruct an Austrian treaty was in the first place directly related to Soviet policy in Germany. Even after the announcement of the founding of the Federal Republic of Germany on 23 May 1949, Stalin still held out hope that the actual formation of the western state might be averted. At the Paris conference Vyshinsky had tried and failed to negotiate a return to four-power control. When the West German Bundestag convened in September, the Soviet Union quickly established the German Democratic Republic. The likelihood of East-West reconciliation with respect to Germany was small.[92]

On its own Austria had never been vital, and in early 1949 its greatest usefulness to the Soviet Union was the economic assets it would provide under the treaty. But events in Germany coupled with developments in the Austrian negotiations shed new light on the smaller country. By October 1949 the best possible source of political leverage for the Soviet Union in the deteriorating German situation was Austria.[93] Large economic concessions in the negotiations had indicated to the Soviet Union that the Western powers were strongly interested in getting an Austrian treaty. It might therefore be wise to maintain the only position in Western Europe in which the Soviet Union now clearly controlled the outcome of East-West negotiations.

The second cause of a major change in Soviet foreign policy in 1949 was the reason most often cited by political pundits of the day: the successful testing of a Soviet atomic weapon in late August.[94] The belief at the time that the Soviet Union aimed to frighten the West into submission or force Western Europe to appease Stalin was exaggerated, but it is no doubt true that possession of "the secret of the atomic bomb" enhanced Soviet self-confidence. Certainly, the breaking of the U.S. atomic monopoly brought the USSR a stronger international position in popular perceptions and formalized the emerging political and military standoff between the United States and the Soviet Union. In the USSR the year 1949 also marked the beginning of a series of new programs to modernize and improve the Soviet armed forces. Conciliation in Soviet foreign policy lasted only a few months, and by the end of 1949 it was replaced by a vigorous national effort to built up the Soviet conventional—and, eventually, nuclear—arsenal.[95] It was not a time conducive to the signing of treaties, the withdrawal of forces, and the ceding of territory.

A third major change was the launching of anti-Tito witch-hunts in Eastern Europe. The economic consolidation of a Soviet empire was essentially completed, with numerous agreements and cooperative industrial ventures in operation by 1949, but in Stalin's eyes Eastern Europe had not yet been politically purified. On 27 September 1949 the USSR repudiated its treaty of friendship with Yugoslavia, and Stalin used the threat posed by "Titoism" as an excuse to launch a wave of terror and purges throughout the new satellite states. The purges lasted from mid-1949 through 1951.[96]

This Soviet-sponsored campaign began in countries bordering Yugoslavia and continued north until each of the new satellites had undergone something reminiscent of the pervasive and horrifying Soviet purges of the 1930s.[97] Romania underwent trials in 1949 designed to rid the country of "deviationists." In June, Albania's communist vice premier, among others, was convicted of being a Yugoslav agent and executed. Bulgaria's communist deputy premier was found guilty of ideological deviation and executed in December. In Hungary communist foreign minister Rajk and other leaders were arrested, tried, and also executed in December, after which a huge number of other Hungarian Communists met the same fate. Poland's Central Committee expelled several senior members for "Titoist" sympathies. Czechoslovakia had been undergoing purges since Feb-

[93]

ruary 1948; in 1950, however, a new series of political trials began. Members of the government were accused of anti-Soviet, pro-Western sympathies, and most Westerners were barred from the country.

It is likely that Stalin, having planned this wave of purges months in advance, decided in late 1949 that it was not desirable to withdraw Soviet troops and thereby risk Western encroachments up to the borders of Czechoslovakia and Hungary.[98] Moreover, it is quite possible that the new Eastern European Communists were themselves worried about the effect of a Soviet withdrawal from Austria on their own tenuous positions. As the Austrian negotiations moved closer to the signing of a treaty, Stalin's new Eastern European minions may have reminded him of the deep historical connections between Austria and Eastern Europe, particularly between the peoples of Austria and Hungary. In late 1949 the fragile communist regimes in Hungary and Czechoslovakia would have been threatened by the political pressure of an independent Western state on their borders. Years later, in fact, it was no coincidence that the Warsaw Pact treaty would be signed on the day before the Austrian State Treaty was signed.

Finally, in late 1949 Soviet foreign policy shifted its focus from Europe to Asia. Europe still retained importance for the Soviet Union, but Soviet policy there was now a matter of consolidation rather than change. With the exception of Austria the lines of East-West division in Europe had become clear by autumn 1949, and events in China held far greater opportunity for the Soviet Union.[99] The Chinese Communists under Mao Tse-tung had taken power without Soviet help. Indeed, throughout most of the Chinese civil war the USSR had maintained proper diplomatic relations with the Kuomintang, and Stalin probably had not expected Mao to win. In an important sense, then, Stalin was *forced* to pay attention to developments in the Orient or risk the appearance of a rift in communist ranks of such massive proportions as to make Titoism seem insignificant.

The People's Republic of China was founded on 1 October 1949. By December, Mao had come to Moscow for a visit that lasted two months. Stalin's attention was clearly diverted from Austria. Sino-Soviet consultations were a portent of events in the Far East that would soon monopolize Western attention as well.

[4]

Stalemate, November 1949–
March 1953

In the late autumn of 1949, after four years of tough negotiations, the goal of Austrian independence began to appear not only elusive but futile. In November, the same month that President Truman signed NSC 38/4 and clarified the importance of a quick settlement, Russian interest in an Austrian treaty had begun to diminish. Although the Western Allies had made important concessions, it soon became obvious that, regardless of terms, the Soviet Union had no intention of signing a treaty. Before 1950 the Soviet Union seemed willing to accept a treaty if the economic terms were advantageous; the Russians might well have been bribed by the West. After 1950, however, the Soviet position changed from stubborn hard bargaining to blatant obstructionism.

The issues raised by the Soviet Union evolved from a primarily economic to a primarily political nature.[1] In the late autumn of 1949 articles began to appear in the Soviet press warning of resurgent fascism in Austria and attacking the fundamental nature of the Austrian government. As the months progressed, ominous warnings of dangerous militarism in Austria gradually replaced complaints about the "dried pea debt." Held in reserve for months, Soviet knowledge of the West's stockpiling of military equipment and plans to arm the Austrian gendarmerie now emerged to justify putting off the treaty. The Western powers no longer wondered why the Russians had stifled their formal complaint at the Allied Council in the spring of 1949, for Soviet accusations about Western military activities appeared in 1950 with an accumulation of evidence and self-righteous justification that would have been impossible in earlier months.

In casting these aspersions on the very nature of the Austrian government and the character of Western support for it, Soviet leaders employed arguments so general that no specific Western concessions or treaty proposals could offset them.[2] Soon there was no common basis for negotiations, and the prospects for a treaty, which had seemed so bright during 1949, evaporated after 1950.

A FRENCH POLICY REVERSAL

The erosion of the basis for negotiation could not, however, be blamed solely upon the Russians. No sooner had the British begun to congratulate themselves upon their success in "persuading" the Americans to make necessary concessions in late 1949 but the French began to show signs of reversing their apparent willingness to sign. The French based their objections to the treaty upon two specific matters: the paragraph dealing with displaced persons in Austria (Article 16, para. 5), and the question of Austrian rearmament. But discussions between the British and French soon revealed that French reservations about the treaty had much deeper roots.

In late November the French deputy to the Austrian treaty negotiations, Marcel Berthelot, informed his British and American colleagues that he could not agree to the Soviet draft of the treaty article dealing with displaced persons. The terms of the proposed draft would not permit the Austrians to provide relief to persons who had collaborated with the Nazis or who were engaged in activities hostile to their countries of origin. The Americans had also had serious qualms about this article, but American deputy Samuel Reber was now under instructions to accept the Soviet draft in order to reach agreement on the treaty. Regardless of extremely strong British pressure both in New York and in Paris, however, the Quai d'Orsay refused to authorize Berthelot to agree to the article until the Russians somehow proved that they really wanted a treaty. On 26 November the exasperated British delegate sent a message to the Foreign Office:

> I hope you will intervene with Schuman himself if necessary in order to get the French Government to withdraw their opposition to Article 16 paragraph 5. No one likes this paragraph, least of all the Americans who have for months strenuously fought the Soviet over this Article but they have withdrawn their opposition in order to make a treaty possible. How do the French expect to have proof that the Russians really want a treaty when the whole point of the operation is that it is *we* who are trying to get the Treaty for reasons which M. Schuman appeared to consider adequate when the Secretary of State exposed them to him and

Mr. Acheson here in New York. Surely it is a little late to decide now that no further concessions can be made to the Russians. It is just petty-mindedness to insist that it is now the turn of the Russians to make a concession. . . .[3]

Discussions were held the next day in Paris between the British ambassador to France, Sir Oliver Harvey, and French foreign minister Robert Schuman, but the the talks disappointed the British. Schuman claimed that for strong personal reasons he could not agree to the article. "[H]e considered that the Vichy Government's surrender of political refugees to the Germans had been one of their most reprehensible acts, [and] he found it difficult to condone a like act," the British ambassador reported. According to Schuman, the Soviet draft of Article 16(5) would raise the number of displaced persons subject to possible return to the Soviet Union from four to forty thousand.[4] Officials in the British Foreign Office recognized the argument on humanitarian grounds but maintained that it was a meagre excuse for delaying the treaty. Whatever the merits of the French case, its last-minute nature angered the British.[5]

At the same time the second French objection emerged, threatening to fracture the Western negotiating position. At the end of November the Quai d'Orsay began to insist that Austrian rearmament be raised with the Russians in New York and terms settled to Western satisfaction in advance of the completion of the treaty. British and American diplomats were extremely averse to this suggestion. The time to approach the Russians regarding an Austrian army was immediately *after* the signature of the treaty, they argued; otherwise the treaty would be indefinitely delayed.[6] This time it was the Americans who pointed out that the French proposal directly contradicted both an agreement reached on 15 September between the three Western foreign ministers and the general tripartite understanding about the need for early agreement to a treaty.[7] However, the French continued to insist that the arrangements be agreed in advance, arguing that the Soviet Union should be given no pretext for refusing to ratify the treaty.[8]

Both issues were familiar, and most Western diplomats recognized that the French arguments had at least some merit. But the timing was poor. Dean Acheson, Ernest Bevin, and Schuman had agreed in their meetings in New York that an early treaty was the first priority and that the concessions necessary to achieve that treaty would have to be made. The sudden French reversal was a surprise to the other Western powers and particularly frustrated the British, who blamed

[97]

the French military for sabotaging the treaty negotiations. Some months later British foreign secretary Bevin presented the Cabinet with the following explanation of French behavior:

> The attitude of the French Government towards the conclusion of the Austrian Treaty had never been a factor of prime importance, and they were generally content to associate themselves with agreed Anglo-American policy. However, no sooner had we at last got American agreement in New York than the French Government raised fundamental objections to concluding the treaty at all. This eleventh-hour initiative was mainly the work of the French military authorities and their supporters, who regard the continued presence of American troops in Austria as a guarantee of French security. The French opponents of the treaty also exploited the personal preoccupation of M. Schuman with the problem of displaced persons and refugees which arises on Article 16, a matter with which he appeared to come in contact for the first time in New York, although it had been before us for nearly three years. I do not doubt that M. Schuman's qualms were perfectly genuine, although we ourselves consider them to be exaggerated.[9]

The British belief about the French military's activity appears to have been justified. At the end of 1949 the weakness and volatility of the French government were encouraging French military interference in foreign policy. Indeed, during October, shortly after the Queuille government collapsed, Berthelot had confided in British Deputy W. I. Mallet his fears that the French military would undermine the Austrian treaty at a time when there was no French government to defend it.[10] Berthelot's fears, though a few weeks premature, were accurate. The French military were skeptical of Austria's ability to maintain its independence after the withdrawal of Western—and particularly American—forces. According to British sources, French military officials were particularly concerned about the status of the Austrian Tyrol in the event of war because they considered the buffer zone of northern Italy and the Austrian Tyrol vital to the defense of France from any threats from the East.[11] The withdrawal of Allied troops would increase the threat of a communist takeover in Austria (similar to what had occurred recently in Czechoslovakia) and would also discourage anticommunist forces in the Soviet satellites and in Western Europe.[12]

Underlying these political and strategic arguments, however, was a profound French distrust of the Austrians themselves and particularly of the Austrians' determination to protect their own independence. This lack of confidence pervaded much of the French government, from the Quai d'Orsay to the Assembly. Citing Austrian behavior between the wars, many French officials believed that the Austrians would never withstand the Russian pressure that would be exerted through the economic terms of the treaty; and they predicted that an independent Austria would eventually become another Soviet satellite.[13] Thus when General Bethouart, high commissioner of the French zone in Austria, began lobbying in Paris at the end of 1949 against immediate conclusion of the treaty, he planted his doubts in fertile soil. At the time of the reversal of French policy in the negotiations, moreover, it was far from clear that the French government could have ratified an Austrian treaty.[14]

General Bethouart explained his views to British Political Representative Harold Caccia in Vienna. After the Western powers withdrew, the Austrians would be responsible for the survival of Austria, General Bethouart observed; "And there, as Bethouart sees it, is the rub. They are, he said, a female race and they are ready to be violated. Last time it was the Germans. The next time it may be the Russians. They are not only female, he went on, but in many ways oriental in their fatalism and readiness to accept what they feel is an irresistable force . . . ."[15] Even if it were to become desirable to agree to an Austrian treaty, Bethouart argued, measures should be taken to ensure the country's continuing independence:

> What, he said, do you do if you want to make a rape more difficult? You keep the woman under constant observation and never allow her alone with her intending despoiler. So, immediately after the implementation of the Treaty, the Austrians should be brought into the Council of Europe and as soon as possible thereafter the permanent seat of the Council should be moved to Vienna. That would make the Austrians and Russians behave more cautiously. At any rate, the main Austrian political parties might hesitate to repeat the follies of the years between the wars and destroy Austria in the their battles with each other. It might also make the Russians risk less.[16]

The British countered French reservations with four arguments. First, while it might be true that the Austrians were not strong at the moment, continued Soviet occupation would probably weaken them still further. In any case, there was certainly no guarantee that in one or two years' time the Austrians would be more self-sufficient. Second, any hint of Western stalling in the negotiations would seriously damage the prestige of the pro-West Austrian government; again, this would not enhance Austria's ability to withstand Soviet pressure.

Third, widespread disillusionment could lead to the resurgence of national socialism in Austria. Finally, if the economic and political status of western Germany continued to improve while that of Austria deteriorated, there could be a rebirth of pan-Germanism in Austria and even a movement toward another Anschluss. Obviously such developments would be extremely damaging to French interests, the British argued.[17]

By January 1950 the British and the Americans had apparently brought the reluctant French back into the fold, but by this time the Russians were clearly obstructing the negotiations. Indeed, the French had raised their objections in late November, at about the same time that Soviet policy changed. The qualms of the French government may have threatened the cohesiveness of the Western negotiating position, therefore, and had certainly irritated the Americans and especially the British, but they had not in themselves prevented the completion of an Austrian treaty in 1949. Soviet behavior in the negotiations clearly indicated that the opportunity of the Paris initiative was already lost.

Austrian officials ruefully observed the behavior of the Western powers and became increasingly disillusioned. They continued to place primary blame for the delay on the Soviet Union, but they believed that the bickering and disunity among the Western powers was contributing to the delay. Plainly speaking, in the negotiations the Austrians had expected the Russians to be obstreperous, but they had had much higher hopes of the Western Allies. In 1949, at least, Austrian hopes were disappointed. In a private interview with a French official President Karl Renner, the aged politician who was largely responsible for Austria's postwar national government, curtly responded to French criticisms and delivered a scathing critique of Western policy:

[Y]ou have sacrificed the Austro-Hungarian Empire in 1919 and have abandoned Austria in 1938 for Czechoslovakia which in turn you abandoned also. These are bad precedents.

Besides, you are weak, you do not agree with one another and you declare that, in the event of an aggression by the Russians, you would defend yourselves on the Rhine, which means that you would abandon us once more.

In these conditions, and even though 90 percent of the population feels, by its culture and its traditions, tied to the Western Powers, how do you want us to adhere to an organization such as the European Union which answers all of our wishes and my own in particular? As a responsible leader of this country I can . . . only recommend a policy of strict neutrality between the two allied blocs.

But the day when I will see the French and the British High Commissioners come into my office and assure me of their agreement between themselves and of their common support and, when behind them, the U.S. High Commissioner guarantees me that he supports them, then I will sign with both hands the request for adherence to the European Union.[18]

Renner's attack was an interesting portent of events to come.

SOVIET DELAYING TACTICS

In January 1950 the Soviet Union was maintaining that no progress could be made toward an Austrian treaty until the Soviet-Austrian negotiations on postwar relief supplies were concluded. Although the foreign ministers' deputies met in London on 9 January 1950, the Soviet deputy had received no information or new instructions from Moscow regarding the "dried pea debt," so progress toward an Austrian treaty was impossible.

Annoyed by the delay, the Western powers instructed their ambassadors in Moscow to lodge a formal protest with the Soviet government. The French, British, and American ambassadors tried to arrange an audience with Foreign Minister Vyshinsky but were informed that he was ill. Instead, they were received by Deputy Foreign Minister Andrei Gromyko. Gromyko was apparently acting under instructions not to be drawn into a lengthy conversation, but the three ambassadors succeeded in keeping him under cross-examination for fifty minutes. Gromyko gave them only evasive replies.[19] Finally the U.S. ambassador, Admiral Alan Kirk, got to the heart of the matter: "How long, Mr. Minister, before we can hope to reach an agreement? This has gone on now for some time." Gromyko replied, "That depends on the value you place on time."[20]

Subsequent meetings of the four deputies also failed to yield any progress. The Soviet delegate refused to discuss any of the few remaining articles of the treaty until the issue of Austrian postliberation debts had been settled. He also refused to indicate how those negotiations were progressing or when they might be finished. In April the Russians tried a different approach, maintaining that an imminent resurgence of Nazism in Austria required an amendment that would

[101]

mandate the Austrian government to take action against all bodies "of a Fascist type." The wording of the proposed amendment was so loose as to permit broad Soviet interpretation of the term "Fascist."

Only eight days later the Russians demanded that a state treaty be contingent upon the resolution of Soviet grievances about allied policy in Trieste. The Western allies were turning Trieste into an Anglo-American base, Soviet delegate Zarubin charged. With such a precedent, how could the Soviet Union trust them with regard to Austria?

Some Western observers believed that the real reason for Soviet concern about Trieste was the port's strategic importance in relation to Austria and Eastern Europe. In Trieste the Western powers held a Mediterranean port with direct access to central Europe. A Red Army withdrawal from Austria would complete the consolidation of Western power on the southern flank of Europe, thereby enhancing the political and military threat to Soviet allies in East Europe as well as complicating any Soviet adventure toward the Rhine.[21]

In any case, this time the Soviet government had chosen an issue that would stall talks indefinitely, because the Trieste controversy had reached impasse. Meetings for the remainder of 1950 were characterized by the repeated Soviet contention that the Trieste question must be resolved before the Austrian treaty could even be considered. Western protests that Trieste was completely irrelevant to the Austrian treaty were ignored.[22] Even the most optimistic observers were discouraged by Soviet behavior. At the end of May 1950 British deputy Mallet informed Foreign Secretary Bevin that "[t]he Soviet Union had now made it abundantly clear that they had no intention of concluding the treaty. . . ."[23]

If during 1950 the Russians were deliberately seeking a breakdown of the Austrian negotiations, Stalin had several reasons for wanting to do so. With four-power control of Austria operating reasonably well, the Soviet Union was holding a forward strategic position at Vienna with very little risk of war. A Soviet presence also gave Stalin political leverage with the Austrian government and some control over the destiny of the country; as an attempted communist putsch in September 1950 later showed, the dictator had not yet abandoned hope of turning Austria into a Soviet satellite. Furthermore, as mentioned earlier, control of the frontiers just beyond Russia's newly converted satellites minimized Western meddling in Czechoslovakia and Hungary and helped guarantee that the countries of the Eastern bloc would not lightly consider the heresy of counterrevolution. Yugoslavia had recently severed ties with the Soviet Union, and eastern Austria was a convenient base both for exerting political and military pressure against Tito and checking the spread of Titoist influence. Indeed, some observers in mid-1950 argued that Stalin would not withdraw his troops from Austria until Tito had been overthrown.[24]

Although the significant economic concessions made by the Western powers in 1949 had tempted Stalin to sign a treaty, nothing was lost by delay: resources collected by the Soviet Union in the interim were not subtracted from the Austrian reparations bill. Besides, Vienna had become the center for Soviet black-market activity in Europe. It was a lucrative outpost, not to be surrendered easily.[25]

Many of these Soviet justifications for remaining in Austria had existed for several years, however. None of them adequately explains why in mid-1949 Stalin had seemed willing to sign a treaty if the price were right, and in 1950 he was not. The critical factor was Germany. The convening of the West German Bundestag in September 1949 had been followed by the establishment of the German Democratic Republic, and within a few weeks the Soviet position in the Austrian negotiations had become blatantly obstructionist. The rapid sequence of events indicated that, in Stalin's eyes at least, the political connection between the two states had outlived the Anschluss.

Shortly after the founding of the Federal Republic, the Western Allies began to believe that the security of Western Europe required the rearmament of West Germany. The prospect alarmed Stalin, and much of Russian foreign policy in the early 1950s focused on preventing a remilitarized Germany. Sometime between October and November 1949 Stalin had decided that Austria's value as a bargaining chip in the struggle for the future of Germany far exceeded its economic and political attractiveness; he hoped to use Austria as a quid pro quo to induce the Western powers to abandon, or at least to limit, West Germany's rearmament.[26] Throughout the early 1950s Austria would be held hostage to Allied policy in West Germany.

WESTERN POLICY TOWARD AUSTRIA

During 1950 relations between the four military regimes in Austria became increasingly tense. In May the Western powers decided to try to ease the situation by instituting reforms, among them the replacement of military high commissioners with civilian diplomats and determined efforts to reduce the burden of occupation costs.[27] Although invited to do so, the Russians refused to do the same.[28]

Western uneasiness about Soviet plans for Austria began to intensify in the first few months of 1950. For example, high-level consideration was given to measures to be adopted by the United States in the event of a Soviet blockade of Vienna. Members of the U.S. National Security Council feared a blockade might put pressure on the Austrian government and drive the Western powers out of the country. A top secret report on the subject, NSC 63/1, instructed American forces in Austria to exercise fully all existing U.S. rights in the Soviet zone, to protest vigorously any interruption of those rights, to consult with British and French colleagues, and to make no threat of force. Finally, the directive warned: "Caution must be taken in preserving the security of these instructions and no steps should be taken which would lead the Soviet authorities or the Austrian population to believe that we are taking precautionary measures in anticipation of their action, thereby providing a pretext for aggressive or probing measures on their part."[29] President Truman approved NSC 63/1, "U.S. Policy in the Event of a Blockade of Vienna," on 17 February 1950.

The Truman administration apparently feared that Vienna might become another Berlin. In Vienna, moreover, the Russians had a much stronger strategic position. The airfield near Vienna allotted to the United States was located in Tulln, seventeen miles outside the city and deep within the Soviet zone. In the early years of occupation the Russians had frequently blocked the road from Vienna to Tulln, and even after a direct rail line was established the route was constantly subject to Soviet disruption. To get to the airport, American planes had to fly through a narrow corridor of Soviet-controlled air space.[30] Even if they wanted to do so, the Americans would have found it extremely difficult—if not impossible—to organize an airlift for Vienna. American leaders apparently recognized the poor Western strategic position in Vienna as well as the city's lesser importance compared to Berlin: the U.S. National Security Council report had no specific prescriptions for breaking a Soviet blockade and stressed above all that no force or threat of force be employed. Evidence indicates that Soviet leaders also understood the strategic circumstances in Vienna. Years later, during the April 1955 Austro-Soviet negotiations in Moscow, Soviet foreign minister Molotov mentioned to the Austrians that the Russians had long recognized how easy it would be to cut off Vienna.[31]

In February 1950, according to available documents, at least some Western policy makers considered the division of Austria a possible result of deteriorating East-West relations. The Western powers did not consider the partition of Austria to be in their interests, and they would do nothing that might encourage such an outcome. Austrian foreign minister Gruber several times repeated his suggestion that the Western powers openly take unilateral action in lieu of a treaty, for example by bringing the agreed articles of the treaty into force and then withdrawing from the Western sectors, but the Western powers resisted his proposal.[32] Without a treaty, there was no reason to believe that the Soviet Union would also withdraw, and the likely result would be partition. The three Western zones of the country were probably more capable than the Soviet zone of surviving economically; they had more natural resources (apart from oil), more industry, and more favorable trading prospects than existed in the east.[33] But conditions in a Western rump state would nonetheless be very difficult.

More to the point, Western analysts believed that Austria, unlike Germany a culturally fragmented nation, would never survive partition. A truncated eastern Austria would quickly be swallowed into the Soviet system and be a continual fount of unrest and refugees to the West. Western Austria would probably dissolve under the strains of provincialism, with the central provinces drawn toward Germany, Vorarlberg toward Switzerland, and Carinthia toward Yugoslavia. The result would be dangerous instability on the continent and a possible rebirth of the kinds of tensions that had already helped bring about two major wars. As one British expert observed, "Such an act of dissection is economically undesirable, but it would be a historical disaster."[34]

In the early 1950s, therefore, Western policy toward Austria was a matter of trying to strike a delicate balance. On the one hand were actions that would improve conditions in the Western sectors, encourage the Austrian people, and thereby enhance the status of the pro-Western Austrian government; on the other hand, the Allies had to eschew any wide-reaching reforms that might evoke a defensive Soviet reaction and thereby precipitate partition of Austria.

Western governments based their policy for Austria largely upon the political and economic tactics intended to strengthen Austria itself as well as the deterrent effect of stationing American, British, and French troops in the Western zones. Contrary to what most Austrians believed, in 1950 the United States and the United Kingdom had no intention of defending Austrian territory against a major Soviet attack. Top secret British documents indicate that, in the event of a sudden assault from the east, the British and American military plans before early 1951 called for the evacuation of occupation forces into Italy as quickly as possible.[35] The Americans and the British apparently believed that northern Italy provided a better strategic position than western Austria for the defense of Western Europe. It would be difficult to defend Austria at the front lines; British and American military planners thus tacitly admitted that in the event of a military emergency, western Austria was not so vital to Western interests as to warrant devoting major military resources to a front-line defense.

But the economic influence that the Western powers—and particularly the United States—now exerted in Austria indirectly contributed to Austrian defense. Austria's trade with its eastern neighbors had declined in the postwar years, to be replaced largely by trade to the West and also to the south.[36] Between 1945 and 1949 the portion of Austria's trade with Czechoslovakia, Hungary, Poland, and Yugoslavia declined from 25.1 percent to 19.5 percent.[37] Marshall funds and other aid gave the United States a tremendous role in Austrian economic policy, with the Americans practically holding a veto over important Austrian economic agreements. In October 1950, for example, when the Austrian government was considering the desirability of a Soviet-Austrian trade agreement, Austrian foreign minister Gruber consulted Secretary of State Acheson for the American viewpoint, "with [the] assurance," Acheson later reported, "that no action w[ou]ld be taken until US views were known."[38] By 1950 Austria's economy was clearly oriented toward the West and subject to the influence of the Western powers, a fact that may have deterred Soviet military action.

Indeed, Soviet leaders were extremely unhappy about the gradual reorientation of the Austrian economy to the West, and in particular about the burgeoning trade between Austria and West Germany.[39] Citing the maxim "Diplomacy follows trade," Soviet analysts warned that the growing economic cooperation between Austria and Germany would encourage pan-German sentiments and eventually lead to another Anschluss. The Russians found particularly worrisome the export of raw materials from Austria to Germany and the building of electrical facilities in the western zone to be shared by the two countries.[40] The Americans, however, were worried far less about trade between Germany and Austria than about trade between East and West blocs; in fact U.S. restrictions on Austrian exports to the East became so annoying to the Austrians that a few years later the Austrian chancellor complained to the British about the American regulations.[41] But whatever the terms, American economic power with all its political and military implications was the single most important factor in the strengthening of Austria as of so many countries in Western Europe after the war.

What of Soviet economic policy in Austria? The cessation of Soviet investment in eastern Austria, which had raised expectations in 1949, was reversed in 1950. Soviet obstruction of the negotiations was accompanied by increased investments in securities and properties in eastern Austria.[42] If financial policy was a barometer of Soviet intentions, then Stalin clearly expected his troops to occupy eastern Austria for some time to come.

THE KOREAN WAR

The outbreak of the Korean War in June 1950 sharply diminished any Western incentive to reach an accommodation with the Russians over Austria. Although today considerable controversy concerns the extent of Soviet responsibility for the North Korean invasion, at the time the United States clearly believed that Stalin had instigated the attack. Throughout 1950 American military leaders were preoccupied with the Far East; they dared not withdraw from Austria and risk a Soviet attack in Europe as well. Even many Austrians saw a correlation between the stiffening of the Soviet position in the treaty negotiations and what they later interpreted as a period of Russian military planning for the Korean campaign; some concluded that they could expect no state treaty until after a Korean armistice.[43] In any case, the Korean War followed recent Soviet attempts to influence Finland's elections, repeated partial blockades of Berlin, and Moscow's support for the communist Chinese.[44] It promoted the general impression in the West that the Soviet Union was untrustworthy, expansionist, and belligerent—certainly not an attractive negotiating partner in settling the future of a small, strategically important, but nearly indefensible state.

During the summer of 1950 neither the Soviet Union nor the Western powers desired or expected progress on the Austrian treaty. Nonetheless, a meeting scheduled for 10 July 1950, only a few weeks after the fighting started in Korea, went ahead as planned.[45] Although the Americans and the British had qualms about meeting the Russians so soon after hostilities had begun, they could not cancel the meeting without giving the Soviet Union a propaganda advantage. During the July 1950 meeting the delegates all carefully avoided the subject of Korea.[46] The Soviet Union again raised the subject of Anglo-American troops in Trieste, however, and no progress was made. With East-West relations so bad, no incentive or reasonable prospect existed for an Austrian treaty. Even Austrian government officials recognized that negotiations were a casualty of the East-West stalemate. In August, Sir Harold Caccia, now British High Commissioner, reported a pessimistic conversation with Austrian foreign minister Gruber: "[Gruber] said that while things were as they are over Korea, not even the most rabid Treaty enthusiast would reasonably expect progress with the Russians. Certainly he did not."[47]

Indeed, it might seem strange that the Western powers would negotiate at all with a state they were accusing of belligerence and aggression elsewhere. The useless session following the outbreak of hostilities in Korea demonstrates that while the Austrian negotiations certainly reflected outside events, the Western powers did not consider the talks important enough in themselves to be used, in turn, as a tool with which to make symbolic gestures to the Soviet Union. The Western powers' major concern seems to have been to satisfy Western (and notably Austrian) public opinion by always appearing willing to negotiate. To the Western powers, the likelihood of results was not as important as the appearance of an unfaltering Western commitment to the process. Thus even when East-West relations virtually guaranteed that no agreement would be reached over Austria, the scheduled meeting went ahead anyway. As the Cold War intensified during the 1950s, the Austrian negotiations came to occupy a unique position in the East-West relationship: peripheral enough for the negotiating process itself to be continued in fits and starts but central enough for any real progress in the negotiations to be stymied.

A Second Attempted Communist Putsch

As the great powers confronted each other elsewhere, conditions within Austria were becoming increasingly tense. A cutback in Marshall Aid funds in the autumn of 1950 led the Austrian government to increase the price of food, coal, and electricity by approximately 30 percent while wages were increased by only 13 percent.[48] This reduction in the standard of living was introduced without warning and without any preparation of Austrian public opinion.[49] Widespread anxiety over economic conditions, compounded by extremely low Austrian morale following the breakdown of four-power negotiations, provided the perfect opportunity for a second and more serious uprising by the Soviet-backed Communist party. Beginning on 26 September 1950 the second communist putsch attempt caught the Western powers preoccupied with Korea and believing Austria safe from the threat of revolution.

The putsch attempt began with a mass demonstration in Vienna, organized by the Communist party, to protest the wage-price agreement. Approximately 6,000 demonstrators gathered in the international sector of Vienna near the Ministry of the Interior, overran police lines, and marched to the Federal Chancellory. The Austrian police attempted to repel the demonstrators with fire hoses but were overwhelmed by sheer numbers. At the Chancellory the 400 police guarding the building were stoned by the protestors.[50]

From within the Chancellory, Austrian federal chancellor Leopold Figl urgently requested U.S. assistance. In response the U.S. high commissioner placed American troops in Vienna on alert and then called a meeting of the Allied Council; but the Soviet representative did not attend the meeting. Following this tripartite session, British and French troops also went on alert. Although Chancellor Figl repeated his request for assistance three times, his minister of the interior insisted that the Austrian police could handle the situation. The Western powers took no action. After a few hours the protestors dispersed, in response to instructions given by their communist leaders.[51]

On the following day communist shop stewards sent an ultimatum to the Austrian government, threatening a general strike if the government did not "reexamine" the wage-price agreement. The threat was more convincing because major factories in several large towns were already on strike.[52] The Austrian government issued a proclamation begging the people to resist the Communists' subversive attempts to overthrow Austrian democracy and asking them not to participate in the strikes and demonstrations. By 28 September, Austrian socialist leaders had organized a counteroffensive against the Communists, and striking workers were returning to work in increasing numbers.[53]

The communist shop stewards nonetheless declared a general strike on 4 October 1950. In response to the declaration, scattered local strikes broke out throughout Austria; they were particularly serious in Greater Vienna and also in some parts of the Soviet zone. Within the eastern zone workers from Soviet-run factories were loaded onto lorries and transported to other, nonstriking factories to pressure other workers to join the strike.[54]

For several days the Austrian government once again feared that the Austrian police could not control the situation; but the Western powers hesitated to use troops to intervene and thereby risk an East-West confrontation. In particular, Lt. General Geoffrey Keyes, U.S. high commissioner, warned the Austrian government that if U.S. troops were to be brought in, their small numbers would force them to rely heavily upon their weaponry. The result would undoubtedly be bloodshed.[55] Torn between a fervent desire for Western help and a deep fear of the consequences should that help be received, the Austrian government continued to depend upon its own small, ill-equipped police force to deal with the disturbances.

To make matters worse, the efforts of the Austrian police were severely hampered by Soviet authorities. The 1950 putsch attempt was more serious than the thwarted takeover of 1947 because the Soviet Union interfered directly in the operations of the Austrian police, thereby violating the control agreement and paving the way for the intended takeover. The U.S. chargé d'affaires in Austria, Walter Dowling, informed the secretary of state on 1 October 1950: "Strikes and demonstrations [during the] past week in Vienna and Eastern Austria, which represent first tangible success of Communists since food riots of 1947, were marked by two salient factors: Overtness of Soviet instigation and assistance . . . and lack of effectiveness of [the] Austrian police."[56] On the day before the disturbances began, the Soviet occupation authorities issued orders restricting the movement of Austrian police in the Soviet zone. The commandant of the Soviet sector of Vienna, Colonel Pankratow, refused to allow police to leave the Soviet sector without the consent of the Soviet authorities; no dismissals or transfers of police officers would occur without Soviet permission. As a result Austrian minister of the interior Oscar Helmer was prevented from using the significant reserves of Austrian police located in the Soviet zone. He complained bitterly to the Americans.[57]

Evidence of a Soviet hand in staging events had ominous overtones within Austria. Wild rumors added to the general panic: Czech troops were amassing at the border, Russian tanks were moving toward Vienna, low-flying Russian aircraft were approaching the border.[58] The Austrian Communist party was weak, but the Romanian Communist party had been even weaker when the Russians placed it in power.[59] In a heightened state of alarm the Austrian government on 5 October addressed an appeal to the Allied Council "to take, immediately, the appropriate measures to enable the Federal Government to accomplish its constitutional duties." It concluded with a "fervent appeal" to each of the four occupying powers to support the Austrian government "in its efforts to maintain order in the country."[60] The three Western foreign ministers immediately issued firm declarations of support for the Austrian government, but the Soviet government gave no reply.

By 6 October order was finally restored by the Austrians themselves, and the general strike ended. There were two reasons why the putsch ended in failure. First, the Austrian Federation of Trade Unions did not support the strike, and the anticommunist Austrian workers refused to participate in the communist-backed general strike. The government proclamation had met with some success among people who had recently witnessed the transformation of neighboring Czechoslovakia and Hungary into communist, Soviet-satellite status. Second, with Western troops in Austria, Stalin dared not send the full military support necessary to ensure the success of the putsch. It was one thing to encourage the activities of the Austrian Communist party or even to interfere with the administration of the Austrian government; it was quite another to commit Soviet troops and risk military confrontation with the Western powers.[61]

APPARENT SOVIET PLANS FOR AUSTRIA

The two Soviet-supported attempts at a putsch in the postwar years indicate that Stalin had had some hope of turning Austria into a communist state. His plans for a communist Austria were unsuccessful, of course, and finally abandoned or at least postponed. The first reason for the failure was that indigenous support for Russian communism and the Communist party was quite low. This is partly explained by the Western orientation of the Austrian people, but is still more attributable to Austrian resentment toward the Soviet Union which began as a result of the liberation, increased under heavy-handed Soviet occupation, and reached a high pitch in response to blatant Soviet obstructionism at the treaty negotiations. Postwar Soviet antipathy to the German-speaking Austrians also played a role: with respect to the Austrian Communists, the Russians remembered first that they were Austrian and only incidentally that they were Communists.[62]

Second, Austria did not become a communist state because the failure of the Communists to enlist the support of the Socialist party, in particular the primarily socialist trade unions, undermined both the May 1947 and the September 1950 attempts at a communist take-over. The third, and most important, reason was the presence of the Western powers, providing support for the Austrian government and supplying aid to the Austrian people. As a result of that presence, finally, Stalin was not willing to challenge the West directly and dared not provide the open military support necessary to place a communist government in power.

When he finally realized that attempts to turn Austria into a communist state were fruitless, the Soviet leader might have considered converting eastern Austria into a separate state like the German Democratic Republic. The Western powers had come to the conclusion that partition would not be in their interests, but there is no reason to assume that Soviet leaders also felt that way. Indeed, given Stalin's aversion to withdrawing from any Soviet-conquered territory, partition may have seemed a logical outcome in terms of Soviet interests.

But even in Soviet eyes the plan involved serious economic and political difficulties. The Soviet sector contained the agricultural heartland of Austria but only about 41 percent of total Austrian production.[63] Separated from western Austria, the Soviet zone would be able to obtain industrial raw materials and electrical power only by shifting its demands eastward to the overburdened economies of the Soviet satellites; interestingly, power stations in the Western zones built with American aid were already supplying electricity to factories in the Soviet zone.[64] With grave problems in its own economy, the Soviet Union did not have the resources to shore up a struggling rump state. Austria's participation in the Marshall Plan might have been a serious embarrassment to the Soviet Union, but for the Soviet Union it was easier to let Western money rebuild the entire Austrian economy and then to worry about changing the government.

By 1950 a strong Austrian national government also deterred any Soviet plans for partition. Formation of an eastern Austrian state would have cleaved the government right down the middle. The Soviet Union had taken an early responsibility for forming that government and ensuring its national character. As a result, transition to Soviet support of a communist government representing only half of the country would be difficult, especially since the new government would earn only meagre indigenous support.

For these reasons the Soviet Union would neither attempt directly to force Austria into the ranks of its East European satellites nor attempt to split the country in two and claim the eastern half. Germany was a country of absolutely vital strategic and political interest to the USSR, worth the economic and political sacrifices; Austria was not. The two situations were integrally related but fundamentally different.

Stalemate in the Negotiations

In the wake of the 1950 putsch attempt prospects for an Austrian treaty went from bad to worse. The foreign ministers' deputies met for the 258th time on 15 December 1950, but the session soon degenerated into a review of the same Soviet complaints regarding Anglo-American troops in Trieste and Austrian denazification which had characterized meetings earlier in the year. The Western powers requested that the meeting be adjourned for three months.[65]

In the meantime the Soviet Union had requested a meeting of the Council of Foreign Ministers to discuss Germany.[66] The foreign ministers' deputies gathered in Paris in March 1951 and spent four months on an agenda for their principals' meeting. At this point the Western Allies seemed even less anxious than the Soviet Union to compromise. As Charles Bohlen, a junior member of the U.S. delegation in 1951, observed, "[I]t was quite obvious that the Western side was not particularly interested in a conference while a war was on in Korea."[67] Although the British delegate at one point expressed his desire to "go very far in meeting Gromyko," the Western Allies were plainly unwilling to go far enough.[68] In June the four-power session adjourned sine die without an agenda. The deputies would not meet on Austria again for the remainder of the year.

In early 1951 the domestic difficulties of both the British and the American governments militated against the extraordinary measures that a treaty would have required. In the British general election held the year before, Clement Attlee's Labour government had earned an extremely small margin of victory. Lacking a convincing mandate from the British electorate, the government lost confidence in its foreign policy. To make matters worse, veteran foreign secretary Ernest Bevin, a long-time champion of an Austrian treaty, became ill and was forced to resign in March 1951. Bevin was replaced by Herbert Morrison; he was inexperienced and held the post of foreign secretary for only a few months. With regard to Austria, then, British foreign policy from Bevin's illness in mid-1950 to the general election of October 1951 was uninspired.[69] Although still desiring a treaty, the British were no longer able to exert the pressure they had in the past applied to their French and American colleagues. Since the British, and Bevin in particular, had been (apart from the Austrians themselves) the prime supporters of the treaty, no progress was made during 1950 and 1951.

The Truman administration, on the other hand, was facing its own unique, but very serious, domestic challenge. In February 1950 Senator Joseph McCarthy announced that there were 57 Communists and 205 communist sympathizers in the State Department. Although never proved, the allegation set off a series of witch-hunts at State and in other branches of government, fueled in part by the Re-

[113]

publican party's angry conviction that the Truman administration had "lost" China to the Communists. The suspicion of communist sympathy was directed at every member of the government, from the lowliest administrator to Secretary of State Acheson himself. As a result, between 1950 and 1952 the foreign policy of the Truman administration was subject to a unique paralysis, prompted by fear that policy makers would be accused of cooperating with the Communists. In the climate of McCarthyism no self-interested American diplomat was willing to offer the Soviet Union any concession whatsoever; indeed, polemical anticommunism proved loyalty. Even if the Soviet Union had been interested in a treaty, the U.S. State Department was in no position to negotiate one. Certainly no American diplomat—including Acheson—would have wanted to be responsible for "losing" Austria.

By the autumn of 1951 the State Department's position with regard to the treaty had hardened considerably. On 4 October 1951 the British ambassador in Washington wired the Foreign Office that the State Department's "mention of the Senate makes us suspect that they are now receding from the position to which we pushed them with so much difficulty two years ago. It is difficult to be sure of their motives . . . but whereas previously they have agreed with us that broadly speaking any treaty would be better than none, their present position seems to come very close to believing that it is better not to have a treaty at all than one on the lines of the present draft."[70]

In the meantime American military equipment in western Austria had been stockpiled at an accelerated rate. The 1951 U.S. Military Assistance Program for Austria allocated funds to equip an initial Austrian security force of approximately 28,000. The equipment was to remain under U.S. control until an Austrian treaty came into force and Congress authorized its transfer to the Austrians.[71] In October 1950 the U.S. Army had assigned the stockpiling program the highest priority for foreign military assistance and assured the secretary of defense that the program would be completed by 1 September 1951.[72]

The Soviet Union's complaints about the "remilitarization" of Austria steadily increased in frequency and stridency throughout 1951. The charges were met by American assurances that no remilitarization was taking place and U.S. complaints about larger-scale Soviet military activity in eastern Austria. On 12 October 1951 Ambassador Walter Donnelly, now civilian U.S. high commissioner in Vienna, met Soviet accusations with a list of counteraccusations at an Allied Council meeting.[73] The United States and the Soviet Union had reached stalemate in Austria; in the atmosphere of charges and countercharges no progress toward an Austrian treaty was likely.

Nonetheless, moved by a request from the Austrian government, the United States managed to arrange a meeting of the deputies for 21 January 1952 in London. Invitations were issued on 28 December 1951, but three days before the scheduled conference the Soviet Union announced that its representative would attend only if the agenda included discussion of Austrian implementation of measures to demilitarize and denazify all four zones, as well as the withdrawal of Anglo-American troops from Trieste. When the Western Allies refused to agree to any preconditions, the Russians boycotted the talks.[74] Thus collapsed the first attempt since December 1950 to discuss an Austrian treaty.

THE ABBREVIATED TREATY PROPOSAL

The Russian refusal to attend the January 1952 meeting gave the Americans an opportunity to redouble their efforts to get British and French agreement to a proposal the Americans had been advocating for months. The State Department wished to put aside the draft treaty on Austria and present to the Soviet Union a new, abbreviated treaty. In September 1951 the U.S. State Department began to argue that a shortened treaty, consisting of only a few general articles that granted Austria independence and omitted any detailed economic restrictions, would be an attractive alternative to the current draft. The shortened draft would not break the continuity of treaty negotiations and would take into account the need for Austrian independence, but more to the point (in American eyes) the old draft no longer represented Western objectives in Austria and was not a satisfactory basis for a settlement.[75]

Secretary of State Acheson first presented this suggestion to the British and the French in tripartite discussions in Washington on 13 September 1952.[76] They greeted it first with surprise, then skepticism, arguing that it was most unlikely that the Soviet Union would ever accept a shortened treaty as the basis for negotiation. Instead of jolting the Russians into progress at the talks, such a demarche by the Western powers would only anger the Soviet leaders and perhaps worsen the situation in Austria. The French in particular feared that the abbreviated treaty would so anger the Soviet Union as to disrupt the four-power arrangements in Austria, arrangements that the

French above all wished to perpetuate as long as there was no treaty.[77] Moreover, the short treaty would not only omit the articles of concern to the Soviet Union, such as Article 35 on German assets, 9 on denazification, and 48(bis) on Austrian postwar debts, it would also omit economic and political clauses of concern to the Western powers. The French particularly objected to the omission of Article 3, Germany's recognition of Austrian independence, 4, a prohibition of Anschluss, and 17, limitations on Austrian armed forces.[78]

The British argued that the short draft would be seen internationally as a provocative move. In a brief written for the new British foreign secretary, Anthony Eden, one Foreign Office official summed up the British view of the situation: "We, the French and the Austrians have serious doubts about this gambit. On points of detail in the existing draft little separates us from the Russians. If they remain unwilling to conclude a Treaty, this will be due to their general policy, which will not be altered by any initiative we may make."[79] In blunter terms a Foreign Office representative elsewhere complained that the Americans "certainly claim that their proposal is a constructive move and not a mere propaganda stunt and I think they have persuaded themselves that this is so, but in their rather woolly state of mind it is not a far cry one to the other."[80]

Nonetheless, the Russian refusal to meet with the Western powers in January 1952 increased the need for the Western powers to take some action; the American case was strengthened. In addition, the Austrians changed their minds about the abbreviated treaty and began to support the American position. The French, under pressure from the Americans, were apparently placated by promises of supplements to an abbreviated treaty, such as an Allied-Austrian declaration against Anschluss to which Germany would adhere.[81] Only the British remained set against the short draft. Faced with American pressure combined with Austrian lobbying, they also began to waver.

A decision to propose the short-draft treaty was finally made in tripartite discussions during NATO Countil meetings in Lisbon, on 26 February 1952. Secretary of State Acheson conceded that the status of the old treaty would remain deliberately blurred and that the new draft would be presented as an alternative, not necessarily a replacement. On this basis the British and the French agreed to the American proposal. To separate the tripartite demarche from any direct association with NATO, the Western powers waited a few weeks after the Lisbon meeting concluded.

On 13 March 1952 the United States, Britain, and France, in identical notes to the Soviet Union, proposed the immediate signature of an abbreviated treaty as "an important step toward the consolidation of peace."[82] The treaty consisted of eight articles, seven of which the Russians had already accepted. The remaining article was, however, the critical one, for it proposed that the Soviet Union and the Western powers renounce all claims to German assets in Austria. As the British, the French, and perhaps also the Americans expected, the Soviet Union rejected the short treaty and refused to consider it a basis for negotiation.

Those historians who have suggested that the abbreviated treaty was never a serious proposal, but an attempt to lay the blame for delay directly on the Russians, are at least partially correct.[83] Only the most optimistic or naive Western negotiators expected that the Soviet Union would suddenly renounce its sweeping economic claims on Austria. The result of the Soviet rejection whether deliberately calculated by the Americans or not, was to focus public disapproval on Russia. In fact the Russians themselves probably anticipated this unfavorable public reaction. They delayed rejection of the short draft for five months, presumably while they tried to find a way to avoid or to mitigate their political embarrassment. In a sense, then, the so-called propaganda stunt was a great success.[84]

But this explanation distorts what declassified American documents reveal.[85] In addition to being an attempt to gain favorable publicity, the abbreviated treaty was a genuine—if futile—attempt by the United States to get rid of the long draft of the treaty.[86] Some officials of the U.S. State Department believed that the long draft contained too many concessions to the Russians, and they hoped to begin afresh with a shortened treaty based on essentials.[87] Perhaps Secretary of State Acheson was personally motivated to escape the assault of the McCarthyites by getting rid of a document he knew they would despise. Or perhaps the proposal was a delayed American reaction to the British pressure that had led to major Western capitulations to Soviet economic demands in late 1949. Whatever the origin of the short-treaty demarche, it is clear that the Americans did not intend it as merely a cynical exercise. For the Americans, the short draft represented a hope that the four powers might extricate themselves from the mire of the treaty negotiations and start over again.

The British, the French, and the more realistic Americans had a related but shrewder purpose in mind when they agreed to propose the short treaty; namely, to make the earlier, longer treaty seem more attractive to the Russians. In this they were successful, for in its 4 August 1952 reply to the Western powers the Soviet government adamantly insisted that negotiations resume only on the basis of the

[117]

original treaty.[88] Indeed, the Soviet attitude to the short draft was public and graphic. In an effort to align Austrian public opinion with current Soviet interests, the Russians plastered the streets of Vienna with propaganda posters contrasting the long and short treaties. A symbol of peace hovering daintily over the long treaty; the Grim Reaper wielded his scythe over the short draft.[89]

In September the United States offered to modify the short draft by adding four articles from the long version. The United States then proposed another meeting of the foreign ministers' deputies in London for 29 September. Demonstrating its unwillingness to negotiate constructively on the basis of any draft, however, the Soviet Union stated that the Western proposals were unsatisfactory and again raised the Trieste question. The Russians refused to attend the meeting.

Austria Approaches the United Nations

The Soviet government was still considering its response to the short draft when Austrian foreign minister Gruber decided that the time had come to extricate Austria from the East-West stalemate and bring international pressure to bear on the treaty negotiations. After consulting with the American, French, and British governments Gruber flew to Rio de Janeiro in July 1952; he asked the Brazilians to sponsor a UN resolution demanding the conclusion of a treaty. Brazil was sufficiently independent of the four powers, the Austrians believed, to act as an unbiased observer and therefore might be able to sway international opinion. Since Austria's application for membership had been vetoed by the Soviet Union, Austria itself had no voice in the United Nations. The Brazilians agreed to present the Austrian case, and on 20 December 1952, despite Soviet attempts to prevent the General Assembly from considering the plight of "an enemy country," a resolution urging the rapid conclusion of an Austrian State Treaty was passed overwhelmingly.

Foreign Minister Gruber had confided to Dean Acheson that he did not think the UN resolution would lead to the conclusion of a treaty. The important thing, Gruber claimed, was to keep the public eye on the Austrian dilemma, to shore up morale at home, and, he later added, to make the Russians feel as uncomfortable as possible about their position in Austria.[90] The UN resolution accomplished precisely these goals and nothing more. Public opinion probably helped induce the Soviet Union to attend a meeting of the deputies in February 1953, but the talks adjourned when the Western allies refused to withdraw the abbreviated treaty. Attempts to meet in May and August were fruitless, with the Russians insisting that the short draft be withdrawn as a prerequisite to their attendance and the Western powers refusing to accept preconditions. The UN resolution provoked a temporary flurry of diplomatic activity, but it left the substance of the negotiations unchanged. Deadlock between the great powers persisted.

At the end of 1952, then, treaty negotiations were completely paralyzed. Indeed, the situation had never been worse: with the Americans insisting on a short-draft treaty that the Soviet Union refused even to consider, the great powers could not even agree on what they were negotiating. Forced against their better judgment to agree to the abbreviated draft, the British and the French found their influence on American policy toward Austria waning. And in the meantime Acheson's State Department was handicapped by McCarthyite hysteria and preoccupied by the Korean conflict, and Stalin's Foreign Ministry was determined above all not to surrender any territorial conquests. Their positions left no room for compromise over Austria.

[5]

Signs of Change, 1953–1954

In January 1953 the "lame duck" presidency of Harry S Truman was replaced by a Republican administration under former general Dwight D. Eisenhower. By the end of 1952 the Truman administration's foreign policy was lame not only because the incumbent was not running for reelection but also in part because frequent assaults by Joseph McCarthy and his followers had taken a heavy toll. The junior senator from Wisconsin had personally attacked Secretary of State Dean Acheson, among others, labeling him the "Red Dean of Fashion" and demanding at various times that he resign, be fired, or be impeached.[1] Furthermore, domestic and legislative support for the Truman administration's foreign policy had crumbled in controversy because of the perceived "loss" of China, the stalemate in Korea, and, perhaps above all, the abrupt dismissal of General Douglas MacArthur. Even had he wished to do so, Acheson possessed neither the congressional support nor the popular approbation at the end of the Truman administration to make any controversial initiatives in American foreign policy. In January 1953 a worn and dissipirited Acheson was replaced by a vigorous new secretary of state, John Foster Dulles.

By 1953 earlier Western concern about Austria's capacity to maintain internal security and protect its own territory had been somewhat alleviated as a result of the training and equipping of the Austrian gendarmerie and the completion of U.S. military stockpiles in western Austria. The more important consideration for the West, therefore, was what relationship an independent Austria would have to the new North Atlantic Treaty Organization. American defense planners had, it seems, long envisioned the small country as a nominal member of NATO, unlikely to be a major participant in joint military exercises but vital to the organization simply by virtue of geographic location. In fact, only a year after the formation of the pact the U.S. Joint Chiefs of Staff had suggested "[i]nclusion of Austria in the protective interest of NATO and the best possible uses of her resources in the common defense."[2] In 1948 and 1949 the U.S. Defense Department had concentrated on the danger that the hasty conclusion of a treaty when Austria had little means of protecting itself could lead to Soviet encroachments and even gradual conversion to satellite status. In the early 1950s, however, after two attempted communist takeovers had failed and the Austrian gendarmerie had been strengthened, Western apprehension shifted to the possibility that an obviously pro-Western Austria would be prevented from participating in the defense of Western Europe. In fact, especially after the Eisenhower administration took office, the American fear that Austria would be "lost to Communism" was replaced by the fear that it would be "lost to neutralism."

STRATEGIC CONCERNS IN THE WEST

Although a communist Austria was still the worst prospect in the Western view, important strategic reasons brought the West to oppose any treaty that might make Austria a neutral state, particularly if that neutrality precluded NATO's use of Austrian territory.[3] Most important, the movement of men and supplies between Germany and Italy would be greatly complicated by the necessity to detour through France. A neutral Austria, bordering neutral Switzerland, would drive a wedge through the center of Western Europe and would certainly be a serious logistical handicap in any East-West conflict. With only a small army, furthermore, an independent Austria without any additional Western troops or security guarantees would tempt Soviet invasion. Postwar political realities dictated that the Austro-German and Austro-Italian borders remain virtually unfortified, and Soviet forces could therefore easily expand both north and south from an Austrian salient. Finally, western Austria had for years been the source of the best American intelligence information concerning the Balkan area and thus the U.S. position was an asset that no prudent security planner would want to relinquish.

Throughout the period the U.S. Defense Department officially deferred in all policy statements to the overriding political considerations involved in the treaty negotiations. But regarding strategic matters, a secret memorandum from the chairman of the Joint Chiefs of Staff to the secretary of defense left little doubt as to the position of the American military:

[121]

> By virtue of its geographical location, Austria is an important strategic
> link in the defense of Western and Southern Europe. Any weakening of
> our present military position in Austria, such as would be brought about
> by a substantial "neutralization" of Austria, the creation of a military
> vacuum in Austria, or, as the most adverse possibility, the communiza-
> tion of Austria, would have a serious impact upon the entire NATO
> defense concept. Therefore, maintenance of the *status quo* would be
> preferable to acceptance of a treaty which would deny to the United
> States its security objectives with respect to Austria.[4]

The official U.S. position, as propounded by the State Department,
remained strongly in favor of a treaty during the early years of the
Eisenhower administration. The Defense Department, however, exerted significant pressure to avoid concluding an Austrian treaty—
particularly a treaty that would require Austria's military neutrality.

But even as strategic concerns were pushing the American bureaucracy away from support of a state treaty, financial concerns were
nudging the British and the French bureaucracies in the opposite
direction. The costs of occupation were becoming a serious burden
for two European powers whose economies had not yet recovered
from the devastation of the war. Their funding of soliders stationed in
a relatively peaceful, remote country such as Austria seemed an out-
rageous luxury when social services and recovery programs were
suffering at home. Most important, the cessation of Marshall Aid
funds in 1952 had removed the security of incoming U.S. dollars; the
British and the French found unreasonable even the suggestion that
they should approach the military and economic commitment of
wealthy America in Austria. In the autumn of 1953, therefore, the
governments of Britain and France each informed the United States
that they wished to withdraw two-thirds of their troops from Austria.
Pentagon analysts were horrified.[5]

By 1953, therefore, disparate political pressures, strategic interests,
and economic realities were causing conflicts among the Western
powers. The British and the French began to favor any treaty that
could get them (and of course the Russians) gracefully and permanently out of Austria. The United States, meanwhile, opposed more
firmly than ever any treaty that required Austrian military neutrality
or excessive economic burdens on Austria.

Yet even as these disagreements were developing among the Western Allies, the Soviet Union continued its obstinate refusal to negotiate an Austrian treaty. The pressure of the UN resolution of December 1952 had compelled the Soviet Union to attend a meeting of
the deputy foreign ministers in February 1953; the meeting soon

deadlocked, however, because the Soviet deputy refused to proceed until the short-draft treaty was completely withdrawn. The Western powers were therefore spared both the embarrassment of appearing to stall on the Austrian treaty and the necessity of settling their differences under pressure. The onus for delay remained firmly on the Russians.

THE DEATH OF STALIN

The difficulties among the Western Allies were insignificant, however, compared to the upheaval occurring in the Kremlin at the same time. On 5 March 1953 Stalin died, and with him passed an era in Russian history when one *vozhd* would exercise complete and direct control of Soviet foreign policy. With the death of the Soviet generalissimo, new hope emerged that Soviet policy toward Austria might be revised. Stalin's passing, combined with a confident new administration in the United States and a strong government in Britain, led to a surge of optimism in Austria. For the first time in three years it seemed possible that the deadlock in the negotiations might soon be broken.

Stalin's death threw the Soviet government temporarily into disarray; but from the initial scramble for power emerged the collective leadership of Georgii Malenkov as prime minister, Vyacheslav Molotov as minister of foreign affairs, and Nikita Khrushchev as Communist party secretary. The contest for power among these leaders continued for three years, and most of the details of that struggle remain a mystery to this day. Between March 1953 and May 1955, however, Soviet policy toward Austria, where Soviet leaders protected appearances less carefully than they did in East Germany, provides a unique insight into the contest for power in the Kremlin.

The collective leadership first ordered a relaxation of the more rigorous policies of the Soviet regime in Austria. The local Soviet authorities waived nearly all controls at the East-West demarcation line, declared an amnesty for Austrian political prisoners, officially ended censorship of the mail, telephone, and telegraph services, and even allowed the resumption of airmail service with Germany and Japan.[6] More remarkably, the Russians agreed for the first time to cover their own occupation costs in Austria and, after a delay of three years, followed the lead of the Western powers in replacing their military high commissioner with a civilian administrator. Other surprising moves in both domestic and foreign policy accompanied these

Soviet actions in Austria. The new leaders reorganized the top Communist party and Soviet government organs, declared a general amnesty for the whole of the Soviet Union, and endorsed Chinese communist proposals to reopen armistice talks in Korea. By April 1953 Western observers were already cognizant of a major change in Soviet foreign policy. They questioned only the permanence of the new approach.[7]

A WESTERN INITIATIVE

At the same time secret plans were being made for an initiative in Western policy. In late April the NATO ministerial council met, and the Western powers discussed, among other things, tactics to ensure the ratification of the European Defense Community (EDC) treaty and the rearmament of West Germany. After the NATO meeting Dulles returned to the United States, and on 28 April he briefed the president and the National Security Council about the situation in Europe. Although generally pleased by the NATO discussions, Dulles spoke of a growing concern among European governments that ratification might not be moving rapidly enough. The EDC treaty had to be ratified quickly, he emphasized, before Stalin's successors had a chance to interfere. Dulles argued that the West should therefore preempt the negotiating field in Europe by moving ahead with the Austrian treaty.[8]

Claiming British and French agreement with his proposal, Dulles suggested that the Western powers and Austria should return to the long-draft treaty as the basis for negotiations. Tactically, the best way to proceed would be to reopen negotiations between the foreign ministers' deputies on the basis of the short draft and then shift to the long draft when compelled to do so. The record of the discussion continues: "We must, however, hurry to give the British and French the green light on resuming the meetings of the Deputy Foreign Ministers. The objective, continued Secretary Dulles, was to stave off a Russian initiative for a Foreign Ministers meeting on the German problem. The Austrian treaty offered the best means to avert this. Time, therefore, was of the essence."[9]

Shortly thereafter the Western powers proposed that the foreign ministers' deputies meet on 27 May; in preparation the State Department planned to withdraw the short treaty if necessary to ensure progress in negotiations. Indeed, progress was given such a high priority that, in a top secret communication, the U.S. assistant secretary of state instructed the U.S. deputy to go beyond the official tripartite policy directive issued earlier:

Paragraph 4 of our telegram indicates that if attempts to revise the long draft negotiations grind to a halt a new tripartite position will be sought. Actually we continue to have the authority to sign the long draft with Article 35 and the Soviet version of the unagreed articles but we are committed in the Government to make every effort to obtain better terms. For obvious reasons it would therefore be best not to communicate our final position to the French, British and especially the Austrians at the present time.[10]

Thus the Soviet Union was not the only power to determine Austria's fate by calculating the state of affairs in Germany. The rearmament of Germany was the most important goal of U.S. policy in Europe. U.S. policy makers in the spring of 1953 planned to sign an Austrian treaty on Soviet terms if it were necessary to preempt a Soviet demarche on Germany. By taking the initiative on an Austrian treaty, the Western powers could divert attention from Germany as it rearmed. They could also prevent the Soviet Union from interfering with European support for the rearmament of Germany.

Western fears that the change in Soviet foreign policy would lead to Soviet initiatives in European negotiations were, however, premature. In May the Russians refused even to attend the scheduled meeting of the foreign ministers' deputies, rendering the Western contingency plan for signing a treaty on Soviet terms irrelevant.

Austrian hopes for a treaty were not completely dashed, however, as the Russians left open the possibility of negotiating through other channels. The Malenkov leadership complained that the four-power council was "not the most suitable instrument" for treaty negotiations; it proposed that all future contacts regarding Austria occur through normal diplomatic channels.[11] Although the complaint seemed unconstructive after seven years of negotiations between the deputies, it was at least directly relevant to the treaty talks. On 12 June the Western powers asked the Kremlin to produce a draft treaty that it felt would be negotiable, but notes from Moscow in July and August responded that the short treaty must be withdrawn *first*; moreover, any solution to the Austrian problem was inextricably linked to a solution of the German problem.[12] By August no new Soviet initiatives had emerged, and the Soviet relaxation of controls in Austria remained to be translated into progress toward a treaty.

THE AUSTRIANS APPROACH THE SOVIET UNION

Meanwhile, as a result of the Austrian elections of 22 February 1953, a new chancellor, Julius Raab, had replaced Leopold Figl. Raab

[125]

was anxious to break the deadlock. Whatever schemes were clandestinely developing in the French, British, or American foreign offices, the public positions of the three Allies seemed inflexible; the Austrians were becoming increasingly frustrated by what many of them perceived to be Western inertia. In the spring of 1953 the Western powers seemed to be missing a golden opportunity to coax the Russians into a treaty. The death of Stalin and subsequent more liberal policies in the Soviet zone held new promise for Soviet cooperation, and by 1953 many Austrians felt that their principal goal must be Russian withdrawal, almost regardless of terms. This view saw no need to fear Soviet attack, for once the Russians had withdrawn their troops, an invasion of Austria would mean a major war between East and West. American interests were sufficiently entangled in the future of this small Western-oriented country to deter any Soviet attack, the argument continued.[13] The Austrians, while acknowledging that the Western powers had been far more sincere than the Soviet Union in their attempts to conclude a treaty, believed that both sides had become mesmerized by calculations of the East-West balance of power and thus had overlooked Austrian interests.

As a result the new Austrian government attempted independent, bilateral negotiations with the Russians. On 30 June, without consulting any of the Western powers, the Austrians discreetly sent a memorandum to the Kremlin. The memorandum strongly suggested that the Austrians would agree to some form of military neutrality, in addition to significant East-West trade concessions, if the Soviet Union would sign a treaty.[14] The Austrians had been encouraged by recent articles in the local communist press to believe that neutrality was in Soviet eyes a sine qua non for a state treaty.[15] Clear Austrian willingness to be neutral would, they hoped, provide the breakthrough needed in the negotiations.

But the Austrians were disappointed by the Soviet response. According to information gleaned by the American State Department, Molotov was uninterested in an Austrian offer to make a declaration of neutrality. Molotov reportedly told the Austrians that a declaration of neutrality was mere words. The Soviet Union wanted something more concrete.[16]

In their independent approach the Austrians probably gambled that the Western powers, publicly committed to supporting Austria, were unlikely to use their considerable political and economic leverage to control the Austrian Foreign Ministry.[17] A State Department intelligence report candidly commented upon the hidden strength of the Austrian position in relation to the paradoxically powerless Western powers:

In pursuing their new Eastern policy, the Austrians have deliberately proceeded without consulting the Western powers. Realizing that the West is, for political and propagandistic reasons, unable to flout policies the Austrians themselves developed to attain important national aspirations, they have practically committed the West to an unqualified support of their policies. Moreover, they may rationalize that the West would be extremely reluctant to apply its already very limited economic aid leverage against Austria. The new policy affords them an opportunity to find out to what extent the U.S. is prepared to underwrite Austria's economic future. Austrian policy makers are, therefore, risking little by their actions. If the new approach succeeds, they can claim credit for having brought about a detente in the cold war. If it fails, the Western powers, in view of their strategic commitments in Central Europe, are judged to be unwilling and unable to castigate the Austrians for their deviation.[18]

The Kremlin's assessment of the situation may have been similar, for one goal of Soviet policy in Austria as in Germany was to lure the Austrians away from the Western powers. Bilateral relations between Vienna and Moscow enabled the Russians to wield more influence with the Austrians and thereby exert greater pressure on the West. The Russians must have known that the threat of a separate agreement, without Western involvement, provided a strong incentive for new Western concessions. Indeed, if Austria's independent approaches to the Kremlin had any effect at all, it was upon Washington, not Moscow. The Western powers soon showed greater flexibility about Austrian independence, but the Russians continued to demand better terms from the Austrians and to refrain from negotiating with the Western powers on the future of Austria.

Developments in East-West Relations

Throughout the summer of 1953 Western Kremlinologists continued their intense scrutiny of Soviet behavior in an effort to divine the future course of Soviet foreign policy after Stalin. On 26 July 1953 a Korean armistice agreement was signed; the Western powers saw the agreement as an indication of goodwill. On 8 August, however, Malenkov declared before the Supreme Soviet that current Soviet foreign policy would soon lead to the disintegration of the Western alliance by exploiting the contradictions inherent in the capitalist bloc. It soon became apparent that Malenkov's stridency was underpinned not only by a fresh interpretation of Stalinist ideology but also by an unprecedented confidence in Soviet strategic strength. His speech coupled a strong, surprising advocacy of negotiations in Europe with the announcement that the Russians had successfully tested a hydrogen bomb.

This was the demarche that the West had anticipated. The Western powers, compelled by the desire to retain (or regain) Austrian confidence—but more importantly by the need to recover the initiative in European negotiations—offered on 17 August to withdraw the short treaty if the Soviet government would agree not to introduce any extraneous issues. By excluding "extraneous issues," the Western Allies especially meant to preclude questions regarding the future of Germany. Once again the Western powers hoped to separate the Austrian and German issues and thereby to offset Soviet interference in the delicate process of ratifying the European Defense Community treaty and rearming West Germany.

But to the men in the Kremlin there were several reasons to avoid negotiations limited strictly to Austria. First of all, the Soviet policy of relaxation in Austria was bearing fruit: discord among the Western Allies was evident in the independent Austrian approach to Moscow and in the British and French movements to withdraw their troops from Austria. Indeed, pressure seemed if anything to be mounting on the United States to make compromises in order to satisfy the Austrians and maintain harmony among the Western powers. In Soviet eyes, events in Austria probably indicated that the time was not yet opportune to strike a bargain. Discord among the Western powers served broader Soviet interests in Europe. Second, during the summer of 1953 strikes and riots had broken out in Czechoslovakia and on a much larger scale in East Germany. Soviet troops had been needed to restore order. Such a heightened sense of unrest in Eastern Europe made August 1953 an inappropriate time for the Soviet Union to negotiate a withdrawal from Austria. Third, it seems that in late 1953 Malenkov was losing ground in the power struggle to Molotov, a hard-liner who insisted that Soviet interests could never be served by considering the Austrian and German questions separately. Molotov was reputedly adamant that no territory bought with Russian lives in wartime be surrendered in peacetime. Finally, and most important, Malenkov's public advocacy of negotiations in Europe had been primarily aimed at Germany. Negotiations strictly limited to Austria—a country that for the reasons given above the Soviet Union had no desire to evacuate anyway—would be counterproductive.

Thus the Soviet leaders refused the Western offer to negotiate strictly about Austria. Meetings scheduled for late August 1953 were canceled. The Western powers had recovered the initiative in European negotiations, but progress toward an Austrian treaty was stymied. The foreign ministers' deputies, whose last session had been held in February 1953, did not meet for the remainder of the year.

THE BERLIN CONFERENCE

On 26 November the Soviet Union suggested a foreign ministers' conference be held in Berlin. The collective leadership tried, as in the past, to impose preconditions on the meeting, including stipulations that the agenda omit the Austrian State Treaty and that the Western powers abandon the rearmament of West Germany. These demands provoked such unified public resentment in the West, however, that the Soviet Union finally proposed that the conference begin without a fixed agenda.[19] On this basis the Western powers agreed to attend, publicly expressing their hopes that the Berlin conference would lead to the reunification of Germany and to the conclusion of an Austrian treaty.[20]

There is every indication that the Western powers, particularly the United States, did not believe that these ambitious goals would be achieved and were reluctant to attend the Berlin conference. On the surface January 1954 seemed a good time for an accord on the future of Europe. The United States, its nuclear superiority still overwhelming, would bargain from a position of strength and thus could afford concessions to the Russians. The Soviet Union had apparently adopted a more cooperative approach in foreign relations, and the time seemed propitious for the West to take advantage of this new atmosphere of accommodation.

But appearances were deceiving. The Berlin conference opened with no secure basis for negotiations between the great powers. As later events confirmed, the Soviet Union was still in the throes of a struggle for succession. In subsequent months the resignation of Malenkov would prove Western suspicions that at the time of the conference no one controlled the Soviet government firmly enough to come to an accord with the West. And although the United States may have been militarily powerful in early 1954, the political position of the Eisenhower administration was unenviable. On the domestic front the hysteria of the McCarthyite era was still in force; any significant concessions to communism would be exceedingly difficult for the president to sell. In Europe, however, the apparent inflexibility of the American position on Austria and Germany had been widely criticized, and many Europeans were beginning publicly to blame the inflexible U.S. foreign policy for the lack of progress.[21] The United States thus had only limited freedom to negotiate, and yet it could not afford to refuse to enter the talks. State Department documents, as mentioned above, indicate that the United States had for some months been deliberately avoiding a foreign ministers' conference on Germany until the European Defense Community treaty could be ratified. During the weeks before the Berlin conference opened, the growing optimism in Vienna was certainly not shared in the corridors of the U.S. State Department.

Secretary of State Dulles was extremely skeptical about the upcoming conference. He would probably have refused to participate had he not believed that the Western alliance and its own international image required the United States to attend.[22] Several days before the session began, he candidly discussed his expectations with President Eisenhower. Dulles saw virtually no chance of achieving Germany's reunification at Berlin; but an Austrian treaty might be possible. Still, it is clear from Dulles's note of the conversation that his hopes lay not in the prospect of an East-West agreement but in strengthening Western unity: "I told the President that I was going to try to play a somewhat inconspicuous role at the conference, giving the leadership to the French so that the French, thus primed, might feel that they had independently arrived at the final conclusions and not been forced into them by the U.S. or that the U.S. was responsible for the failure of the conference."[23]

The Berlin conference began on 25 January 1954. On Dulles's initiative the three Western powers decided to throw the Soviet delegation off balance by agreeing almost immediately to accept the Soviet Union's agenda, which placed a proposal for a five-power conference (including China) on Indo-China and consideration of the German situation before discussion of an Austrian treaty (which actually began on 12 February).[24] The agenda itself dimmed prospects for an Austrian treaty, because sharp disagreements between the great powers over Germany had already set a very negative tone. On the first day of the talks Molotov presented a proposal that would prohibit Austria from joining any military alliances or allowing any foreign bases on its territory; "in order to prevent any attempt at a new *Anschluss*," moreover, Allied occupation forces would remain in Austria until the German peace treaty was signed.[25] On Molotov's two conditions focused the remainder of the debate on Austria.

Regarding the first condition, that Austria refrain from joining military alliances, there seemed to be room for negotiation. On the day following Molotov's proposal U.S. secretary of state Dulles went so far as to commit himself to the principle of neutrality on the Swiss model, as long as the Austrians freely chose that neutrality. To the surprise of the Austrian delegates, full participants in the negotiations for the first time, Dulles stated:

> A neutral status is an honorable status if it is voluntarily chosen by a nation. Switzerland has chosen to be neutral, and as a neutral she has achieved an honorable place in the family of nations. Under the Austrian State Treaty as heretofore drafted, Austria would be free to choose for itself to be a neutral state like Switzerland. Certainly the United States would fully respect its choice in this respect, as it fully respects the comparable choice of the Swiss nation.
>
> However, it is one thing for a nation to choose to be neutral. It is another thing to have neutrality forcibly imposed on it by other nations as a perpetual servitude.[26]

The Austrians regarded Dulles's statement as an especially significant outcome of the Berlin conference, for the leader of the Western powers had gone on record as supporting Austrian neutrality as long as that neutrality was freely chosen.[27] After the conference Austrian chancellor Raab privately concluded that only a legal commitment to neutrality freely undertaken by Austria would provide the four powers with the reassurance necessary to induce them to withdraw their troops.[28]

Whatever his personal feelings about neutrality, Dulles had publicly insisted at Berlin that the choice belonged to the Austrians alone; but he did not forswear attempts to influence the Austrian choice. During the conference the Austrians considered (to prevent another Soviet postponement) formally declaring their willingness not to become involved in any military pacts. When he got wind of the plan, Dulles had a late-night meeting with Austrian state secretary for foreign affairs Bruno Kreisky and Austrian foreign minister Leopold Figl. Dulles argued that an Austrian declaration of neutrality would be senseless and even dangerous, for it would invite Soviet interference in Austrian affairs. Only the help of the Western powers could prevent the Soviet Union from taking advantage of the Austrians.

The two Austrian officials told Dulles that they had no choice but to make some declaration of military neutrality for Austria, in order to avoid partition. Kreisky remembers the conversation as follows:

> So I said, "Yes, I admit that I am ready to accept the idea that a small

[131]

country has to have strong friends. But [in] the case of Austria, it would only be possible for half of Austria. Because if we would accept a pact or military alliance with the West, we could only get it for half of Austria. The other half would be aligned with the East. And the main goal of our policy is to preserve the unity of Austria. Therefore we cannot envisage such a development."

And it was astonishing for me to see that Dulles could be convinced it was possible.[29]

So it was that Dulles stood by as the Austrians stated several times at the conference that they would join no military alliances and would allow no foreign bases on their territory. They avoided the actual use of the word "neutrality" in order to avoid compromising their sovereignty within the terms of the treaty; still, Austria conformed exactly to the terms of Molotov's first condition. In Foreign Minister Figl's words, "I have stated unambiguously that Austria will do everything to keep herself free from foreign military influence."[30] To the disappointment of the Austrians, however, the statement seemed to have no effect upon the Soviet position.

It was not neutrality but troop withdrawals that caused the breakdown of the conference. The Western powers were all incensed by Molotov's second condition, that occupation troops remain in Austria until a German peace treaty were signed; and even the Austrians felt that it was intolerable. As there was no reasonable prospect of a German peace treaty, the second condition effectively allowed Russian garrisons on Austrian soil indefinitely. Molotov's argument, that troops were necessary to prevent another Anschluss, seemed to the Western powers illogical: after a German treaty was signed, a united Germany with its own national army would prove a far greater threat (or inducement) to Austria than a divided, disarmed Germany without a treaty could ever be.[31]

Nor did the proposal make sense in the context of the Austrian treaty negotiations. The Soviet Union seemed to indicate that, whether or not an Austrian treaty was signed, it would maintain its position in Austria as a safeguard until the fate of Germany was settled to Soviet satisfaction. Such a caveat made the treaty useless to the Austrians; indeed, most observers could hardly believe that the suggestion was serious.

Khrushchev later confided to Bruno Kreisky that Molotov had been personally responsible for the Soviet proposal. In consultations in Moscow before the Berlin conference, Khrushchev reported, Molotov had not exactly opposed the Austrian treaty but had insisted that the Soviet Union could not give up a country that it had conquered in war. Khrushchev claimed that he eventually stopped trying to convince Molotov otherwise and said, "All right, you go to the Berlin Conference and try to give the Austrians the state treaty while keeping Soviet soldiers there." And that, according to Khrushchev, is precisely what Molotov was trying to do when he proposed that Soviet troops remain in Austria until a German peace treaty was signed.[32]

Whether or not Khrushchev's self-serving explanation is true, the Soviet proposal was unacceptable to the West. In a top secret telegram sent to Washington on the morning after Molotov's proposal, Dulles informed the president that "Molotov's original presentation last night regarding Austria seemed to destroy last lingering hope of any substantial agreement here. It turned the clock back on Austria and cut heart out of proposed treaty by providing for indefinite Soviet occupation so that treaty would not be treaty of liberation but of servitude."[33] In the telegram Dulles did not even mention the neutrality issue.

The next day, 14 February, the United States made an unusual attempt to gain Soviet approval of what the West considered a reasonable Austrian treaty. Secretary Dulles, with the support of the Austrian, French, and British foreign ministers, offered to accept the long-draft treaty as last negotiated in 1949, including the Soviet version of the five remaining unagreed articles, on the condition that the treaty be signed within four days. Internationally, the offer was seen as an impressive move. Although a few observers pointed out that the treaty carried a considerable economic burden for Austria, most applauded an earnest attempt to reach accomodation with the Russians. Initially, Molotov seemed stunned; but falling back on the old, worn-out references to the "dried pea debt," Anschluss, and Trieste, in addition to the new neutrality and withdrawal conditions, he flatly rejected the offer.[34] Destroyed by Russian intransigence, the Berlin conference ended in failure.

Although the U.S. delegation may have been disappointed by the failure of its bold initiative, recently declassified American records indicate that the outcome might have been expected and even planned. An internal working document entitled "Austrian Tactical Considerations," for example, recommends that if the United States were unable to get a suitable Austrian treaty, it should "[o]ffer to sign the long draft treaty including the Soviet version of the unagreed articles on condition the offer is accepted at the Conference and no additional difficulties are raised and exploit advantage to full when Molotov refuses."[35] It therefore seems unlikely that the Americans believed that their surprising proposal would actually be accepted. The proposal was intended less as a basis for agreement than for domestic, Austrian, and Western European audiences.

Considerable attention has focused on the Western attitude toward neutrality. One important interpretation of the Berlin conference claims that the Austrians offer to assume neutral status was the crucial breakthrough, because neutrality was the vital basis for agreement which the Soviet Union had long awaited.[36] Indeed, the argument often continues so far as to assert that had it not been for Western pressure on the Austrians to refuse a written neutrality commitment, the treaty might have been signed in 1954. The strength of this hypothesis is that it is easy to document Western, and especially American, opposition to the idea that Austria should be "neutralized."[37] State Department briefing papers written before and during the Berlin conference speak candidly of the need to reject Soviet efforts to include a neutralization article in the treaty and even discussion of the "extraneous issue" of Austrian neutralization.[38]

This evidence, however, is somewhat misleading. The true position of the Eisenhower administration is not entirely clear. Even as some lower-level American planners opposed neutrality for Austria, others accepted it as a final bargaining chip.[39] Policy directives drawn up before the Berlin conference indicate that the State Department's official position on neutrality was ambiguous. More important, the highest levels of American foreign policy making were showing a surprising flexibility. For example, Dulles, in his notes on a breakfast conference with Eisenhower a few days before the start of the conference, recorded the following policy statement: "With reference to the Austrian Treaty, the President said he could see no objection to the neutralization of Austria if this did not carry with it the demilitarization. If Austria could achieve a status somewhat comparable to Switzerland, this would be quite satisfactory from a military standpoint."[40] Had the Berlin conference depended on the question of neutrality alone, the records of this secret strategy session imply that neutrality might have been accepted in 1954 as a price for the treaty, as it was eventually accepted in 1955.

It is surely no coincidence that the formula for neutrality which Dulles presented at Berlin followed closely the president's views regarding Austrian neutrality; whatever Dulles's personal reservations, he conformed to the wishes of the president during the conference. And the British and the French followed the American lead on neutrality at Berlin. Western policy with respect to Austrian neutrality did not prevent the signing of an Austrian treaty at the conference.

[134]

More to the point, Western intentions on neutrality were irrelevant to the outcome of the conference, for neutrality was not the crucial issue. The Austrian foreign minister's statement that Austria would avoid foreign military influence may have been more explicit than the Western powers wished, but it was not a stunning breakthrough. Leading Austrian politicians had for years been advocating Austria's military neutrality. Moreover, Austria had dropped hints of its willingness to be neutral in its attempts at independent bilateral negotiations with the Soviet Union a few months before the conference opened. Whatever the Western reservations, it was the Russians who did not pursue the issue of neutrality in the negotiations. The failure of the Berlin conference with respect to Austria was caused not by Western refusal to agree to Austrian neutrality but by disagreement on the question of troop withdrawals.

Nonetheless, the impending failure of the session did not seem to discourage Dulles; indeed, the spirits of the entire American delegation were if anything extremely high during the Berlin conference. In a personal letter C. D. Jackson, a member of the American delegation, made the following observations: ". . . [John] Foster [Dulles] has been absolutely superb. I suspect that this is the kind of existence he loves and because he is enjoying it, his personality is blossoming. He has supplied real generalship to the group—he works harder than anyone else. He has stiffened the wavering spines of Bidault and Eden time after time. I think he has proved a more formidable adversary than anyone Molotov has met in a long time."[41]

In fact the Berlin conference was, strictly speaking, a limited success for Dulles personally, as well as for the United States. The State Department's first priority, bringing the Western Allies together, had certainly been achieved. As British foreign minister Anthony Eden later wrote, "The efforts of the Western powers at the Berlin Conference . . . had been closely coordinated and well worked out. Despite some difficult periods, we managed always to keep in line."[42] The French foreign minister, Georges Bidault, even reportedly defended Dulles's behavior at the meetings: "He was considerably more moderate than was generally understood. It is true that he was very firm on principle. He was also sometimes very rough and rigid. But the truth is that he carefully avoided being the one to close the door to Molotov."[43]

Indeed, in 1954 Western unity was not an easy goal to attain. The Berlin conference was the apex of the cooperation between Dulles and Eden. The U.S. secretary of state and the British foreign secretary did not like each other personally, and their mutual antipathy helped put an end to the close British-American cooperation established in wartime.[44] Britain's influence on American policy with regard to Austria never regained its strength under Foreign Secretary Bevin. The pressure exerted by the British during the 1949 Paris initiative, for example, could not be repeated in subsequent years. After Bevin's resignation in March 1951 American policy had grown increasingly independent of British policy on Austria. By the time Dulles had taken full control of the State Department, the British were no longer exercising the avuncular advisory role they had so deftly filled in earlier years. In the context of Anglo-American relations—dominated by two personalities as strong and as uncomplementary as Dulles and Eden—the appearance of Western unity at the Berlin conference was no small achievement.

The second U.S. goal, signing an Austrian treaty, had not been possible; but the Russians could be blamed. The Western position on neutrality had never been put to the test because the suggestion that the Red Army remain in Austria beyond the signature of the treaty was clearly objectionable. Thus the third goal—to place the onus for failure squarely on the Soviet Union—had been accomplished with ease. U.S. interests may have benefited indirectly, but with respect to Austria the Soviet Union was responsible for destroying the Berlin conference. In February 1954 the Russians decided that it was not in their interest to give up Austria. The promise of a new approach in Soviet foreign policy evaporated as the old arguments and the old rhetoric surfaced once again. At Berlin, Molotov controlled the Soviet position; Dulles may have been "a formidable adversary," but the Austrians did not profit by it.

THE LINK TO GERMAN REARMAMENT

Soviet foreign minister Molotov's insistence at Berlin that troop withdrawals from Austria depend upon a German peace treaty satisfactory to Moscow erased any remaining doubts about the link between Austria and Germany in Soviet foreign policy. For the remainder of 1954 the future of Germany eclipsed Austria's grievances for the Soviet Union and the Western Allies alike. Indeed, as matters stood at the close of the Berlin conference, there seemed to be little promise for negotiations about Austria. Molotov was still demanding that Soviet troops remain in Austria even after an Austrian treaty was signed, Dulles that further negotiations were useless until the Soviet Union set a specific date for withdrawal. With two of the world's

[136]

most stubborn negotiators now publicly committed to contrary positions, an Austrian treaty seemed distant.

Talk of Austria's independence on the basis of Austria's own needs now seemed sadly irrelevant. It became increasingly obvious during 1954, as the Russians launched a vigorous propaganda crusade, that an Austrian treaty was to be used to help dissuade the Western electorate from rearming West Germany. Until some durable solution on Germany or some change in Soviet leadership dramatically altered East-West relations in Europe, the Soviet Union was unlikely to surrender Austria, its valuable bargaining chip.

Political conditions within Austria degenerated as local bitterness over Soviet intransigence at Berlin caused increased tension between the Russians and the Austrians.[45] The improvements in Soviet occupation policy instituted in 1953 were reversed after the conference ended.[46] By the spring of 1954, for example, film censorship had been reintroduced, Soviet unilateral actions against the press had increased, and spot checks on traffic crossing the demarcation line had begun anew.[47] The Soviet crackdown included deliberate intimidation of the Austrian government. On 17 May 1954 the Soviet high commissioner summoned the Austrian chancellor and vice-chancellor to his office and delivered a lengthy condemnation of the Austrian government, ending with the threat that if the Austrians did not stop anti-Soviet behavior in Austria then the Soviets themselves would take the necessary measures.[48] By the end of May articles in the Soviet press were attacking the Austrian government in increasingly scathing terms.[49] To the alarm and disappointment of the Austrians, the post-Stalin thaw in Austria appeared to have ended.

Meanwhile the foreign ministers of Britain, France, the United States, the Soviet Union, and the People's Republic of China were meeting in Geneva to discuss Indo-China and Korea. The Geneva conference had been planned at the Berlin conference and was one of its very few obvious by-products. On 20 July 1954 the Geneva conference settled the terms of armistice for Vietnam and divided the country into two parts, split at the seventeenth parallel. These Geneva agreements evoked very mixed reactions in Austria. Although encouraged by a slight relaxation in East-West relations, Austrian officials were concerned that the formula applied to Indo-China might be contemplated for Austria. On the day the Geneva agreements were announced, Austrian vice-chancellor Adolf Schaerf curtly stated that any attempt to solve the Austrian question by partition would bring with it the danger of a fresh war.[50]

The Austrian government attempted to take advantage of the apparent improvement in East-West relations by suggesting the formation of a five-power commission (including Austria) in Vienna. In part to avoid offending the Americans, whose secretary of state had publicly refused to negotiate until the Russians modified their demands, the Austrians asked that the commission deal with "alleviation of the current situation in Austria" rather than with the question of a treaty. In sidestepping the controversial question of a treaty, the Austrians hoped to separate their own problems from larger East-West controversies.

The government seemed desperate to get discussions going, even if only about collateral issues, in order to provide some sign of progress for its discouraged constituents. Only too aware of the precedent of Indo-China, the government may also have felt compelled to try to increase its hold on all four zones of Austria. In any case the originator of the plan, Bruno Kreisky, believed that Austrian national sovereignty might be incrementally restored through a five-member commission, even without a treaty.[51]

Although always inclined publicly to support measures that would improve the situation for the Austrians, the Western powers were concerned lest the five-member commission undercut the authority of the Allied Council, thereby weakening the control agreement. From the beginning of occupation all four great powers had deliberately avoided measures that might undercut the legal instrument of control in Austria and thereby increase the degree of uncertainty and the danger of confrontation between them. The Americans, furthermore, felt that current East-West tension made it unlikely that the five-member commission would accomplish anything substantive. Nonetheless, in order to demonstrate to the Austrians that every effort was being made on their behalf, as well as to forestall bilateral Austro-Soviet negotiations, the Western powers decided that the Austrian five-power proposal must be supported.[52]

But the Soviet Union refused to participate in the Vienna commission. The Russians argued that they remained quite willing to sign a treaty as long as discussions continued on the basis of the Russian proposal at the Berlin conference. By the summer of 1954 many Austrian intellectuals, encouraged by Soviet-sponsored communist propaganda, were beginning to suspect that the Soviet Union had been prepared to sign at Berlin but the Austrians, subservient to the whims of the Western powers, had missed their opportunity. The indeterminate presence of occupation troops "to prevent an *Anschluss*" was scarcely mentioned. By the autumn of the year the Austrian government had lost almost all hope for a treaty, and in a climate of per-

vasive pessimism Chancellor Raab reportedly gave serious consideration to allowing a few Soviet regiments to remain on the soil of an
independent Austria. The idea was apparently rejected, for the chancellor soon declared his unwillingness to sign any treaty that did not
call for the complete evacuation of Austria. Still, the Russians must
have considered their diplomatic and propaganda tactics a success,
for the deepening despondency of the Austrians increased pressure
on Britain, France, and the United States to conclude a treaty immediately and on Soviet terms.[53]

In the meantime international attention was directed to the question of Western Europe's future defense needs and, in particular, the
rearmament of West Germany within the European Defense Community. The French National Assembly had not yet endorsed the European Defense Community charter. To halt the momentum toward
French ratification, the Soviet Union urged a conference on a collective security system for all of Europe and then proposed a September
four-power meeting to lay the groundwork.[54] As an incentive the
Russians even modified their position on the Austrian treaty. West
Germany's adherence to an all-European collective security treaty—
that is, one with the stabilizing influence of the Soviet Union and
Eastern Europe—would, they conceded, be as satisfactory a prerequisite to Soviet evacuation of Austria as signature of a German peace
treaty.

The combination of alternatives to German rearmament and hints
of future Soviet concessions seemed to have some effect. On 30 August 1954 the French Chamber of Deputies rejected the European
Defense Community treaty. Soviet leaders took this rejection as proof
of success for their propaganda and diplomacy campaign, and they
barely disguised their contentment with the setback to Anglo-American diplomacy.

Soviet satisfaction was short-lived, however, for within two
months a new set of treaties was drafted to replace the abortive defense community. The Paris agreements, signed in October 1954,
provided for the direct admission of the Federal Republic of Germany
to full membership in NATO, a prospect that was even worse, in
Soviet eyes, than Germany's restricted membership in the EDC. Once
again, however, the treaties would not take effect until the signatory
governments ratified the agreements; thus the Soviet Union started a
new drive against ratification, directed particularly at the French and
German legislatures.

The Soviet crusade was very similar to the summer campaign except that, incentives, including offers of alternative all-European se-

curity arrangements, were this time coupled with threats of the detrimental consequences to ratifying the Paris accords. On 23 October, the day the Paris agreements were signed, the Soviet government proposed a conference in Vienna of the four great powers plus Austria, to discuss the conclusion of an Austrian treaty.[55] Anxious to take advantage of any opportunity for progress, the Austrian government had already indicated to the Soviet Union its willingness to take part in a Vienna meeting. Austria's agreement added pressure on the Western powers; nonetheless, they did not respond immediately to the Soviet note. On 13 November 1954 the Soviets sent another note to the United States, Britain, and France, this time proposing a conference to begin two weeks later, on creating a system of collective security in Europe.[56] Once again the Western powers did not immediately respond.

The Austrians viewed the Soviet proposals with some hope. Chancellor Raab visited the United States on 21 November and broached the question of the Western response to the Soviet demarche and its implications for Austria. Dulles assessed Soviet policy and outlined a Western response in the following terms:

> Once the London and Paris accords are complete to the point where it is clear that there will be no turning back, the Secretary said, it will be more useful to have a conference with the Soviets. He said it is the main Soviet objective to prevent the ratification of those accords and so long as that is possible any conference on any subject would be used by the Soviets only as a means of blocking ratification. After ratification, the Secretary believed that a useful conference on Austria and Germany would be possible.[57]

In line with this strategy the United States, Britain, and France simultaneously answered the two Soviet notes on 29 November, insisting that a quadripartite conference would be pointless. The Western powers, having already indicated their willingness to sign the long-draft treaty, could not understand what questions the Soviet Union could wish to discuss. With regard to the second Soviet proposal, the Western powers questioned Soviet motives in proposing a collective security conference, claiming that the Soviet Union "openly and explicitly aimed at delaying or preventing the ratification of the Paris agreements."[58] Clearly, the Western powers were determined not to risk meeting with the Soviet Union while German rearmament still hung in the balance—unless they could be certain that the meeting would achieve some positive result. To throw responsibility for progress back upon the Soviet leaders, the Western powers asked for a Soviet guarantee of good intentions in advance of any meeting. The foremost sign of good faith requested was a Soviet commitment to sign the Austrian State Treaty.[59]

On the day that the Western powers responded to the two Soviet notes, Russian leaders convened a European security conference in Moscow. Although all European powers and the United States were invited, only Eastern bloc countries attended. The Soviet Union publicly announced after the conference that participants had agreed to form their own security organization to offset NATO if the Paris accords were ratified. Having now shifted from incentives to threats, the Russians also warned that they would abrogate the Anglo-Soviet and Franco-Soviet treaties of 1942 and 1944 if the Paris agreements came into effect.[60]

During the ratification debate the Western powers had eliminated one of the issues that the Soviets had used for years as a pretext for refusing to sign an Austrian treaty. In the autumn of 1954 Trieste was divided between Yugoslavia and Italy. The settling of the issue enabled British and American troops to withdraw shortly thereafter, belying Soviet accusations that the city had become a permanent Anglo-American base.

December 1954 brought more vehement Soviet threats, specifically tying the future of Austria to the ratification debate. A Soviet note to the Western powers on 9 December stated that ratification "could not contribute to achievement of agreement" on the Austrian question. On 17 December another note warned that plans to rearm Germany would result in "new impediments for the final settlement of the Austrian question."[61] Later in the month the Soviet government made its most serious threat to the future of Austria. On 21 December the Soviet high commissioner took the unprecedented step of requesting a special session of the Allied Council. When the other three commissioners had assembled, he launched an attack on the United States for jeopardizing Austrian unity by stationing its troops in the French zone. The complaint stunned the Western powers, for the 300 American soldiers, who were occupied with administrative duties on the lines of communication between Italy and the American zone in Germany, had been in the French zone for eight years without Soviet objection.[62] Suddenly, the Russians pointed to the offense as if it were tantamount to deliberate partition of Austria. The unanticipated harangue seemed a scarcely veiled attempt to indicate that Moscow was considering partition and would probably implement it if West Germany were rearmed.[63]

This time Soviet tactics were apparently less successful, for on 30 December the French Chamber by a small margin endorsed the Paris accords. However, ratification by the more capricious French Council of the Republic was still needed. The Soviet Union redirected its efforts to persuade members of the council that German rearmament was no longer necessary. Threats became incentives once again; the Soviet government offered to discuss the reunification of Germany and, in a surprising turnabout, even suggested the possibility of holding free all-German elections and beginning atomic disarmament if only the West refrained from enacting the Paris agreements.[64]

By this time intellectuals in France, Germany, and even Britain were receiving Soviet pleas favorably. Leading political figures in the socialist parties and in liberal circles began to argue that ratification of the Paris accords should be postponed, at least until a conference between the heads of government could ensure that no more peaceable solution existed to the dispute between the Soviet Union and the Western powers.[65] At the same time voices from more conservative Western quarters countered that the Russians had already proved disingenuous negotiators in both Germany and Austria and that the only hope for a peaceful future lay in Western unity and a Western European defense system. Moreover, concern that the United States might reduce its role in Western Europe if the Paris agreements were not passed—a fear heightened by Dulles's ominous warning that failure to ratify would force the Americans to conduct an "agonizing reappraisal" of their role—strongly militated against further negotiations with the Soviets. The arguments raged through the early months of 1955; Austria's future hung in the balance, paradoxically entwined with the fate of a state with which Austria was forbidden to align itself.

[6]

The Soviet Reversal, 1955

As controversy over the Paris agreements continued in the West, evidence of a leadership struggle was emerging in the East. Soviet policies toward Austria, which had wavered between reasoned accommodation and scathing rhetoric during 1953 and 1954, even led to Western speculation that the military had taken command in Moscow.[1] In 1955, while the Western powers were still trying to determine the nature of the new leadership in Moscow, a policy change by the Kremlin had a profound effect upon the future of Austria.

Although events in the Kremlin probably will always remain a mystery to outsiders, by 1954 three protagonists in the power struggle appear to have had a significant influence on Soviet foreign policy. Premier Malenkov was apparently Stalin's chosen successor; his foreign policy speeches of 1953 and 1954 confirmed him as an advocate of relaxation on the international front.[2] Foreign Minister Molotov, seasoned veteran of the Stalin era and orthodox Soviet communist, had a visceral aversion to giving up any military positions. Communist party leader Khrushchev, a skillful opportunist, appeared to be temperamentally in favor of international coexistence but willing to adapt his ideology to suit his goals.

During 1954, it seems, Malenkov gradually began to lose control of foreign policy. Molotov's insistence at the Berlin conference that Soviet troops remain in Austria seemed inconsistent with the more moderate stand in Austria that Malenkov had supported immediately after Stalin's death. Indeed, the uncertain and sometimes incoherent policies during the remainder of the year seemed to reflect a dispute in the Kremlin over how best to use Austria in the heightening conflict with the West. The Soviet Union might offer incentives to the Western powers, including eventually an Austrian treaty, as a token of Soviet desire for détente. Austria was politically, historically, and militarily much less important than Germany to the Soviet Union, and a Soviet accommodation of the West might forestall the nightmarish prospect of an armed Germany controlling a unified Western Europe. Initially Malenkov and later Khrushchev seem to have advocated this course.[3] Or the Soviets might hold onto gains already achieved, to threaten the West with dire consequences should an anti-Soviet defense organization be formed and, in particular, to use Austria as a hostage to be ransomed only by appropriate Western behavior. This was the course of action apparently supported by Molotov. Throughout the year these two approaches had been used alternatively, and sometimes even simultaneously, much to the confusion of the Western governments.

By September it had become apparent to the West that Malenkov was losing the battle. Malenkov was missing, for example, from an important delegation to China, led by Khrushchev and his crony Nikolai Bulganin. The premier's demise was probably caused as much by the jealousies of his colleagues and his own ineptitude in the struggle for power as by his specific policies, but it was nonetheless in the debate over Soviet policy toward Europe that he lost ground rapidly to Molotov.[4] The decay of Malenkov's position coincided with the shift from mainly offering incentives to the West in October and November, to issuing threats and even considering partition of Austria in December. In late 1954 Khrushchev shrewdly allied himself with Molotov and other hard-line forces in order to bring down Malenkov. The alliance was more than the premier could withstand, and Molotov's hawkish approach soon began to prevail.[5]

The veteran foreign minister, nicknamed the "iron behind" by Lenin, clung to his belief that Austria would never be truly neutral. Most of all he feared that after the Russians withdrew, the small country would be wholly incorporated in the anti-Soviet defense system. Although the Austrians had formally announced their intention to join no military alliances and allow no foreign bases on their territory, Molotov evidently deemed such an offer of neutrality worthless. The Austrian people had already shown themselves to be economically and politically oriented toward the West. What good were promises easily circumvented by secret basing and transit agreements operative in times of war? Only a small amount of pressure from the United States would induce the Austrians to allow the Western Allies to reoccupy, the argument continued. The Soviet Union, on the other hand, with few friends in Austria, could enter Austria only by force. A Western presence might be a treaty violation, but a Soviet presence would be an invasion. The rearmament of West Germany would only exacerbate the problem. For these reasons Molotov and his sympathizers vehemently opposed evacuation, seeing continued occupation and the threat of partition as the only possible guarantees against the country's complete military incorporation into the Western bloc.[6]

By the early months of 1955, however, the campaign of threats against German rearmament seemed to be bringing about what it was designed to prevent. Ratification of the 1955 Paris accords appeared likely, and Austria's incorporation into NATO seemed ever more possible. The "marriage of convenience" being no longer useful, Khrushchev began to challenge Molotov. Confronted by the apparent failure of his hard-line approach to the West, Molotov was forced to yield to Khrushchev, who was disturbed by deteriorating relations between the Soviet Union and the West. Ideology and external interests aside, Khrushchev needed a period of international relaxation in order to introduce the economic and military programs that would consolidate his own domestic power. Furthermore, Khrushchev argued, Soviet interests were broader than the East-West struggle in Europe. He thus advocated a course bolder than anything Malenkov had dared espouse: to use an Austrian agreement primarily as a relatively cheap price for an East-West rapprochement, secondarily as a last-ditch attempt to prevent German rearmament, and finally as the symbolic beginning of a new Soviet approach to the "uncommitted" nations of the Third World.

MOLOTOV ANNOUNCES THE REVERSAL

The surprising Soviet about-face on Austria was announced by Molotov himself on 8 February 1955, in a speech before the Supreme Soviet. After fulminating against the deplorable situation in international affairs, Molotov announced that the Soviet Union would consider signing an Austrian treaty even without a German peace treaty, provided that there was a firm guarantee against Anschluss and that a conference on both Germany and Austria be convened without delay. In parts Molotov's address was confusing and inconsistent, probably because Khrushchev forced some last-minute editing upon him.[7] At the same session of the Supreme Soviet, Malenkov tendered his resignation from the premiership, citing particularly his inexperience in "local work" (which just happened to be Khrushchev's forte).[8] The session was obviously a victory for Khrushchev, and in detaching the German and Austrian treaties it broke the deadlock over Austria.

Aside from using Austria in the latest twist of Kremlin intrigue, Khrushchev and his supporters also looked to delay passage of the Paris agreements. By holding out the prospect of an Austrian treaty but requiring that a four-power conference on Germany and Austria meet first, the Soviet leaders calculated that the Austrians would pressure the Western powers to agree to a conference. Ideally, German rearmament would then be buried in Allied squabbles over the Western negotiating position. The goal, in any case, was to entice the Austrians to lobby for the conference before the French Council of the Republic could ratify the Paris accords.[9]

The immediate Western reaction to the speech was, however, surprisingly subdued. It has been argued that Western speculation about Malenkov's resignation overshadowed interest in Molotov's statements on Austria.[10] More likely, as available documents indicate, Western leaders (particularly Dulles) had long before gleaned Soviet intentions and were determined to frustrate them.[11] Coming so late in the movement toward ratification of the Paris accords, Molotov's proposal posed no tremendous threat; however, the goal of Western policy remained as it had been since the Berlin conference, to put off Soviet negotiating initiatives in Europe until German rearmament was completely assured.

In any case, the Soviet foreign minister found it necessary one week later to summon the Austrian ambassador, Norbert Bischoff, to his office and reemphasize the relevant portions of the address. Molotov particularly stressed the need for a strong guarantee against Anschluss. Two days later, while Bischoff was consulting with his government, the West German Bundestag ratified the Paris agreements. With a new sense of urgency Molotov again met with Ambassador Bischoff on 2 March. The ambassador expressed gratitude for the Soviet initiative, informed Molotov that the Austrian government could not unilaterally negotiate about a guarantee, and asked the Russians to clarify their position. An indignant Molotov claimed that the Soviet position was quite clear and asked the Austrians, in turn, to clarify their own position. The ambassador, somewhat perplexed, again contacted Vienna.

While the Austrians were consulting amongst themselves and with the Western allies, Molotov became increasingly frustrated by the lack of progress. His speech had not elicited the desired response; ratification of the Paris accords drew nearer with as yet no sign of a four-power conference or any other change of plans. To push the issue still further, Molotov summoned the entire Moscow press corps to his office on 12 March and once again reiterated the proposal he had made in his speech a month earlier.[12]

By now there was virtually no chance that the vote on the Paris accords by the French Council of the Republic, scheduled for later in March, could be forestalled. Too much time had elapsed, and any thought of organizing a conference before the question was decided was plainly futile. It is also quite possible that in the month after Molotov's speech the Western powers were secretly discouraging any quick Austrian response. In any case, it is quite clear that the Allies, particularly the United States, deliberately muted their response to suggestions of a four-power conference until French ratification of the Paris accords was assured.

THE AUSTRIAN GOVERNMENT RESPONDS

The Austrian government finally gave an official response to Molotov's speech in a note dated 14 March. Welcoming every guarantee for their independence, the Austrians repeated their intentions to join no military alliance and allow no foreign soldiers on their soil. They still avoided mentioning "neutrality," however. First of all, the Russians had in the past shown hostility toward neutral states. Second, the Western powers, particularly Britain and the United States, as a matter of principle continued to oppose a neutrality clause that would restrict Austria's sovereignty. Indeed, the Austrians themselves worried that such a restriction might eventually threaten the Austrian state.

More generally, the concept of neutrality was an ambiguous one, and the Austrians had no way to ensure that their understanding of the term coincided with the Soviet definition. The Austrian had for some time been willing to become militarily neutral, strictly in the sense that Austria would deliberately avoid joining any military alliances and would refuse to allow foreign bases upon Austrian soil. But they had no desire to be "neutralized," that is, barred from establishing political and economic ties with whatever states they chose and prevented from developing a strong national army.[13] Particularly aware of the precedent of Finland, the Austrians were afraid to allow the Soviet Union to define their neutrality.[14] When they reiterated their willingness to abjure military alliances and foreign bases on their territory, they were in fact describing their own conception of neutrality without using the word.

The Soviet government studied the Austrian note and, after some uncertainty (apparently regarding the issue of neutrality), responded favorably. In a letter of 24 March, Molotov dropped the prerequisite of a four-power conference and invited Austrian chancellor Raab to Moscow for bilateral discussions on a treaty. Three days later the French Council of the Republic ratified the Paris agreements, but the Russians did not interrupt their plans for an Austrian visit in April.

Those historians who argue that the Russians could not have intended their volte-face on Austria directly to prevent ratification of the Paris accords have a very strong case.[15] Molotov's crucial speech came too late to affect what had begun to seem an irreversible process. Had the Soviet Union announced its initiative a few months earlier, the concession on Austria might have caused irresolution in European governments. As it was, by February 1955 European opinion firmly supported German rearmament.

Still, Molotov's unprecedented and almost frantic reiterations of the new Soviet terms—terms that he himself would have adamantly opposed a few months earlier—reveal something about Kremlin activities. Molotov's own post in the Politburo was becoming increasingly tenuous during the early months of 1955. On 10 March, two days before he summoned the Moscow press corps to his office, Molotov was openly attacked in *Pravda*.[16] Ratification of the Paris accords was sure to weaken his position further, since Molotov's earlier hard line would be blamed for the foreign policy failure. Aware that he might well become Khrushchev's scapegoat, Molotov pursued the new Soviet line on Austria with the tenacity of a desperate man. It is unlikely that Khrushchev, on the other hand, ever intended an Austrian treaty or a four-power conference primarily to forestall German rearmament; indeed, his support for the treaty had more to do with his need for a breathing space in which to launch his own internal reforms. He was willing to let Molotov take the risks, however; it was not until long after the treaty was signed that Khrushchev began to take credit for the Soviet initiative. But Molotov had staked his reputation on preventing German rearmament, and in the face of overwhelming evidence that he had failed, he was willing to try anything, even an Austrian treaty.

Of course, his last-minute efforts were of no use, and in the months after the passage of the Paris accords increasing evidence attested to Molotov's loss of power. Career Soviet ambassadors in Eastern Europe, supporters of Molotov, were one by one replaced by Communist party functionaries, Khrushchev's men. In May, Molotov was excluded from the Soviet delegation to Yugoslavia; his place was taken by Dmitri Shepilov, who later succeeded him. By July he was openly attacked at the Central Committee meeting and blamed for all previous failures in Stalinist foreign policy.

Khrushchev's idea of using Austria as the first of a series of relatively easy Soviet concessions to initiate an East-West détente, or what he called "peaceful coexistence," was a prominent rationale for a treaty.[17] However, Molotov's hopes of saving himself by averting German rearmament must also be recognized. Self-centered and self-serving as their origins were, however, both primary motives ultimately benefited the Austrians most of all.

SOVIET-AUSTRIAN NEGOTIATIONS IN MOSCOW

On 11 April a delegation led by Austrian chancellor Raab of the People's party arrived in Moscow. Molotov immediately expressed the Soviet Union's desire for a quick agreement, and as talks progressed, there was no doubt that Molotov, confirmed Stalinist though he was, now earnestly desired a treaty. He seemed anxious to appear responsible for the Soviet turnaround and concentrated upon the positive aspects of the talks. He played down his demand for a guarantee against Anschluss and instead gave central importance to the question of Austrian neutrality.

For both sides the stumbling block was the precise words in which to express Austria's future status. The Soviet Union conceded that the neutrality pledge could come as a separate declaration of Parliament, enacted after the signing of the treaty, in order to protect Austrian sovereignty and demonstrate that the decision to become neutral was freely chosen. The declaration, however, had to contain the word neutrality or it would be unacceptable to Moscow. Since the Austrians had already effectively stated their intention to remain apart from military alliances, Chancellor Raab saw no objection to calling this condition "neutrality." But Vice-Chancellor Adolf Schaerf and State Secretary for Foreign Affairs Bruno Kreisky, both members of the coalition Socialist party, opposed the term because the Russians might later exploit its vagueness to make false accusations against some future Austrian government. Would not, they asked, the expression "freedom from alliances" suffice? Molotov rejected it firmly. Would Molotov accept a "foreign policy based on the principles of neutrality"? Once again the Soviet response was a firm negative. Finally, the Austrian delegates agreed to use "neutrality" on the condition that it be clarified within the declaration. "Neutrality after the

Swiss model" became the agreed formula, and from the time that phrase was approved, negotiations proceeded smoothly.[18]

With the question of neutrality settled, Molotov seemed more pliable than ever on the issue of Soviet troop withdrawals. First proposing six months for withdrawal, Molotov allowed the Soviet position to inch progressively closer to that of the Austrians until the two sides agreed that all troops should be withdrawn ninety days after the treaty came into force or 31 December 1955 at the latest. The remaining economic issues were somewhat more difficult to settle, but after some very hard bargaining by Deputy Prime Minister Anastas Mikoyan the Soviet Union agreed to reduce the Austrian oil deliveries and financial obligations to a mutually satisfactory level.[19] A date was also set for the repatriation of hundreds of Austrian prisoners of war still in Soviet camps. In the course of the negotiations the Austrians gained the clear sense that the Politburo had resolved to sign a treaty, and they pushed for all the Soviet concessions they could get.[20] In the space of a few days the Austrians and the Russians settled all the disagreements that had for years seemed impossible to resolve.

For the most part the Austrians were pleased by the course of the negotiations; however, some members of the delegation still had reservations about the neutrality arrangements. At the end of one day of talks Mikoyan approached Kreisky and asked, "Why are you looking so sorry? Are you sorry? What's happened? We had a good day." Kreisky ruefully answered, "Yes, but I am wondering what our Western friends may say." And Mikoyan retorted, "Listen, they cannot say no, because they [have] promised you the State Treaty for such a long time, now that the State Treaty will come, they cannot say no."[21]

On 15 April 1955 the Austrian delegation and the Soviet government summarized their agreements publicly in what became known as the Moscow memorandum. Both governments stated that the earliest conclusion of the state treaty was desirable. The Austrians "gave assurances that the Austrian Republic, in the spirit of the declaration made at the Berlin Conference in 1954, intends not to join any military alliances or permit military bases on her territory and will pursue a policy of independence in regard to all states which should insure the observance of this declaration." The Soviet leaders agreed that the occupation forces of the four great powers would be withdrawn by 31 December 1955. Oil refineries and other properties currently held by the Soviet Union would be transferred to Austria under terms they had agreed.[22]

Khrushchev, in a state of buoyant good humor at the close of the negotiations, gave Chancellor Raab this advice: "Follow my example

[150]

and turn Communist. . . . But if I really can't convince you then for God's sake stay as you are!"[23]

The Soviet-Austrian meeting in Moscow was the result of a shift in Soviet policy. It was caused not by any Western proposals made in the treaty negotiations nor by evidence of Austria's willingness to become neutral on the Swiss model.[24] Between 1949 and 1955 the Soviet Union did not really negotiate over Austria, because Soviet leaders had no intention of withdrawing from Austrain territory unless wider considerations indicated clearly that such an uncharacteristic action was in broader Soviet interests. In his famous "Chance for Peace" speech of 1953, Eisenhower had called for an Austrian treaty as a concrete example of peaceful Soviet intentions, and the Soviet leaders had taken note. In 1955 Khrushchev and his supporters decided that the time had come to oblige the president and initiate a thaw in the Cold War. The startling reversal of Soviet policy apparently resulted from Khrushchev's desire for an East-West détente in Europe, from the Soviet need to offset German rearmament, and from Khrushchev's plan to initiate a new Soviet policy with respect to the Third World.

The decision to sign an Austrian treaty signaled a change in Soviet foreign policy doctrine with respect to neutrality. As Harold Macmillan remarked in his memoirs, the Swiss must have been wryly amused by the sudden elevation of "neutrality after the Swiss model" to a Soviet-supported political principle. During the war the Soviet Union had repeatedly denounced the "pro-fascist," "cowardly" Swiss.[25] Indeed, the Moscow memorandum was the first official Soviet document to recognize and confirm Swiss neutrality.[26] It seems that the Russians, having failed in their attempt to prevent German rearmament, now tried to make the best of a difficult situation by acknowledging a legitimate third approach to the East-West conflict. In Europe the sudden change of Soviet policy was largely a defensive response, designed to limit the political effects of the new Western alliance.

The specific goal in Europe, difficult as it might have been, was to convince the West Germans that only military neutrality could bring about German reunification. Although both outcomes were undesirable in Soviet eyes, a neutral, reunified Germany was a slightly less undesirable prospect than an anti-Soviet, Western-supported West

Germany. In 1955 the Soviet fear that the Western powers would rearm West Germany and then launch an attack on the USSR was apparently more immediate than the threat posed by a reunified and militarily neutral Germany. Soviet propaganda after the signature of the treaty leaves no doubt that the Soviet leaders wanted a neutral Austria to serve as an example for Germany.

Indeed, the most optimistic Soviet thinkers might even have hoped that the new policy would result in a neutral corridor on the Soviet Union's Western frontier, from Finland and Sweden through Germany, Austria, and Switzerland down to Italy and Yugoslavia.[27] Certainly, the signing of the Austrian State Treaty was followed closely by Soviet attempts to improve relations with neutral or "uncommitted" states in Europe, including a Soviet trip to Yugoslavia, the return of the Porkkala naval base to Finland, and an invitation to West German chancellor Konrad Adenauer to visit Moscow. At the very least, the Soviet leaders probably calculated, the Austrian example over a long period of time would weaken Western resolve, encourage rifts in the Western alliance, and pave the way for good diplomatic relations with West Germany.[28]

But the truth was that in Europe Soviet policy, its primary aim to prevent German rearmament, had already failed, and failed miserably. Khrushchev hoped that the new Soviet position on neutrality would be favorably received in the Third World where, unlike Western Europe, many young countries still reserved judgment on Soviet communism. With its East European empire now intact, the Soviet Union under Khrushchev began to propagate a new, peace-loving image; the change in attitude toward neutrality added a touch of reasoned conciliation to an ideology that had begun to seem little more than ancient Russian expansionism. Eventually, of course, the Soviet leaders hoped to convince neutrals that only through cooperation with the Soviet Union could true peace be achieved.[29] There was always a risk that the countries of the Third World would view the Soviet reversal as a setback to Soviet communism, but in 1955 Khrushchev was willing to take that gamble.[30] The unprecedented success of Soviet Third World policies in subsequent years proved it was a worthwhile risk.

Another risk for Soviet leaders was that countries already under Soviet rule might also seek to become independent neutral countries.[31] Indeed, the Warsaw Pact was formed with this possibility in mind, not only to be a counterpart to NATO but also to ensure that Soviet troops would remain in Hungary and Romania. By their presence Soviet troops emphasized that Eastern Europe, proclaimed by the USSR a socialist fortress against "Western hostility," was entirely different from capitalist Austria. As events in Hungary during the following year suggested, however, Khrushchev's calculations in this regard were less accurate.[32]

More mundane factors also militated against continuation of the Soviet occupation. By 1955 the Russians had already extracted most of the economic and political benefits they could expect to gain from controlling Austria. When the Soviet leaders decided to grant the small state independence under a pledge of neutrality, they were actually sacrificing very little.[33]

It had long become apparent that in giving up Austria, the Soviet Union would not be compromising ideological principles. The Austrians had convincingly demonstrated that they were not inclined to become Communists, and only large-scale military intervention could ultimately bring the country into the Eastern bloc. With Western occupation troops sharing the country, the Russians dared not risk direct conflict. The failure of two putsches, the obviously Western orientation of the Austrians, and the extreme unpopularity of the Russian troops had for several years indicated that a communist Austria was, for all practical purposes, a lost cause.

Strategic calculations also favored a Soviet withdrawal in 1955. Although the Russians had been threatening for months that enactment of the Paris agreements would make negotiations on Austria impossible, in fact the opposite proved to be true. West German participation in NATO gave the Russians a greater incentive than ever to ensure a militarily neutral Austria. As William Lloyd Stearman observed, "What the Paris Agreements had joined together, the State Treaty, at least partly, put asunder."[34] The Russians were entirely aware of the anxiety of the American Joint Chiefs of Staff that a neutral Austria would with Switzerland form a wedge in the center of NATO. In the wake of their failure to stave off the formation of the Western defense pact, the Soviet leaders sought to hinder NATO's logistical capabilities. For the Russians it was hardly a sacrifice to split NATO's northern and southern flanks.

Moreover, Austria's topography rendered it logistically easy for the Soviet Union to reoccupy the eastern zone in time of war. Unlike the mountainous regions to the west, eastern Austria is a wide, open plain, extremely difficult to defend. Even today Austrian officials unofficially admit that the Soviet Union could reclaim the Soviet zone in half a day.

By 1955, moreover, the Soviet Union no longer needed the Austrian occupation as a legal rationale for keeping Soviet troops in Hungary and Romania. The original legal pretext for stationing troops in both countries had been to maintain lines of communication with Soviet troops in Austria. With the apparent consolidation of communist control in Hungary and Romania, however, the pretext was unnecessary. In case Soviet military leaders (or, indeed, the satellite countries themselves) had any doubts, the formation of the Warsaw Pact on the day before the final signing of the Austrian State Treaty gave the Russians an even better rationale for stationing troops on the territory of all of the Eastern European satellites.[35]

In his memoirs Khrushchev describes the Soviet desire to "give our comrades the benefit of all reasonable doubt" in settling economic terms with Austria and other countries.[36] But any suggestion that the Soviet Union magnanimously forfeited economic advantages when it signed the Austrian treaty is erroneous. In 1955 the Soviet Union had more to gain economically in signing the treaty than in continuing the status quo.

The Soviet-controlled USIA factories in Austria, for example, were no longer yielding tremendous profits; they had become more of a liability than an asset. Part of the decline was due to poor management. Run by Communist party functionaries who rarely had any technical expertise, the plants were rife with inefficiencies. As early as 1947 the Austrians secretly informed the American government that under Austrian management, they estimated, the current total production of $61 million from Soviet-run factories could easily be increased to $109 million.[37] In addition to management problems, moreover, the industries suffered from the Soviet Union's refusal to install new equipment or make any form of capital investment. What little capital was available in the USSR after the war was consigned to industries within the Soviet Union. Soviet leaders obviously planned to extract as much from Austria as they could, and by early 1953 this shortsighted policy had begun to take its toll. The USIA empire began to decline, and the downturn continued until the occupation ended. The Soviet-run concerns could not compete with neighboring Austrian factories, and even a system of illegal black market USIA stores dealing in smuggled East European goods failed to salvage the network. By their last year of operation the USIA industries were operating with a deficit of about 40 percent of their total production. Bankruptcies had become commonplace. When the Austrian government undertook in Moscow to buy back the entire USIA complex for $150 million worth of goods, a figure almost four times the estimated worth of $40 million (not including necessary repairs and investments), it was hardly against Soviet interests to agree.[38]

As for the Austrian oil industry, the Soviet Union had been extracting two-thirds of total oil output for its own purposes and selling the remainder back to the Austrians at a hefty profit. The terms of the treaty entitled the Russians to ten million tons of oil over ten years—one-third of total capacity if the high production rate could be continued (which was doubtful).[39] The Soviet Union was thus guaranteed its allotment regardless of actual production or reserves. By 1955, moreover, the Russians had developed their own domestic oil industry to the point where they no longer particularly needed Austrian oil.[40] Giving up control of the Austrian oil industry was therefore not a major concession.

One important incentive for signing an Austrian treaty was subsidiary benefits for the Soviet Union's relationship with Yugoslavia. Although Molotov was strongly apprehensive, Khrushchev was very interested in a reconciliation with Tito. In the ten years since the war Austrian-Yugoslav relations had evolved rapidly. From initial animosity over territorial issues, the two countries had progressed to a state of friendly relations. Shortly after the Cominform denounced Yugoslavia in 1948, the Austrians and the Yugoslavs signed a trade agreement and began to discuss frontiers and reparations.[41] In 1951 Yugoslavia declared an end to its state of war with Austria and relaxed restrictions along the border.[42] The next year the Austrian foreign minister visited Belgrade. Inspired by these friendly ties, and undoubtedly motivated by the desire to remove Soviet troops from its northern flank, Yugoslavia made it clear in early 1955 contacts with the USSR that an Austrian treaty would enhance prospects for future Soviet-Yugoslav relations.[43] It was likewise significant that in October 1954 the Trieste dispute had been ameliorated and American and British troops subsequently withdrawn, thereby eliminating another of the Soviet Union's excuses for delay. It was certainly no accident that Article 23 of the final four-power treaty on Austria granted only Yugoslavia the right to seize Austrian property within its territory; by the autumn of 1955 the Austrians and the Yugoslavs were busy with independent negotiations for the return of Austrian assets. It was also no coincidence that shortly after the signing of the Austrian State Treaty Khrushchev, Bulganin, and Shepilov—but not Molotov—paid an unexpected and highly publicized visit to Belgrade, where both sides made crucial statements about the basis of Soviet-Yugoslav relations. Khrushchev's desire to enhance his own prestige in the Yugoslav capital played its part in the Soviet decision to invite the Austrians to Moscow.[44]

The Moscow memorandum was a breakthrough, but the Western Allies' suspicions, especially the personal misgivings of Secretary of State Dulles, were not entirely assuaged. According to the American ambassador in Moscow, Charles Bohlen, Dulles was particularly wary of Foreign Minister Molotov's sudden desire for quick action, maintaining that the Western powers must not be "stampeded" into a premature peace conference. Dulles personally insisted on a preliminary meeting at a lower level, to prevent the Russians from manipulating the Western powers in the public spotlight.[45] In addition, although this aspect was never widely publicized, French, British, and American companies had their own economic interests in Austria, and all three Western governments wanted to ensure that the treaty would provide adequate compensation to their companies. When the Soviet government proposed a foreign ministers' conference to sign the treaty, therefore, the Western powers agreed but insisted that the four ambassadors in Vienna plus the Austrians meet first, to scrutinize the final terms. The Soviet Union complied with the request, and on 2 May 1955 the ambassadors' conference convened.

During his two years in office John Foster Dulles had slowly come to accept that the solution to the difficult situation in Austria would almost certainly have to be Austrian neutrality. Indeed, by 1955 he must have recognized that he had little choice but to underwrite Austrian neutrality: the French had almost completely withdrawn their forces from Austria in 1954, and the British had cut their strength down to one batallion.[46] The United States could not singlehandedly occupy all three Western zones without risking a dangerous confrontation with the Russians. He therefore resigned himself to some form of Austrian neutrality—Dulles may have been famous for his brinksmanship, but in Austria the stakes were not high enough.

In Germany, however, the stakes *were* substantial. Dulles's major concern in accepting Austrian neutrality was that the Germans might find the formula attractive. The Western powers, before agreeing to the foreign ministers' conference, had sought assurances from the Bonn government—and Dulles personally from his close friend Adenauer—that Austrian neutrality would not affect West Germany.[47] On 26 April 1955 Adenauer had even publicly stated that Western misgivings about Germany's position in light of the Austrian State Treaty were unfounded.[48] After the treaty was signed, Dulles particularly stressed that Austria's status was one of armed neutrality

[156]

and that Germany's situation was entirely different: "It is all well to talk about neutrality for a country such as Austria, a small country with 7 million people," he said. "But I do not believe that anybody realistically believes that the German people, 70-odd million of them, are destined to play the role of a neutral country."[49]

Even after he had signed the Austrian treaty, Dulles showed no sign of endorsing the abstract concept of neutrality, except in luring East European satellites out of the Soviet camp. In a closed session of the Senate Foreign Relations Committee Dulles asserted, "I do think [the treaty] is going to have a very profound effect upon the adjacent satellite countries, such as Czechoslovakia, where it opens up a new border with freedom, and in Hungary, where it opened up for the first time a border with freedom; and I believe there is a chance, at least, that the Soviets must know that and are reconciling themselves to granting a larger measure of freedom and independence to some of these satellite countries."[50] Dulles apparently considered the withdrawal of Soviet troops from Austria an encouraging success for his "rollback" policy in central Europe.[51] When asked at a news conference whether the United States would favor armed and noncommitted states from the Baltic to the Adriatic, Dulles replied: "Well, I couldn't say we are committed to any such policy; but anything which increases the national independence of the [Soviet] satellite states is along the lines of U.S. policy."[52]

Dulles reluctantly acknowledged that neutrality was a policy of survival for small countries such as Austria and Sweden, so close to overwhelming Soviet military strength. But Dulles's statement at the Senate hearing on the Austrian State Treaty proves that he did not fully accepted the concept: ". . . I think that one can recognize that in the case of small countries such as Austria and her neighbor, Switzerland, there is a legitimate place for independent neutrality. I do not think the principle is a sound one for general application."[53]

THE VIENNA CONFERENCE OF AMBASSADORS

The Vienna Conference of Ambassadors began cordially but soon degenerated into open disagreements. Acting upon Austria's request the Western powers opposed Article 16, which provided for the repatriation of displaced persons, and on their own initiative pressed for the elimination of Article 17, which limited the size of Austria's army. Both articles had been included in the long-draft treaty.[54] The Russians, committed to their treaty initiative, were for the first time thrown seriously off balance. After lengthy and heated debate the Soviet ambassador, acting on fresh instructions from Moscow, suddenly agreed to eliminate the two articles. Other arguments erupted over the date of departure for Allied troops, the restitution of British, American, French, and Dutch oil concerns, and the disposal of UN property in Austria. In all cases the Western powers obtained compromises or concessions either from the Russians or, as in the case of their oil interests, from the Austrians themselves.[55] Word came on 14 May of the final ratification of the Paris accords, but the last-minute negotiations over Austria continued uninterrupted.

The most serious disagreement concerned the long-contested Article 35, which dealt with the issue of German reparations. The Western powers wanted to include in the treaty the economic agreements that the Russians and the Austrians had reached in Moscow, thereby to ensure that Soviet leaders would not renege on the promises made in the Moscow memorandum. The Russians, however, angrily pointed out that the Western powers had earlier accepted the existing provisions of Article 35. Bilateral terms arranged between the Austrians and the Russians were a private matter.[56] By now it was 10 May and the imminent foreign ministers' meeting, with its treaty ceremony scheduled for 15 May, added urgency to the Soviet imperative not to allow the treaty initiative to fail. To increase the pressure Dulles, informing Eisenhower that "[t]he Soviets are very sticky and following their usual tactics of holding out to the last in hopes of getting some slight dividend," made it clear that he would not fly to Vienna until the economic issues were settled.[57]

Finally on Friday the thirteenth the Russians broke the suspense, agreeing to state in the treaty that Article 35 had been amended by the economic provisions of the Moscow memorandum. Dulles flew to Vienna, and the final ceremonies went ahead. At the end of the ambassadors' conference the four powers had deleted eleven articles from the treaty, eliminated three annexes, and modified three other articles.[58] The final Austrian State Treaty was far more favorable to the Austrians than the draft over which the great powers had quibbled for eight years.

With a treaty finally assured, the five foreign ministers assembled in Vienna for last-minute discussions on 14 May. In a gesture of goodwill foreign ministers Macmillan, Molotov, Pinay, and Dulles agreed to grant Austrian foreign minister Figl's request that the anachronistic "war guilt" clause, which stated that Austria bore some responsibility for fighting on the side of the Nazis, be deleted from the treaty. Molotov then proposed that the four great powers sign a declaration guaranteeing the territorial integrity of neutral Austria—a final attempt, albeit indirect, by Molotov to achieve his long-sought guarantee against Anschluss. But although the Austrians supported the idea neither the British nor the Americans were willing to risk a repetition of the Polish guarantee of 1939.[59] Molotov let the proposal die without a protest.

Meanwhile a separate treaty ceremony took place in Poland, where the Soviet Union and its six Eastern European satellites signed the Warsaw Pact agreements. And on the evening of the same eventful day Molotov informally agreed to the first postwar four-power summit conference, to be held in Geneva during July. The Russians were now practicing their own version of American-style stick diplomacy.

The Signing of the Austrian State Treaty

The next morning, 15 May 1955, the treaty ceremony commenced at the Belvedere Palace in Vienna. The streets of the capital were lined with over 500,000 joyful Austrians, and Dulles would later remark that the outpouring of emotion was one of the most moving experiences he had ever had. Each of the Western foreign ministers made a very brief statement after affixing his signature to the treaty, but Molotov, much to Dulles's special distaste, spoke for half an hour. Figl then suggested that Macmillan, Dulles, and Pinay each appear separately on the balcony of the palace to acknowledge the deafening cheers of the crowd. Molotov, apparently trying to avoid measuring the Soviet Union's relative popularity in decibels, bounded to the side of each of his colleagues and appeared on the balcony three times.[60] The Americans noted it, but by most observers the inelegant behavior of the Russian foreign minister went unnoticed. Goodwill was abundant in Vienna that day, for the Austrians had finally come to the end of a seventeen-year struggle for independence.

Conclusion

The signing of the Austrian State Treaty in 1955, after eight years of frustrating and nearly fruitless negotiations between the four powers, was hailed at the time as a great success for Western diplomacy. Yet as much as the diplomats deserve credit for heroic tenacity, the final breakthrough for a treaty had very little to do with what was happening at the bargaining table. The Soviet decision to sign could not have been based upon Western negotiating proposals, for the final treaty was much more favorable to Austria than the draft treaty that had been passionately debated for so long. The Russians agreed, for instance, to drop limitations on the size of an Austrian army, and they accepted economic terms more liberal to Austria than any they had previously considered. The end of Soviet obstruction of the negotiations was principally the result not of skillful Western diplomacy but of internal Soviet considerations and events outside Austria.

Examining Soviet Policy

Critical to the Soviet decision was the course of events in postwar Germany. Stalin and his successors were preoccupied by events in Germany and, particularly after the founding of the Federal Republic in November 1949, they hoped to use Austria as a bargaining chip against the rearming of West Germany. The Soviet campaign against ratification of the Paris accords tied Austrian independence specifically to the outcome of the rearmament debate. Moreover, Soviet insistence that a German peace treaty be prerequisite to an Austrian treaty made the link that Soviet foreign policy drew between Austria and Germany absolutely clear. Had Soviet threats concerning the future of Austria succeeded in putting off German rearmament, the Austrian State Treaty would probably not have been signed in May 1955. But Soviet tactics failed. The campaign of threats helped unify the West and, paradoxically, facilitated passage of the Paris accords. Austria lost its usefulness as a hostage against Western behavior.

With German rearmament virtually assured, a Kremlin struggle over Soviet policy toward Austria ensued. Evidence indicates that Molotov was responsible for the uncooperative Soviet stance in the treaty negotiations during 1954 and for the campaign of threats against the West. The imminent passage of the Paris agreements almost certainly weakened Molotov's position on the Politburo and enabled Khrushchev to exert greater influence on Soviet Foreign policy. The decision to sign the Austrian State Treaty directly resulted from Khrushchev's plan to use the treaty to initiate an East-West détente in Europe. A period of peaceful coexistence would enable Khrushchev to launch the domestic reforms that, he hoped, would consolidate his position as leader of the Soviet Union. Furthermore, a lessening of East-West tensions would permit him to shift the focus of Soviet diplomacy from the problematical European theatre to more promising regions in the Third World.

Molotov, realizing that he was soon to become Khrushchev's scapegoat, personally announced the turnaround in Soviet foreign policy toward Austria and then pursued a treaty. The veteran foreign minister may have nurtured some hope of halting the momentum of German rearmament; but if so, he was greatly disappointed. After the enactment of the Paris accords Molotov was attacked in the Central Committee and held accountable for all failures in Stalinist foreign policy. Khrushchev, on the other hand, got the breathing space he wanted for domestic reforms. He consolidated his power sufficiently to meet the three Western leaders at the Geneva summit conference in July 1955.

Thus the rearmament of West Germany removed the most compelling Soviet rationale for holding onto Austria; but the specific decision to sign a treaty was the unintended consequence of a power struggle between Molotov and Khrushchev, of Khrushchev's need for an East-West détente, and of his desire for a new Soviet approach to the Third World. The four-power treaty negotiations were irrelevant to the Kremlin decision to sign a treaty.

Other, more specific factors contributed to make the Austrian State Treaty attractive to Soviet policy makers. Soviet leaders were convinced that the Austrians were not inclined to become Communists, and the Russians were unwilling to risk direct conflict with the West. The Soviet Union thus did not sacrifice a potential convert to communism, and indeed, a pact of neutrality was a convenient solution to a difficult political situation. Strategic arguments favored signature of a treaty. Austria's military neutrality prevented its incorporation into Western defense plans and split the northern and southern flanks of NATO. Shortly before the treaty was signed, furthermore, formation of the Warsaw Pact reduced the Soviet need for a forward strategic position in Austria. Economically, the Soviet Union in signing a treaty probably gained more than it lost. On political, strategic, and economic grounds, therefore, the signing of the Austrian State Treaty was no great sacrifice for the Russians.

The Austrian State Treaty signified an important doctrinal shift in Soviet ideology, to an open acceptance of the concept of neutrality for states outside the Soviet communist realm. In the wake of the Truman Doctrine, the Marshall Plan, the formation of NATO, and the rearming of West Germany the Soviet Union was on the defensive in Europe. By endorsing Austrian neutrality, the Soviet leaders hoped first of all to convince the Germans that military neutrality was the only means to achieve German reunification. Within a month of the signing of the Austrian State Treaty, the Soviet government invited Chancellor Adenauer to Moscow and suggested the establishment of diplomatic relations. Second, the Soviet Union hoped to strengthen its position in Europe by improving relations with other "neutral" or "uncommitted" states. The return of the Porkkala naval base to Finland and the overtures to Yugoslavia were additional elements of the new conciliatory policy.

But whatever the European reaction, a favorable reception was likely to greet the new official Soviet attitude toward neutrality outside Europe. The Berlin blockade and the Prague coup had poisoned the cause of Soviet communism west of the Berlin Wall, but the peoples of the less developed countries, many of them alienated from their former imperialist masters, were more receptive to new ideas. Recently the Chinese Communist Revolution of 1949, an exciting successor to the Bolshevik Revolution, had begun to capture the admiration of many nonaligned countries. Acknowledging a third way between East and West added a new touch of reasoned conciliation to post-Stalin Soviet ideology; by the end of 1955 Khrushchev and his followers had effected a dramatic Soviet demarche, including state visits to India, Burma, and Afghanistan, flamboyant denunciations of Western "colonialism," and offers of technical and agricultural assistance to any underdeveloped Arab or Asian country. The Austrian State Treaty was the first step in a long-term international campaign to project a fresh, peace-loving image of the Soviet Union to the Third World.

The difficulty for Khrushchev was that this fresh new Soviet image in some cases proved attractive to the wrong people. The Hungarians, for example, were culturally and historically tied to the Austrians; a Hungarian uprising occurred almost exactly twelve months after the Austrians declared permanent neutrality. Some Austrians believe that their example contributed to the incentives for a Hungarian uprising, but on that we can only speculate. Clearly, however, the crushing of the Hungarian revolt by Soviet troops in November 1956 made obvious the limits of the new Soviet approach to independence and neutrality; and repeated condemnation by the United Nations of the Soviet action in Hungary tainted the new, peace-loving image of the Soviet Union.

Quadripartite negotiations were not decisive in the settlement of the Austrian problem, but the behavior of the Soviet Union during the eight years of talks encourages several observations about Soviet negotiating tactics. First, Soviet representatives tended to avoid making concessions in order to save up bargaining points for future use. They thus made the smallest concession or change of policy look more significant than it was and gained maximum benefit from it. Unlike the Western delegates, Soviet negotiators were quite willing to appear publicly unreasonable if doing so served their long-term plan. The Western powers, responding much more directly to public pressure, tended to make concessions as demonstrative gestures, regardless of whether or not the Soviet Union was likely to match the concession in the negotiations.

Second, the Soviet Union seemed to enter each session of talks with a preconceived notion of the outcome it considered to be in the best Soviet interest. Before the end of 1949 this preferred outcome was closely tied to the economic provisions Stalin hoped to gain from Austria itself; thereafter the outcome was connected to the long-term political uses that the Soviet Union hoped to make of its Austrian occupation. When, particularly after 1949, an inflexible Soviet stance bore no relation to a negotiable position, Soviet delegates preferred to take the blame for causing negotiations to fail rather than alter their preconceived position. A successful round of negotiations was not in itself a Soviet goal. Only in 1955, after the Soviet leaders had unilaterally decided to sign a treaty, was the Soviet Union concerned about successful negotiations. The unusual concessions that the Russians made to the Austrians in Moscow gave evidence of that concern. By contrast, the Western powers' imperative was not to appear responsible for the failure of negotiations; when failure was imminent, they were more likely than the Soviet Union to try to avoid blame by compromising their predetermined negotiating position.

Finally, the negotiations were not a catalyst to Soviet action. By clearly bearing the responsibility for the continued oppression of Austria, Soviet leaders maneuvered themselves into a position of strength with regard to Austria. The Western powers had no involvement in the Soviet demarche that led to the treaty; the decisive negotiations occurred bilaterally, between the Austrians and the Russians in Moscow. Soviet negotiating intransigence in the end gave Soviet leaders the power to determine when the treaty would be signed.

Indeed, Anastas Mikoyan's candid assessment of the Western powers' predicament in 1955 was correct: once the Soviet Union decided to sign a treaty on the understanding that Austria would be militarily neutral, the three Western powers had little choice but to concur. Britain, France, and the United States had been publicly endorsing the treaty for years, laying full blame for delay at the feet of the Soviet Union, presenting themselves as champions of Austrian independence, and enjoying the public approbation that accompanies a valiant effort against an obvious villain. Once the Soviet Union decided to change policy and the Austrians agreed, the Western powers were powerless to resist—even if they had wanted to do so. Their refusal to make concessions and their years of unreasonable behavior gave the Soviet leaders all the cards. The Western powers, apart from handing Austria over to permanent Soviet occupation, had no more concessions to make; they had agreed to accept Soviet economic terms for the treaty as early as 1949. In a curious twist of logic, by 1955 the Soviet Union's intransigent refusal to negotiate had given it control of the negotiations over Austria.

Once the Soviet Union announced in the Moscow memorandum its intention to sign the treaty, however, negotiating advantage shifted back to the Western powers. Britain, France, and the United States could not refuse to sign the treaty or oppose the Austrian declaration of neutrality; but they could, and did, ensure that the specific terms of the treaty were as favorable as possible to Western and Austrian interests.

The achievement of a treaty in May 1955, therefore, was the result of an abrupt change in Soviet foreign policy. The specifics of the treaty resulted from the policies of the Austrians and the Western powers.

[164]

THE EVOLUTION OF WESTERN POLICY

Unlike that of the Soviet Union, the policies of the three Western powers toward Austria underwent a traceable evolution over the eight years of negotiations. Western claims always to have been religiously seeking a treaty since negotiations started in 1947 were not entirely true. The public image—unified Western powers are repeatedly stymied in their earnest quest for Austrian independence—was carefully cultivated but not always accurate. The British came closest to the image, supporting a treaty throughout the years of the negotiations; but that support was motivated increasingly by domestic economic and political needs rather than by sober calculations of Austria's long-term interests.

Bearing the lion's share of the responsibility for Austria's security and its economic recovery, the Americans in particular harbored secret misgivings about signing a treaty: in the late 1940s because Austria had no indigenous army to protect itself from Soviet encroachments, and in the mid-1950s because a treaty of neutrality would seriously complicate NATO defense planning. Indeed, it was primarily because of American misgivings that an Austrian treaty was not signed on Soviet terms in 1949.

The bureaucratic battle over the American position in 1949 affords an unusual insight into the formation of American foreign policy. The State Department and the Defense Department argued for months over the American negotiating position for the Austrian talks, and U.S. national policy was gradually lost in the quagmire of middle-level bureaucratic squabbles. Even the heads of the two departments, responding to signals from below as much as they directed departmental policy from above, could not reach agreement. Because Austria's future was not central to American foreign policy, moreover, the president was not aware of this lower-level controversy. Only when President Truman learned of the bureaucratic stalemate was a decision quickly reached and American policy clarified in accordance with his wishes.

While the U.S. Defense and State departments were haggling over American policy, the British and the French were facing economic realities that undercut their interest in political and strategic issues. The Western powers diverged in the later years of the negotiations as the British and the French withdrew most of their troops from Austria without a treaty, leaving still more of the burden of the occupation on the United States.

[165]

Events outside Austria also preoccupied the Western powers and reduced their interest in a treaty. The Korean War helped bring progress in the negotiations to a standstill; the Western powers were unwilling to negotiate with the Russians when their attention and resources were devoted to the "Soviet-sponsored" invasion of South Korea. American domestic considerations, particularly the anticommunism of the McCarthy era, limited both the Truman and the Eisenhower administrations' freedom to compromise with the Russians. In 1954 and early 1955, furthermore, the Western powers were primarily concerned with events in Germany, where they hoped to accomplish rearmament before Soviet conciliatory gestures could weaken Western resolve.

Perhaps most interesting of all is what the Austrian government was telling the Western powers during the years of occupation. Despite their public statements the Austrians themselves were not always unreservedly in favor of a treaty. The economic terms negotiated between the four powers in the late 1940s would have been extremely burdensome for Austria and may have precipitated the downfall of the government. British and American documents contain clear evidence of occasional Austrian reluctance to take on sole responsibility for payments to the Soviets. Sometimes the Austrians pressed the Western powers not for immediate signature of the treaty but for changes in occupation policy to strengthen the Austrian government and encourage the Austrian people.

Only during the early 1950s, when a complete lack of progress in the negotiations encouraged fears that Austria might be partitioned, did the Austrians clearly tell the Western powers that they had to have a treaty immediately. And at that point the Austrians' frustration with the slow pace of negotiations and Western preoccupation with other international problems led them to initiate independent bilateral contacts with the Soviet Union. At the time these contacts seemed to have far more effect on the Western powers than on the Soviet Union, encouraging Britain, France, and the United States to make fresh overtures in the negotiations.

Although Austria never controlled its own fate, in the early 1950s the Austrians occasionally exercised a leverage with respect to the Western powers which was out of proportion to the small country's strength. Signs of Austrian discontent seriously embarrassed the Western powers, whose international image as champions of the beleaguered Austrians was itself several times challenged. Moreover, the Western powers realized that bilateral discussions between the Austrians and the Russians gave the Soviet Union increased control

[166]

over Austria's fate. It was, in fact, through just such bilateral channels that the Soviet Union, after its shift in foreign policy, eventually initiated the events that led directly to the treaty.

Happily for the Western powers, the Soviet Union did not make the decisive move toward an Austrian treaty until German rearmament was essentially assured. Nonetheless, it is interesting to speculate about what might have happened had the Soviet Union agreed to grant Austria neutral status and withdraw the troops one year earlier. Molotov's refusal to conclude such an agreement at the Berlin conference of 1954 may have been a tactical error. A well-timed Soviet diplomatic gesture in the months before Germany's inclusion in the Western alliance might conceivably have nudged volatile French and even German public opinion away from support of a rearmed Germany.

But such speculation is of limited value, for only in hindsight is it clear that the Soviet campaign against rearmament was destined to fail. John Foster Dulles was certainly worried that the Soviet Union might succeed in undermining the Western defense effort, and the refusal of the French National Assembly to ratify the European Defense Community charter seemed to confirm his worst fears. By the time that Soviet leaders, preoccupied by their own domestic leadership struggle, recognized that their complicated calculus of threats and incentives was going to fail in Western Europe and changed policy, it was too late to reverse the tide of German rearmament. The Soviet volte-face over Austria occurred only after it was apparent that the Western alliance was gathering strength.

Whatever the long-term strategic significance of the Austrian State Treaty, the timing of the Soviet demarche was very fortunate for unity in the Western alliance. At the time the treaty was signed, the Soviet withdrawal from Austria could be hailed as a success for Western diplomacy without seriously threatening Western defense goals in Europe. After giving varying degrees of support over the years to the Western diplomatic effort, France, Britain, and the United States finally came in 1955 to a clear consensus for a treaty.

LESSONS OF AUSTRIAN NEUTRALITY

The Austrian State Treaty was an instrument that legally formalized Austrian statehood and independence. On 5 November 1955, after the last foreign soldier had left Austrian soil, a constitutional law establishing Austria's permanent neutrality came into effect. The Austrians thus demonstrated that they had themselves chosen military neutrality as state policy and that it had not been forced upon them.

It is not my purpose to argue that the Austrians were forced to become neutral; there is no question that the Austrians in the end acted of their own free will in choosing permanent neutrality. There were, however, important international circumstances that enabled the Austrians to make such a choice. The identification of those international circumstances may make it possible to determine whether the Austrian solution might be more generally applicable to states caught in conflicts of interest between major powers.

After the Soviet Union had consolidated its Eastern European position and the Western powers had formed an alliance under American leadership, the dispute over Austria became essentially bilateral. In abstract terms, then, by 1955 the struggle over Austria had evolved to the point where there were two major actors and four possible outcomes. First, one great power could take over Austria because it needed Austrian territory for some larger purpose. However, in practice neither major actor considered Austria vital or was willing to take the risk of incorporating the entire country. Second, one great power could take over all of Austria in order to prevent the other from doing so. Once again, neither major actor considered this option worth the risk. The two remaining possibilities were partition and neutral unity.

In theoretical terms, then, why was Germany partitioned and Austria left unified and neutral? The Austrian experience indicates that there are at least six conditions necessary for a state to declare itself neutral between opposing power blocs. Germany met none of them.

First, the territorial boundaries of the state must be clearly agreed, both by the great powers and by the smaller state itself.[1] Early great power agreement upon Austria's 1937 boundaries and the Austrians' clear lack of expansionist ambitions or capabilities satisfied this requirement. While Germany's territorial boundaries appeared clear, on the other hand, the recently expansionist ambitions of the Third Reich undercut any faith the great powers (and particularly the Soviet Union) had in a unified Germany's adherence to those boundaries.

Second, the state in question must have a single national government capable of undertaking to guarantee its own neutrality. Austria had a national government from the earliest months of the occupation, and that government gradually gained strength and legitimacy with the passage of time. Germany never had a single national government after the war.

Third, the state must not allow foreign actors to use its territory for military purposes. Austria satisfied this condition after the troops of the four powers withdrew, by undertaking not to participate in foreign military alliances and by developing an Austrian army to deter the ambitions of any stronger power. Germany could not undertake to prevent foreign powers from using its territory, particularly after the Federal Republic became a member of NATO.

Fourth, the great powers must be able to save face and maintain prestige when a country chooses neutrality between them. The unusual thing about the withdrawal from Austria was that both major actors gained public approbation: the United States (and its allies, France and Great Britain) claimed a diplomatic and moral victory while the Soviet Union earned diplomatic benefits by making a seemingly dramatic concession. The situation with respect to Germany was entirely different. The Soviet Union was unwilling to give up East Germany, and the United States and its allies were determined to have a West Germany rearmed and in NATO.

Fifth, there must be clear agreement between the great powers and the country itself about the defensive posture of a potentially neutral state. Will it be armed or unarmed? Will there be limits on armaments? No agreement could be reached on this matter with respect to Germany. Regarding Austria, however, both sides wanted the country to be armed. Complicated motives, East and West, led to this consensus: the Western Allies saw Austrian defenses pointed east, the Soviet Union saw Austrian defenses pointed north, and the Austrians, officially anyway, maintained a tactful silence.

Finally, the country itself cannot be of such absolutely vital strategic, historic, or economic importance to any great power that it would risk war over it. By 1955 Austria fit this description; Germany did not.

These six conditions are necessary requirements for neutrality, but they may not be sufficient in themselves to guarantee a successful neutral policy. As in the case of Germany, additional international circumstances often complicate the position of any particular state. The Austrian experience shows, however, that only a state that meets all of the above conditions will be able to assume a position of neutrality between opposing great powers.

IMPLICATIONS FOR POSTWAR DIPLOMACY

One alternative to the years of fruitless negotiations might theoretically have been to refer the problem of Austria's future to UN arbitration. Indeed, at the 1947 Moscow council of foreign ministers,

U.S. secretary of state George Marshall went so far as to propose turning the problems of Austria over to the United Nations, and during the early years of the negotiations quite a few U.S. State Department officials supported this course of action. For a number of reasons, however, the action was never taken.

None of the four occupying powers showed any sincere belief that UN arbitration would be superior to four-power negotiations, and all apparently feared a loss of control over the outcome. Even the American support for UN involvement was influenced in no small part by the belief that any UN solution would accord closely with U.S. interests and that UN involvement would be popular domestically. The British and the French were never enthusiastic about the idea; the British privately considered even Austrian foreign minister Karl Gruber's brief resort to the United Nations in 1953 more of a propaganda stunt than a useful contribution to the negotiations. The Soviet Union publicly resisted all suggestion of UN involvement. The Russians vetoed the 1947 Austrian application for UN membership, and they kept the Austrians out of the organization until after the treaty was signed. That Austria was not a member of the United Nations prevented the Austrian government from appealing for greater UN involvement during all the years of great-power bickering over its future.

The Austrian negotiations were just the sort of great-power morass that the new international organization might have been expected to help resolve. The irrelevance of the United Nations to the Austrian treaty negotiations helped demonstrate the inadequacy of that organization where the interests of the major powers conflicted. Although the former wartime allies ostensibly supported this new, global institution for settling disputes, in practice the postwar negotiations over Austria were in some ways reminiscent of the nineteenth-century Concert of Europe. To be sure, twentieth-century European diplomacy had undergone an important historical transition, for unlike their earlier counterparts the new great powers certainly did not share common values; nonetheless, the postwar negotiations echoed an earlier era of European diplomacy.

One basis of the Concert of Europe had been a conception common to all of the great powers of the European international system.[2] While World War II had thrown Europe into flux, by 1955 the leaders of the United States and the Soviet Union had come, reluctantly or not, to a new shared conception of postwar Europe. In early 1955 the division of Germany was assured, and the consolidation of the Western alliance and a more tightly controlled group of Soviet client-states had drawn a line through the continent. Soviet leaders sought to finalize and formalize the U.S. and Soviet spheres of influence just as the Western alliance was gathering strength. Austria was the final "grey area" between the two spheres, ideologically and culturally part of the West but still within the grasp of the Soviet Union. Complete, unqualified relinquishment of all Soviet control over Austria would have meant, in Soviet eyes, extension of Western influence to the borders of Hungary and Czechoslovakia. The Soviet Union found it far more advantageous to deny the country militarily to the West than to cling to the eastern portion of Austria.

With the signing of the Austrian State Treaty in 1955, the U.S. and Soviet spheres of influence in postwar Europe were finally drawn, and despite Western hopes (Dulles's especially) of rollback in Eastern Europe, those spheres have endured. Most Eastern Europeans have come to realize through harsh experience, in Hungary in 1956 and Czechoslovakia in 1968 for example, that while the West earnestly espouses universal principles of freedom and democracy, the importance of the division of Europe and the tremendous implications of any military intervention over the East-West line have thus far proved paramount. As in the microcosm of the Austrian occupation, neither side will lightly risk global war in order to impose Soviet communism upon an unwilling people west of the European demarcation or to liberate the restive groups currently under Soviet control.

The East-West line of demarcation on the continent of Europe, established in its current form in May 1955, has endured. Whether that division will be challenged or altered in the near future is beyond the scope of this book. Nevertheless, 1955 was a watershed in the Cold War. It separated the immediate postwar years of uncertainty from the clear East-West status quo that Europe has known ever since. Fortunately for the Austrians, that bilateral status quo has been a stable and prosperous one.

Notes

1. André Fontaine, *History of the Cold War from the Korean War to the Present*, trans. Renaud Bruce (New York: Random, 1969), p. 126.

2. The best of these accounts available in English are Cary Travers Grayson, Jr., "Austria's International Position, 1938–1953: The Reestablishment of an Independent Austria" (diss., Etudes d'Histoire Economique Politique et Sociale, Geneva, 1953); William Lloyd Stearman, *The Soviet Union and the Occupation of Austria: An Analysis of Soviet Policy in Austria, 1945–1955* (Bonn: Siegler, 1962); and William B. Bader, *Austria between East and West, 1945–1955* (Stanford: Stanford University Press, 1966).

3. Gordon Shepherd, *The Austrian Odyssey* (London: Macmillan, 1957), pp. 237–40.

4. Philip E. Mosely, "The Treaty with Austria," *International Organization* 4 (February 1950): 220.

5. Karl Gruber, *Between Liberation and Liberty: Austria in the Post-War World* (London: Deutsch, 1955), p. 43.

6. The term "great power" here refers specifically to the United States, Great Britain, the Soviet Union, and, more loosely speaking, France, between the years 1945 and 1955.

7. For those who read German, I highly recommend the following excellent historical accounts: Gerald Stourzh, *Geschichte des Staatsvertrages, 1945–1955: Österreichs Weg zur Neutralität* (Graz: Styria, 1980); Manfried Rauchensteiner, *Der Sonderfall: Die Besatzungszeit in Österreich 1945 bis 1955* (Graz: Styria, 1979); and Stourzh, *Kleine Geschichte des Österreichischen Staatsvertrages* (Graz: Styria, 1975).

1. The "Liberation" of Austria, 1945–1946

1. M. Gousev, Soviet Embassy, London, to Sir William Strang, Foreign Office, with enclosures: "Declaration of the Soviet Government on Austria," and "Marshal Tolbukhin's Appeal to the People of Vienna," 9 April 1945, F.O. 371/46614(C1392), Public Records Office, Kew (hereafter PRO).

2. U.S. Headquarters, Forces in Austria Advanced, Vienna, to War Department, PV 7521, 18 September 1945, R.G. 218, Records of the Joint Chiefs of Staff, Modern Military Records Division, National Archives, Washington, D.C. (hereafter NA).

[173]

3. Allied Forces Headquarters, Caserta, Italy, to War Department, F 94530, 17 June 1945, R.G. 218, Records of the Joint Chiefs of Staff, NA.

4. Gordon Shepherd, *The Austrian Odyssey* (London: Macmillan, 1957), p. 242.

5. For example, this polite note of objection was sent in April 1945: "His Majesty's Government are sure that the Soviet Government will agree that our common purpose might well be prejudiced by unilateral action on the part of any one of the occupying Powers in regard to the removal of industrial plant and equipment, regardless of whether or not this was German owned. . . ." Text contained in a letter to the prime minister from Sir Anthony Eden, 12 July 1945, F.O. 371/46610(C3945), PRO.

6. See, inter alia, John Mair, "Four-Power Control in Austria, 1945–46," in Royal Institute of International Affairs, *Survey of International Affairs, 1939–1946*, ed. Arnold Toynbee (London: Oxford University Press, 1956), p. 298.

7. Interview with Professor Stephan Verosta, professor of international law (emeritus), University of Vienna, in Vienna, 6 December 1983.

8. Richard Hiscocks, *The Rebirth of Austria* (London: Oxford University Press, 1953), p. 24. Indeed, memories of the early days of Soviet occupation remain so vivid in Vienna that the huge statue of a Red Army soldier which stands in Schwarzenbergplatz is still known as "the unknown rapist." Milton Colvin, "Principal Issues in the U.S. Occupation of Austria, 1945–1948," in *U.S. Occupation in Europe after World War II: Papers and Reminiscences from the April 23–24 Conference Held at the George C. Marshall Research Foundation, Lexington, Virginia,* ed. Hans A. Schmitt (Lawrence: Regents Press of Kansas, 1978), p. 106.

9. See, inter alia, Karl Gruber, *Between Liberation and Liberty: Austria in the Post-War World* (London: Deutsch, 1955), pp. 19–27; Carl Travers Grayson, Jr., "Austria's International Position, 1938–1953: The Reestablishment of an Independent Austria" (diss., Etudes d'Histoire Economique Politique et Sociale, Geneva, 1953), pp. 70–71; and Mair, "Four-Power Control," pp. 300–303.

10. Telegram, Churchill to Truman, no. 25, 30 April 1945, R.G. 218, U.S. Joint Chiefs of Staff Chairman's File, Admiral Leahy, 1942–1948, Box 1, Folder 2, NA.

11. Ibid. It should be noted that the first independent British protest to Moscow occurred on 28 April 1945; see Manfried Rauchensteiner, *Der Sonderfall: Die Besatzungszeit in Österreich 1945 bis 1955* (Graz: Styria, 1979), p. 73. Since the protest had apparently been ineffective, Churchill was extremely anxious to make a joint Anglo-American approach to Stalin.

12. See Harry S Truman, *The Memoirs of Harry S Truman*, vol. 1: *Year of Decisions, 1945* (London: Hodder & Stoughton, 1955), pp. 135–36, and Winston S. Churchill, *The Second World War*, vol. 6: *Triumph and Tragedy* (London: Cassell, 1954), pp. 451–52. Indeed, in the earliest days of his administration President Truman complained to Eleanor Roosevelt that his difficulties with Churchill were almost as irritating as those with the Russians. Harry S Truman to Eleanor Roosevelt, 10 May 1945, cited by Joseph P. Lash, *Eleanor: The Years Alone* (New York: Signet/NAL, 1972), pp. 18–19.

13. Telegram, Churchill to Stalin, relayed in a telegram from Churchill to Truman, no. 29, 1 May 1945, R.G. 218, U.S. Joint Chiefs of Staff Chairman's File, Admiral Leahy, 1942–1948, Box 1, Folder 2, NA.

14. Telegram, Truman to Churchill, no. 41, 16 May 1945, R.G. 218, U.S. Joint Chiefs of Staff Chairman's File, Admiral Leahy, 1942–1948, Box 1, Folder 2, NA.

15. Mark Clark, *Calculated Risk* (London: Hamilton, Panther ed., 1956), pp. 410–11, and Robert L. Ferring, "The Austrian State Treaty of 1955 and the Cold War," *Western Political Quarterly* 21 (December 1968): 654.

16. Message, Allied Forces Headquarters, Caserta, to War Department, F94530, 17 June 1945, R.G. 218, U.S. Joint Chiefs of Staff Chairman's File, Admiral Leahy, 1942–1948, Box 1, Folder 2, NA.

17. Quoted in the *Times*, 22 June 1945; also cited by Mair, "Four-Power Control," p. 308.

18. Mair, "Four-Power Control," p. 308.

19. Churchill, *Triumph and Tragedy*, p. 524.

20. See, for example, Ferring, "Austrian State Treaty of 1955," pp. 653–54.

21. U.S. Department of State report on the "Political Situation in Austria," forwarded by Joseph C. Grew, acting secretary of state, to President Truman, 4 May 1945, President's Secretary File, Harry S Truman Library, Independence, Missouri.

22. Clark, *Calculated Risk*, pp. 414–15.

23. Anthony Eden, *The Memoirs of Sir Anthony Eden: Full Circle* (London: Cassell, 1960), p. 305.

24. Guy David Douglas Stanley, "British Policy and the Austrian Question, 1938–1945" (diss., University of London, 1974), p. 314.

25. Philip E. Mosely, "The Treaty with Austria," *International Organization* 4 (May 1950): 228–30.

26. The United States and the French each had separate individual sectors of Vienna, but the Russian and the British sectors were split and not contiguous. All four powers were represented in the international sector.

27. Richard Hiscocks, *The Rebirth of Austria* (London: Oxford University Press, 1953), p. 23.

28. Mair, "Four-Power Control," p. 300. The government was composed of ten representatives from the Socialist party, nine from the People's party, seven Communists, and three independents.

29. The text of the declaration can be found in *Red-White-Red Book: Descriptions, Documents and Proofs to the Antecedents and History of the Occupation of Austria (from Official Sources)* (Vienna: Austrian State Printing, 1947), pp. 211–12.

30. "Reasons for British Failure to Recognize the Renner Government," U.S. Army OSS Report, 30 September 1945, R.G. 226, No. XL18806, Modern Military Records Division, NA.

31. Top secret briefing book, Naval Aide Files of Harry S Truman, Box 1, Folder: Berlin Conference, vol. 1, Agenda Proposed by the Department of State, 30 June 1945, Truman Library. (At the time the Potsdam Conference was also referred to as the Berlin Conference, because of the proximity of Potsdam to Berlin.)

32. Elisabeth Barker, *Austria, 1918–1972* (London: Macmillan, 1973), p. 157.

33. Top secret briefing book, Naval Aide Files of Harry S Truman, Box 1, Folder: Berlin Conference, vol. 1, Agenda Proposed by the Department of State, 30 June 1945, Truman Library.

34. "Information Concerning the Renner Government," U.S. Army OSS Report, 16 August 1945, R.G. 226, No. L58495, NA.

35. Mosely, "The Treaty with Austria," p. 220.

36. Gruber, *Between Liberation and Liberty*, pp. 28–32, and Barker, *Austria, 1918–1972*, p. 161.

37. U.S. Central Intelligence Agency, "The Current Situation in Austria," ORE 56-49, published internally 31 August 1949, President's Secretary File, Truman Library.

38. Barker, *Austria, 1918–1972*, pp. 161–62.

39. See, inter alia, a paper drafted by the German Political Department dealing with the future prospects for Austria with particular reference to the question of an Austrian

treaty, cover letter signed by J. A. M. Marjoribanks, 24 September 1947, F.O. 371/64101(C12784), final version, F.O. 371/64102(C12938), PRO.

40. Sven Allard, *Russia and the Austrian State Treaty: A Case Study of Soviet Policy in Europe* (University Park: Pennsylvania State University Press, 1970), p. 99.

41. Message from Civil Affairs Division, Operations Division, War Department, to commanding general, U.S. Forces Austria, Vienna, WAR 88638, 20 May 1946, R.G. 218, Joint Chiefs of Staff Chairman's File, NA.

42. Clark, *Calculated Risk*, pp. 427–28.

43. "Russian Interference in Austrian Politics," U.S. Army OSS Report, 13 March 1946, R.G. 226, NA.

44. British Embassy, Washington, to Department of State, "Proposal for reduction of forces of occupation in Austria," 28 November 1945, F.O. 371/46636(C9325), PRO.

45. Telegram, Earl of Halifax (British ambassador to the United States) to Foreign Office, London, No. 8007, 30 November 1945, F.O. 371/46635(C9028), PRO.

46. Telegram, British Delegation, Mosow, to Foreign Office, London, no. 42 Worthy, 19 December 1945, F.O. 371/46637 (C9862), PRO.

47. Memorandum, Lt. General McCreery, commander-in-chief, British troops in Austria, to General Anderson, London, Subject: "Future arrangements in Austria," 24 October 1945, F.O. 371/46634(C7790), PRO.

48. "Austria: Discussions between Mr. Bevin, General McCreery and Mr. Mack" (with Foreign Office Minutes), Foreign Office, London, 15 November 1945, F.O. 371/46634(C8360), PRO.

49. Ibid.

50. Telegram, acting secretary of state to the U.S. ambassador in the United Kingdom (Winant), no. 623, 19 January 1946, and telegram, U.S. ambassador (Caffery), Paris, to Department of State, no. 455, 29 January 1946, in *Foreign Relations of the United States, 1946*, vol. 5: *The British Commonwealth; Western and Central Europe*, p. 298.

51. Memorandum, Mr. Riddleberger, U.S. Department of State, regarding meeting with Mr. D. D. Maclean, first secretary of the British Embassy, conveying Russian reply to British approach in Moscow, ibid.

It should be noted that "D. D. Maclean" was the notorious British spy, Donald Duart Maclean. Maclean was posted to Washington as acting first secretary in the British Embassy in 1944 and he remained until 1948. The apparent accuracy of Soviet information about Anglo-American communications during those years may not have been coincidental. According to one account, "[Maclean's] new position in the Embassy [in Washington] was that of chief administrative officer. He saw most of the documents received and despatched, and at this time they included a vast amount of correspondence and memoranda of the highest scientific and political importance. British and American scientists had worked in close cooperation on the atomic bomb that blasted Japan out of the war, and in the years that followed, the secrets of that bomb were the subject of delicate diplomatic negotiation between Britain and America . . . [therefore] the Soviet agents were making desperate efforts to discover not only the scientific processes but the political policies of the Western atomic powers. Maclean was thus in a unique position to help them, as, many years later, M.I.5 came to suspect that he had done." Anthony Purdy and Douglas Sutherland, *Burgess and Maclean* (London: Secker & Warburg, 1963), pp. 98–99.

52. Telegram, U.S. military commissioner in Austria, General Clark, to the Joint Chiefs of Staff, No. P-3605, 26 February 1946, in *Foreign Relations of the United States, 1946*, vol. 5: *The British Commonwealth; Western and Central Europe*, pp. 312–14; also

telegram, U.S. military commissioner in Austria, General Clark, to the Joint Chiefs of Staff, No. P-6000, 4 April 1946, ibid., pp. 324–35.

53. "Austria: Discussions between Mr. Bevin, General McCreery and Mr. Mack" (with Foreign Office Minutes), Foreign Office, London, 15 November 1945, F.O. 371/46634(C8360), PRO.

54. "Memorandum reviewing situation in Austria and suggesting course of action to combat spread of communism," Foreign Office, London, 5 April 1946, F.O. 371/55257(C4097), PRO.

55. Telegram, Foreign Office, London, to British Embassy, Washington, no. 4908, 22 May 1946, F.O. 371/55152(C5255), PRO.

56. "Long-Term Policy towards Austria—Strategic Implications," Report by the Joint Planning Staff, Chiefs of Staff Committee, United Kingdom, 17 June 1946, F.O. 371/55258(C7116G), PRO.

57. Minutes by B. A. R. Burrows on a telgram from Mr. Mack, U.K. political representative, Vienna, to Mr. Bevin, secretary of state, Foreign Office, London, no. 161, 21 February 1946, minutes dated 27 February 1946, F.O. 371/55256(C2150), PRO.

58. Telegram, Earl of Halifax, U.K. ambassador to the U.S., to Foreign Office, London, no. 1349, 2 March 1946, F.O. 371/55256(C2521), PRO.

59. Civil Affairs Division, Operations Division, War Department, Washington, to commanding general, U.S. Forces Austria, Vienna, no. WAR 88638, 20 May 1946, R. G. 218, U.S. Joint Chiefs of Staff, Chairman's File, Admiral Leahy, 1942–1948, Box 1, Folder 2, NA; and telegram, secretary of state to the U.S. political adviser for Austria (Erhardt), 24 May 1946, in *Foreign Relations of the United States, 1946*, vol. 5: *The British Commonwealth; Western and Central Europe*, pp. 342–44.

60. Barker, *Austria, 1918–1972*, pp. 172–73.

61. "Recent Soviet Policy in Austria, July–September 1946," draft paper by Lord Jellicoe, Foreign Office, September 1946, F.O. 371/55259(C10458), PRO.

62. Barker, *Austria, 1918–1972*, pp. 179–81.

63. Mosely, "The Treaty with Austria," pp. 221–22.

64. Ware Adams, "The Negative Veto—A Breakthrough," in *The Austrian Solution: International Conflict and Cooperation*, ed. Robert A. Bauer (Charlottesville: University Press of Virginia, 1982), pp. 81, 82.

65. Ware Adams, "The Miracle of Austria—A Diplomatic Success Story," *Foreign Service Journal* 48 (June 1971), p. 27, cited by Martin F. Herz, "Allied Occupation of Austria: The Early Years," in Bauer, *The Austrian Solution*, p. 35.

66. Barker, *Austria, 1918–1972*, pp. 173–75.

67. Robert E. Clute, *The International Legal Status of Austria, 1938–1955* (The Hague: Nijhoff, 1962), pp. 34–36, 132. In his book Clute presents an excellent case for the existence of Austria not merely as a sovereign state (albeit under foreign occupation) after the June 1946 control agreement but as an independent and functioning political entity. He asserts that the Austrian State Treaty of 1955 was simply a formal recognition of what was internationally considered to be the status quo, as far as Austria's statehood was concerned, after the war. Of course, the point that this formality led to the withdrawal of the troops of the four occupying powers must not be overlooked!

68. U.S. Department of State, Bureau of Public Affairs, *Foreign Relations of the United States, 1946*, vol. 2: *Council of Foreign Ministers*, p. 97, and James F. Byrnes, *Speaking Frankly* (London: Heinemann, 1947), pp. 162–64. It is interesting to note that the French also had privately expressed some anxiety to the British about placing the American draft of the Austrian treaty on the agenda because they were afraid that it might delay

consideration of the German question. The strength of French concern was never tested, however, because the Russians ensured that the draft stayed off the agenda. See Bernard Burrows, Office of the British Delegation to the Council of Foreign Ministers, Paris, to Jack M. Troutbeck, Foreign Office, London, 2 May 1946, F.O. 371/55247(C4881), PRO.

69. U.S. Department of State, Office of Intelligence Coordination and Liaison, OCL 3521.1A, "Comments on a Draft Treaty for the Reestablishment of an Independent and Democratic Austria (Revision)," 8 January 1947, in R & A Reports File, Diplomatic Documents Division, NA.

70. Telegram, U.K. Delegation to Conference of Foreign Ministers, Paris, to Foreign Office, London, 13 July 1946, F. O. 371/55249(C7960), PRO.

71. Bevin to Byrnes, 22 June 1946, F.O. 371/55146(C7165), PRO.

72. "Austria and the Peace Conference: Speech at the Plenary Session, August 17, 1946," in *U.S.S.R. at the Paris Peace Conference (July–October 1946): Selected Speeches of A. Y. Vyshinsky, Deputy Minister for Foreign Affairs of the U.S.S.R. and Member of the Soviet Delegation at the Conference* (London: Soviet News, n.d.), pp. 18–23; see also A. Solodovnikov, "The Austrian Problem," *New Times* no. 8 (21 February 1947), pp. 12–15.

73. For English text, see *Department of State Bulletin* 15 (21 July 1946), p. 123.

74. Clute, *International Legal Status of Austria*, p. 37.

75. "Notes on the Political Situation in Austria," minutes of a conversation between Mr. Marquand, U.K. Board of Trade, and Mr. John Hynd, secretary of state for trade, transmitted to Mr. Bevin, Foreign Office, 17 September 1946, F.O. 371/53019(UE4337), PRO. According to the Russians, Austrian allegations that nationalization was prevented by the Soviet Union were unfounded (see Solodovnikov, "The Austrian Problem," p. 14). The Soviet representative on the Allied Council opposed the nationalization law and asserted that the law would never be applied in the eastern zone of Austria. But the Austrian realization that they did not have enough resources and that the Western powers were not at all enthused by the idea also contributed to the Austrian decision to reconsider the action. In the end they did not repeal the law but instead exempted UN interests from its effects. Thus the claim by the Austrians—and the Western powers—that the Soviet Union prevented the nationalization was neither wholly true nor wholly false, but it certainly could be faulted for being misleading.

2. The Negotiations Begin, 1947–1948

1. W. H. B. Mack, U.K. political representative, Vienna, to Sir Oliver Harvey, Foreign Office, London, 9 January 1947, F.O. 371/64008(C907), Public Records Office, (hereafter PRO).

2. Mack quotes Kurasov's remark, ibid.

3. Conclusions of a meeting of the cabinet held at 10 Downing Street, S.W.1, London, on Thursday, 2 January 1947, Minute no. 3, Subject: "Austria: Preparation of Peace Treaty," C.M. 47(1), Cabinet Office Records, vol. Cab. 128/9, PRO.

4. For example, former Austrian foreign minister Gruber has written of his hope in 1947 that Austria might slip through a "loophole" in the East-West conflict. Karl Gruber, *Between Liberation and Liberty: Austria in the Post-War World* (London: Deutsch, 1955), p. 102.

5. "Opening Speech at the Moscow Session of the Council of Foreign Ministers, March 10, 1947," *Speeches and Statements Made at the Moscow Session of the Council of*

Foreign Ministers, March 10–April 24, 1947, by V. M. Molotov, Minister for Foreign Affairs of the U.S.S.R. (London: Soviet News, 1947), p. 5.

6. William B. Bader, *Austria between East and West, 1945–1955* (Stanford: Stanford University Press, 1966), p. 189.

7. Gruber, *Between Liberation and Liberty*, p. 104.

8. "Austrian-Yugoslav Frontier: Statement made at the Evening Session on April 19, 1947," *Speeches and Statements Made . . . by V. M. Molotov*, pp. 103–4.

9. John Foster Dulles Papers, Category VIII, Council of Foreign Ministers—Moscow, Reports, March 10–April 24, 1947, vol. 2, pt. 2, p. 403, cited by Bader, *Austria between East and West*, p. 189.

10. "Austrian Treaty: 36th Meeting of the CFM," British record of the Thirty-Sixth Meeting of the Council of Foreign Ministers, held at Aviation House, Moscow, on 19 April 1947, F.O. 371/63962(C6231), pp. 3–4, PRO.

11. "German Assets in Austria: Statement made on March 27, 1947," *Speeches and Statements Made . . . by V. M. Molotov*, pp. 47–49.

12. Quoted by Martin Blumenson, *Mark Clark* (New York: Congdon & Weed, 1984), pp. 257–58.

13. In the papers of Pierson Dixson, 18 April 1947, cited by Victor Rothwell, *Britain and the Cold War, 1941–1947* (London: Cape, 1982), p. 345.

14. John Foster Dulles Papers, Category VIII, Council of Foreign Ministers—Moscow, John Foster Dulles Personal and Miscellaneous Papers, vol. 1., p. 98, cited by Bader, *Austria between East and West*, p. 189.

15. Gruber, *Between Liberation and Liberty*, pp. 110–12.

16. Quoted in Daniel Yergin, *Shattered Peace: The Origins of the Cold War and the National Security State* (Harmondsworth: Penguin, 1977), pp. 300–301.

17. Isaac Deutscher, *Stalin*, 2d ed. (London: Oxford University Press, 1966), pp. 574–75.

18. "Moscow Meeting of the Council of Foreign Ministers: Discussion of German and Austrian Draft Treaties," Statements by the secretary of state, *U.S. Department of State Bulletin* 16 (4 May 1947), pp. 793–94.

19. U.S. Department of State, *The Austrian State Treaty: An Account of the Postwar Negotiations Together with the Text of the Treaty and Related Documents*, released April 1957, European and British Commonwealth Series 49, D.O.S. Publication 6437, pp. 11–12.

20. Telegram, Sir H. Mack, U.K. political representative, Vienna, to Foreign Office, London, 26 September 1947, F.O. 371/64101(C12717), PRO.

21. Minute to the secretary of state [Bevin], Foreign Office, London, from Sir George T. Rendel, U.K. representative on the Austrian Treaty Commission, F.O. 371/64101(C12796), PRO.

22. Ibid., pp. 4–5.

23. Sven Allard, *Russia and the Austrian State Treaty: A Case Study of Soviet Policy in Europe* (University Park: Pennsylvania State University Press, 1970), p. 97.

24. U.S. Forces Austria, Vienna, to War Department for JC/S pass to State Department, P-0078, 19 June 1946, R.G. 218 Modern Military Records Division, National Archives, Washington, D.C. (hereafter NA).

25. Philip E. Mosely, "The Treaty with Austria," *International Organization* 4 (May 1950): 221–22.

26. Bader, *Austria between East and West*, pp. 191–92.

27. Telegram, Mr. W. H. B. Mack, U.K. political representative, Vienna, to Foreign Office, London, 6 May 1947, F.O. 371/63973(C6695), PRO.

28. Allard, *Russia and the Austrian State Treaty*, p. 101.

29. Telegram, Mr. W. H. B. Mack, U.K. political representative, to Mr. Bevin, For-

eign Office, London, 10 May 1947; distributed within the Foreign Office under the title "Demonstration in Vienna against Ration Scales: Threat to State Security," F.O. 371/63973(C6936), PRO.

30. Ibid. According to British documents, Austrian foreign minister Karl Gruber and Austrian vice chancellor Adolf Schaerf reported these things to British political representative W. H. B. Mack, in Vienna, a few days after the attempted putsch.

31. Ferenc Nagy, *The Struggle behind the Iron Curtain* (New York: Macmillan, 1948), p. 381.

32. Paper drafted by the German Political Department dealing with the future prospects for Austria with particular reference to the question of an Austrian Treaty, cover letter signed by J. A. M. Marjoribanks, 24 September 1947, F.O. 371/64101(C12784), final version, F.O. 371/64102(C12938), PRO.

33. Heinrich Siegler, *Austria: Problems and Achievements since 1945* (Bonn: Siegler, n.d.), p. 13.

34. Cary Travers Grayson, Jr., "Austria's International Position, 1938–1953: The Reestablishment of an Independent Austria" (diss., Etudes d'Histoire Economique Politique et Sociale, Geneva, 1953), pp. 110, 111.

35. A. H. Lincoln, Foreign Office, to Sir Desmond Morton, Brussels, 20 November 1946, F.O. 371/53126(UE5243), PRO.

36. See, inter alia, U.K. Delegation Brief no. 8, Paris Meeting, 19 April 1946, F.O. 371/55247(C4418/G); D. D. Maclean, British Embassy, Washington, to J. M. Troutbeck, German Department, Foreign Office, 14 March 1946; and B. A. B. Burrows, Foreign Office, to J. H. Walker, 10 March 1947, F.O. 371/64064(C3218), PRO.

37. Minute by M. F. Cullis regarding Burrows to Troutbeck, letter dated 15 May 1946, minute dated 17 May 1946, F.O. 371/55247(C5461), PRO.

38. D. D. Maclean, British Embassy, Washington, to J. M. Troutbeck, German Department, Foreign Office, 14 March 1946, F.O. 371/55283(C3256), PRO.

39. Extract from a dispatch to the *New York Times* dated 6 March 1946 from London correspondent Herbert Matthews, in Telegram for General Distribution, Earl of Halifax, British ambassador (Washington) to Foreign Office, Washington, 9 March 1946, F.O. 371/55283(C2754), PRO.

40. Minute by M. F. Cullis regarding Burrows to Troutbeck, letter dated 15 May 1946, minute dated 17 May 1946, F.O. 371/55247(C5461), PRO.

41. Memorandum for the secretary of defense from Frank C. Nash, assistant to the secretary for international security affairs, 15 February 1952, Subject: "Pay-as-you-go Program in Austria," R.G. 330, Records of the Office of the Secretary of Defense, Assistant Secretary of Defense (International Security Affairs), Office of Foreign Military Affairs, European Section, Subject File, 1949–52, Folder: Austria, October 1949–May 8, 1952, Modern Military Records Division, NA.

42. Telegram, Soviet Ministry of Foreign Affairs to the Austrian government, Reply to Austria's request for reduction of occupation costs, June 1948, in F.O. 371/70445(C4685), PRO.

43. See, for example, Foreign Office minute from Mr. P. Dean, "Austrian Occupation Costs: British Attitude and Future Action," addressed to Mr. M. Dean, 8 June 1948, F.O. 371/70446A(C5825), PRO.

44. Telegram, Foreign Office to the Austrian government, June 1948, F.O. 371/70445(C4721), PRO.

45. Telegram, French government to the Austrian government, reply to Austrian government's request for reduction in occupation costs, June 1948, in F.O. 371/70445-(C4766), PRO.

46. See, for example, Foreign Office Minute by Mr. Mallet, "Extract from a record of a meeting with Mr. George Perkins of the U.S. State Department," 16 February 1951, F.O. 371/936002(CA1071/12), PRO.

47. W. H. B. Mack, U.K. political representative, Vienna, to British foreign secretary Bevin, Foreign Office, London, 2 June 947, F.O. 371/64113(C7980), PRO.

48. U.S. Department of State, *The Austrian State Treaty*, p. 13.

49. The French proposal granted the Soviet Union half of Austria's oil production, one-third of the exploration rights in oil-prospecting areas, and the external assets of the Danube Shipping Company. Grayson, "Austria's International Position," p. 141. This proposal came to be known as the Cherrière Plan, after General Cherrière, the French deputy on the Austrian Treaty Commission.

50. "The London Meeting of the Council of Foreign Ministers: November 25–December 15, 1947," Report by George C. Marshall, Secretary of State; broadcast on 19 December 1947; reprinted in *Department of State Bulletin* 17 (28 December 1947), pp. 1244–49.

51. Memorandum, Oliver Harvey to the secretary of state [Bevin], Subject: "Tactics for Austrian Treaty at Council of Foreign Ministers," 18 November 1947, F.O. 371/64146(C14790), PRO.

52. Foreign Office Memorandum by James Marjoribanks, 24 November 1947, Subject: "Report of informal conversations with American and French experts on Austrian Treaty," F.O. 371/64147(C16375); final official version of the memorandum for distribution within Foreign Office, F.O. 371/64147(C15293), PRO.

53. Harry B. Mack, U.K. political representative, Vienna, to Bevin, Foreign Office, London, 16 October 1947, F.O. 371/63975(C13901), PRO.

54. Gruber, *Between Liberation and Liberty*, p. 143. The Cominform was established in October 1947 with the purpose of coordinating Communist party activities throughout Europe. At this time of unrest in Europe the Cominform was seen as a particular threat to the West European democracies.

55. U.S. Department of State, Bureau of Public Affairs, *Foreign Relations of the United States, 1947*, vol. 2: *Council of Foreign Ministers: Germany and Austria* (Washington, D.C., 1977), p. 751.

56. U.S. Department of State, *The Austrian State Treaty*, pp. 13–14, and Grayson, "Austria's International Position," p. 142.

57. Grayson, "Austria's International Position," pp. 144–45.

58. Gruber, *Between Liberation and Liberty*, p. 149.

59. See, inter alia, Bader, *Austria between East and West*, pp. 194–95.

60. Patricia Blythe Eggleston, "The Marshall Plan in Austria: A Study in American Containment of the Soviet Union in the Cold War" (diss., University of Alabama, 1980), p. 115.

61. K. W. Rothchild, *The Austrian Economy since 1945* (London: Royal Institute of International Affairs, 1950), p. 67.

62. Gruber, *Between Liberation and Liberty*, pp. 154–55.

63. U.S. delegate to London deputy foreign ministers' meeting (Douglas) to Under Secretary of State Lovett, 771, 27 February 1948, Files of the Office of the Secretary of Defense, NA.

64. U.S. Department of Defense, Report by the Joint Strategic Survey Committee to the Joint Chiefs of Staff on "The Austrian Peace Treaty—Military Implications," 4 March 1948, Records of the Secretary of Defense, NA.

65. Bader, *Austria between East and West*, pp. 193–94.

66. Gruber, *Between Liberation and Liberty*, p. 150.

67. A Report to the National Security Council by the secretary of defense, Louis Johnson, on "Future Course of U.S. Action with Respect to Austria," 16 June 1949, NSC 38/1, President's Secretary File, Harry S Truman Library, Independence, Missouri.

68. Robert A. Lovett, undersecretary of state to James Forrestal, secretary of defense, 14 December 1948, R.G. 330, Records of the Secretary of Defense, NA. In 1961 William Bader suggested a connection between the breakdown of the London negotiations and the equipping of the army, but at the time he did not have access to secret American documents. Newly declassified documents suggest that he might well have been right. Bader, *Austria between East and West*, p. 195.

69. Gruber, *Between Liberation and Liberty*, p. 150.

70. Record of a conversation with Dr. Gruber, by P. A. Wilkinson, British Legation, Vienna, 8 June 1949 (conversation took place on 7 June 1948), F.O. 371/70411(C4648), PRO.

71. Telegram, Sir B. Jerram, Vienna, to Foreign Office, 19 June 1948, F.O. 371/70460A(C4869), PRO.

72. Gruber, *Between Liberation and Liberty*, p. 146.

3. *The Paris Initiative, 1949*

1. Gordon Shepherd, "Why Soviet Troops Are Still on Austrian Soil," *Daily Telegraph*, 22 May 1950, and Shepherd, *The Austrian Odyssey* (London: Macmillan, 1957).

2. In a note to Secretary Acheson, Chip Bohlen interpreted the Soviet campaign as a propaganda maneuver to affect U.S. public opinion and not a serious move toward settlement. "U.S.S.R. Communist Peace Offensive," note to Secretary Acheson from Chip E. Bohlen, Records of C.E.B., 1942–1952, R.G. 59, Box 4, Folder: Memos (C.E.B.), 1949, Diplomatic Documents Division, National Archives, Washington, D.C. (hereafter NA).

3. Report to the National Security Council by the Department of State, NSC 38, "The Austrian Treaty in the Council of Foreign Ministers," 8 December 1948, President's Secretary File, Harry S Truman Library, Independence, Missouri.

4. "Report of discussion with Mr. Reber," Foreign Office Minute by Mr. Cullis, 25 January 1949, F.O. 371/76435(C686), Public Records Office, Kew (hereafter PRO).

5. Cary Travers Grayson, Jr., "Austria's International Position, 1938–1953: The Reestablishment of an Independent Austria" (diss., Etudes d'Histoire Economique Politique et Sociale, Geneva, 1953), p. 145.

6. Memorandum by the U.S. deputy for Austria at the Council of Foreign Ministers (Reber), Washington, 11 May 1949, in U.S. Department of State, Bureau of Public Affairs, *Foreign Relations of the United States, 1949*, vol. 3: *Council of Foreign Ministers; Germany and Austria*, (Washington, D.C., 1974), p. 1094.

7. Grayson, "Austria's International Position," p. 145.

8. Ibid., p. 146; Foreign Office Minute by J. Marjoribanks, 6 April 1949, F.O. 371/76439(C3102/G), PRO.

9. Memorandum by the U.S. deputy for Austria at the Council of Foreign Ministers (Reber), Washington, 11 May 1949, in U.S. Department of State, Bureau of Public Affairs, *Foreign Relations of the United States, 1949*, vol. 3: *Council of Foreign Ministers: Germany and Austria* (Washington, D.C., 1974), p. 1094.

10. Article 6 of the North Atlantic Treaty.

11. Minutes of the treaty negotiations by James Marjoribanks, 13 April 1949, F.O. 371/76439(C3302/G), PRO.

12. Report to the National Security Council by the Department of State, NSC 38, "The Austrian Treaty in the Council of Foreign Ministers," 8 December 1948, p. 4, President's Secretary File, Truman Library.

13. Report to the National Security Council by the secretary of defense, Louis Johnson, "Future Course of U.S. Action with Respect to Austria," NSC 38/1, 16 June 1949, p. 7, President's Secretary File, Truman Library.

14. Telegram from Mr. Cheetham, Vienna, to Foreign Office, 11 February 1949, F.O. 371/76470(C1252/G), PRO.

15. Report to the National Security Council by the secretary of defense, Louis Johnson, "Future Course of U.S. Action with Respect to Austria," NSC 38/1, 16 June 1949, p. 7, President's Secretary File, Truman Library.

16. Foreign Office Minute by Mr. Mallet addressed to the secretary of state, 14 June 1949, F.O. 371/76470(C5305/G), PRO.

17. Telegram from Sir B. Jerram, Vienna, to Foreign Office, 25 March 1949, F.O. 371/76470(C2569/G), PRO.

18. Report to the National Security Council by the secretary of defense, Louis Johnson, "Future Course of U.S. Action with Respect to Austria," NSC 38/1, 16 June 1949, p. 7, President's Secretary File, Truman Library.

19. Federal Chancellor Figl to the Allied Commission for Austria, regarding the urgent need for an improvement in the equipment of the police forces and submitting proposals by the Federal Ministry of the Interior, 8 May 1947, F.O. 371/64033(C7167), PRO.

20. See the following *Pravda* articles: "Military Construction in Austria," 24 March 1949, p. 3; "Military Construction in the American Occupation Zone of Austria," 14 May 1949, p. 4; "Formation of a Secret 'Military Committee' in Austria," 29 June 1949, p. 3; and "American Authorities Train Cadres for Future Austrian Army," 25 July 1949, p. 4.

21. "Is This Not the Reason for the Delay?" *New Times* 16 (13 April 1949): 17. See also A. Shatilov and Y. Borisov, "Militarization of Austria," *New Times* 50 (12 December 1951), pp. 27–29.

22. Allied Commission for Austria, Executive Committee, Report by the Soviet Element of the Military Directorate, "Militarization of Training in Austrian Gendarmerie Schools," 1 June 1949, F.O. 371/76470(C4997), PRO; and *Proceedings of the Allied Commission*, EXCO/P(49)86; EXCO/M-(49)140, pp. 3–4; ALCO/M(50)121, pp. 2–4, cited by William B. Bader, *Austria between East and West, 1945–1955* (Stanford: Stanford University Press, 1966), p. 106.

23. Roy Medvedev, *All Stalin's Men*, trans. Harold Shukman (Oxford: Blackwell, 1983), pp. 97–101.

24. As early as February 1949 the British had evidence of Soviet intentions to drop Yugoslav claims. Sir C. Peake, British ambassador to Yugoslavia wrote: "At a lunch party yesterday the Political Director at the Ministry of Foreign Affairs who talked to me with less of his customary reserve, betrayed considerable nervousness about Soviet attitude towards Yugoslav claims on Carinthia and even went so far as to ask me my opinion as to whether the Soviet Government would now throw Yugoslavia over. I told Mr. Prica that I did not think he would have long to wait before finding out." Telegram, Sir C. Peake, Belgrade, to Foreign Office, 11 February 1949, F.O. 371/76436(C1255), PRO.

25. Conversation between the secretary of state (Bevin) and the Austrian foreign

minister (with attached Foreign Office Minutes), Subject: Situation in Austria and Need for Treaty, 7 June 1949, F.O. 371/76442(4897), PRO, on which I also base the next two paragraphs.

26. On U.S. initiative see Memorandum by the secretary of state for foreign affairs, E. Bevin, to the Cabinet, 11 April 1950, C.P. (50)66, Cabinet Office Papers 129/39, PRO.

27. Ibid., and U.S. Department of State, Bureau of Public Affairs, *Foreign Relations of the United States, 1949*, vol. 3: *Council of Foreign Ministers; Germany and Austria* (Washington, D.C., 1974), p. 1097.

28. "Note of the Soviet Government to the Yugoslav Government," *Pravda*, 24 July 1949, p. 2, trans. and commented upon by British Foreign Office officials, 26 July 1949, F.O. 371/76443(C5372), PRO. Further accusations were published in *Pravda*, 31 August 1949, p. 2, and *Izvestia*, 31 August 1949, p. 2; in English, "Note of the Soviet Government to the Yugoslav Government," supplement to *New Times* 37 (7 September 1949), pp. 1–7.

It is possible that the Soviet government's knowledge of the postwar British-Yugoslav negotiations was related to Donald Maclean's assignment as chief administrative officer in the British Embassy, Washington, between 1944 and 1948. The close intelligence relationship between Britain and the United States during those years probably meant that the American government was kept abreast of the progress of the talks; because Maclean saw virtually all of the cable traffic between London and Washington, it is possible that the Soviet Union also received periodic bulletins about the talks.

29. "Austrian Treaty: Soviet Policy in 1947," Foreign Office Minute by M. F. Cullis, German Political Department, 16 August 1950; minute concerns an account given to Cullis by M. Milutinovic, first secretary of the Yugoslav Embassy in London, regarding Soviet policy toward the Austrian treaty in general, and the Yugoslav claims on Austria in particular, during the Moscow Conference of the Council of Foreign Ministers in April 1947; F.O. 371/84907(C5213), PRO.

30. "Austrian Hopes Fade," *Scotsman*, 7 February 1950.

31. Memorandum for the executive secretary, National Security Council, from Secretary of Defense Louis Johnson, Subject: "Future Course of U.S. Action with respect to Austria," 16 June 1949; part of NSC 38/1, "A Report to the National Security Council by the Secretary of Defense on Future Course of Action with Respect to Austria," 16 June 1949, President's Secretary File, Truman Library.

32. Secretary of Defense Louis Johnson to Secretary of State Dean Acheson, 14 June 1949, Attachment B of NSC 38/1, "A Report to the National Security Council by the Secretary of Defense on Future Course of Action with Respect to Austria," 16 June 1949, President's Secretary File, Truman Library.

33. Telegram, Secretary of State Acheson, Paris, to [Department of State], Washington, no. DELSEC 1916, 18 June 1949, Attachment A of NSC 38/2, "A Report to the National Security Council by the Secretary of State on Future Course of U.S. Action with Respect to Austria," 1 July 1949, President's Secretary File, Truman Library.

34. Secretary of State Dean Acheson to Admiral Sidney W. Souers, executive secretary of the National Security Council, 1 July 1949, part of NSC 38/2, "A Report to the National Security Council by the Secretary of State on Future Course of U.S. Action with Respect to Austria," 1 July 1949, President's Secretary File, Truman Library.

35. Agenda for the National Security Council's 43d Meeting, The White House, agenda dated 1 July 1949, meeting held on 7 July 1949, President's Secretary Files, Truman Library.

36. Secretary of Defense Louis Johnson to Secretary of State Dean Acheson, 14 June

1949, Attachment B of NSC 38/1, "A Report to the National Security Council by the Secretary of Defense on Future Course of Action with Respect to Austria," 16 June 1949, President's Secretary File, Truman Library.

37. Foreign Office Minute by Mr. Mallet addressed to the Secretary of State, 14 June 1949, F.O. 371/76470(C5305/G), PRO.

38. Memorandum [of conversation at the National Security Council meeting of 7 July 1949], "Training of Austrian Army" [by Secretary of State Dean Acheson], 7 July 1949, Papers of Dean Acheson, Truman Library.

39. "Notes on the Security Council Meeting Relative to Austrian Peace Treaty," p. 2, 20 October 1949, dictated by Tracy S. Voorhees, under secretary of the army, R.G. 330, Records of the Office of the Secretary of Defense, Military Documents Division, NA.

40. Memorandum [of conversation at the National Security Council meeting of 7 July 1949], "Training of Austrian Army" [by Secretary of State Dean Acheson], 7 July 1949, Papers of Dean Acheson, Truman Library.

41. Secretary of Defense Louis Johnson to Secretary of State Dean Acheson, 14 June 1949, Attachment B of NSC 38/1, "A Report to the National Security Council by the Secretary of Defense on Future Course of Action with Respect to Austria," 16 June 1949, President's Secretary File, Truman Library.

42. Minutes of the 43d Meeting of the National Security Council, The White House, 7 July 1949, President's Secretary File, Truman Library.

43. Grayson, "Austria's International Position," p. 147.

44. U.S. Department of State, *The Austrian State Treaty: An Account of the Postwar Negotiations Together with the Text of the Treaty and Related Documents*, released April 1957, European and British Commonwealth Series 49, D.O.S. Publication 6437, pp. 16–17, and memorandum by the secretary of state for foreign affairs, E. Bevin, to the Cabinet, 11 April 1950, C.P. (50) 66, Cabinet Office Papers 129/39, PRO.

45. Coburn B. Kidd, Division of Austrian Affairs, to the acting chief of the division (Williamson), dated 29 July 1949, in U.S. Department of State, Bureau of Public Affairs, *Foreign Relations of the United States, 1949*, vol. 3: *Council of Foreign Ministers: Germany and Austria* (Washington, D.C., 1974), pp. 110–11.

46. Telegram, Foreign Office to Vienna, 6 August 1949, F.O. 371/76446(C6274), and letter from Mr. Mallet, British deputy to the Austrian treaty talks, to E. E. Tomkins, private secretary to the secretary of state, 6 August 1949, F.O. 371/76446(C6353), PRO.

47. Telegram from Sir B. Jerram, Vienna, to Foreign Office, 13 August 1949, F.O. 371/76446(C6417), PRO.

48. Secretary, Chiefs of Staff Committee, to the Foreign Office, 13 December 1947, F.O. 371/70388(C199/G), PRO.

49. Chiefs of Staff Committee, Joint Planning Staff, "Withdrawal of Allied Forces from Austria; Report by the Joint Planning Staff," 5 December 1947, F.O. 371/70388-(C199/G), PRO.

50. [Record of conversation between Mr. Mallet and the secretary of state], Foreign Office minute by M. F. Cullis, 19 August 1949, F.O. 371/76447(C6548), PRO.

51. Foreign Office minute to the secretary of state [Bevin] by Mr. Mallet, 22 August 1949, F.O. 371/76447(C6731/G), PRO.

52. Conversation between the secretary of state [Bevin] and the Austrian foreign minister [Gruber], 25 August 1949, F.O. 371/76496(C8543), and telegram, Foreign Office [Bevin] to Vienna, 25 August 1949, F.O. 371/76447(C6771), PRO.

53. "Conversation between the Secretary of State [Bevin] and the United States Ambassador [Douglas]: Austrian Treaty Negotiations," 26 August 1949, F.O. 371/76496(C8543), PRO.

54. Ibid.

55. Telegram from Foreign Office [Bevin], to Washington, 26 August 1949, F.O. 371/76447(C6771/176/3), PRO.

56. "Deputies on Austrian Treaty to Reconvene in New York," *Department of State Bulletin* 21 (3 October 1949): 509.

57. Record of conversation between Major General Winterton and Vice Chancellor Schaerf, 1 September 1949, F.O. 371/76448(C7067/G), PRO.

58. Telegram, Sir B. Jerram, Vienna, to Foreign Office, 7 September 1949, F.O. 371/76448(C7043), PRO.

59. Telegram, Foreign Office to Vienna, 25 August 1949, F.O. 371/76447(C6771), PRO.

60. In the Soviet press see "Western Powers Violate Council of Foreign Ministers Decisions," *Pravda*, 8 September 1949, p. 3, and "On the Results of the London Negotiations on the Draft Austrian Peace Treaty," *Izvestia*, 8 September 1949, p. 4.

61. Foreign Office minute by M. F. Cullis to Sir I. Kirkpatrick, 9 September 1949, F.O. 371/76448(C7901), PRO.

62. Acting chief of the Division of Austrian Affairs (Williamson) to the minister in Austria (Erhardt), 4 October 1949, in U.S. Department of State, Bureau of Public Affairs, *Foreign Relations of the United States, 1949*, vol. 3: *Council of Foreign Ministers; Germany and Austria* (Washington, D.C., 1974), pp. 1171–72.

63. Telegram, Foreign Office to Washington, 14 September 1949, F.O. 371/76449-(C7204), and memorandum by the secretary of state for foreign affairs [Bevin] to the Cabinet, 11 April 1950, C.P. (50) 66, Cabinet Office 129/39, both in PRO.

64. Acting chief of the Division of Austrian Affairs (Williamson) to the minister in Austria (Erhardt), 4 October 1949, in U.S. Department of State, Bureau of Public Affairs, *Foreign Relations of the United States, 1949*, vol. 3: *Council of Foreign Ministers; Germany and Austria* (Washington, D.C., 1974), p. 1172.

65. Ibid., p. 1171.

66. Telegram from Foreign Office to Washington, 14 September 1949, F.O. 371/76449(C7204), PRO.

67. Memorandum of conversation, "Tripartite Position on Austrian Treaty," 15 September 1949, U.S. State Department Papers of Dean Acheson, Truman Library.

68. Acting chief of the Division of Austrian Affairs (Williamson) to the minister in Austria (Erhardt), 4 October 1949, in U.S. Department of State, Bureau of Public Affairs, *Foreign Relations of the United States, 1949*, vol. 3: *Council of Foreign Ministers; Germany and Austria* (Washington, D.C., 1974), pp. 1171–72.

69. "As for the French, you can imagine that Berthelot, without a Government, is not a very constructive colleague. . . ." Mallet, New York, to Sir Ivone Kirkpatrick, 24 October 1949, F.O. 371/76451(C8274), PRO.

70. British record of a meeting of the three Western foreign ministers to discuss the Austrian treaty, held at the Wardorf Astoria Hotel at 4:00 P.M. on Thursday, 29 September 1949, F.O. 371/76451(C7755), PRO.

71. Bevin to Dean Acheson, 1 October 1949, F.O. 371/76451(C7962), PRO.

72. British record of a meeting of the three Western foreign ministers . . . , 29 September 1949, F.O. 371/76451(C7755), PRO.

73. Bevin to Acheson, 1 October 1949, F.O. 371/76451(C7962), PRO.

74. "Continuing Soviet Tactics Block Austrian Treaty Negotiations," statement by Secretary Acheson in *Department of State Bulletin* 22 (6 March 1950), and U.S. Department of State, *The Austrian State Treaty*, p. 17.

75. Acting chief of the Division of Austrian Affairs (Williamson) to the minister in

Austria (Erhardt), 4 October 1949, in U.S. Department of State, Bureau of Public Affairs, *Foreign Relations of the United States, 1949,* vol. 3: *Council of Foreign Ministers; Germany and Austria* (Washington, D.C., 1974), p. 1171.

76. "Notes on the Security Council Meeting Relative to Austrian Peace Treaty," 20 October 1949, dictated by Tracy S. Voorhees, under secretary of the army, R.G. 330, Records of the Secretary of Defense, Military Documents Section, NA.

77. Memorandum from Tracy S. Voorhees, deputy to the secretary of defense as to occupied areas, to the secretary of defense, 20 October 1949, Subject: "Austrian Treaty Negotiations—NSC/38, 38/1, and 38/2," R.G. 330, Records of the Office of the Secretary of Defense, NA. On reactions at State see Chief of the Division of Austrian Affairs (Williamson) to the minister in Austria (Erhardt), 24 October 1949, in U.S. Department of State, Bureau of Public Affairs, *Foreign Relations of the United States, 1949,* vol. 3: *Council of Foreign Ministers; Germany and Austria* (Washington, D.C., 1974), pp. 1184–85.

78. Statement by General Keyes contained in memorandum from Tracy S. Voorhees, deputy to the secretary of defense as to occupied areas to the secretary of defense, 20 October 1949, Subject: "Austrian Treaty Negotiations—NSC/38, 38/1, 38/2," R.G. 330, Records of the Office of the Secretary of Defense, NA.

79. Chief of the Division of Austrian Affairs (Williamson) to the minister in Austria (Erhardt), 24 October 1949, in U.S. Department of State, Bureau of Public Affairs, *Foreign Relations of the United States, 1949,* vol. 3: *Council of Foreign Ministers; Germany and Austria* (Washington, D.C., 1974), p. 1184.

80. Memorandum of conversation, meeting of the secretary of state Dean Acheson, Secretary of Defense Louis Johnson, and President Truman, "Austrian Treaty," 26 October 1949, in the Papers of Dean Acheson, Truman Library.

81. Minute addressed to the private secretary by A. G. Gilchrist, 26 November 1949, F.O. 371/76453(C9155), PRO.

82. Report to the President by the National Security Council on "Future Courses of U.S. Action with Respect to Austria," NSC 38/4, 17 November 1949, approved by the president on 18 November 1949, President's Secretary File, Truman Library.

83. Telegram, Sir. A. Cadogan, New York, to Foreign Office, 19 November 1949, F.O. 371/76542(C8871), PRO.

84. U.S. Department of State, *The Austrian State Treaty,* pp. 17, 18.

85. Karl Gruber, *Between Liberation and Liberty: Austria in the Post-War World* (London: Deutsch, 1955), pp. 174–75.

86. Minute addressed to the secretary of state by I. Kirkpatrick, 12 December 1949, F.O. 371/76457(C9642), PRO.

87. Grayson, "Austria's International Position," pp. 148–50.

88. Memorandum by the secretary of state for foreign affairs [Bevin], to the Cabinet, 11 April 1950, C.O. (50) 66, Cabinet Office Papers 129/39, PRO.

89. British record of a meeting of the Three Western Foreign Ministers to discuss the Austrian Treaty, held at the Waldorf Astoria Hotel at 4:00 P.M. on Thursday, 29 September 1949, F.O. 371/76451(C7755), PRO.

90. Cf. ibid.

91. Medvedev, *All Stalin's Men,* p. 100.

92. Bader, *Austria between East and West,* p. 198.

93. There had also been a great deal of speculation in the press about a Truman-Stalin summit meeting. It might have crossed Stalin's mind that he should retain Austria as a bargaining counter with which to extract concessions from Truman. Philip E. Mosely, "The Treaty with Austria," *International Organization* 4 (May 1950): 219.

94. See, for example, Joseph Alsop, "Matter of Fact," *New York Herald Tribune,* 10

April 1950. There seems to be a dispute about whether the Soviet atomic explosion was in late August or September. Thomas W. Wolfe claims that the first known test of a Soviet atomic weapon occurred on 29 August 1949: Wolfe, *Soviet Power and Europe, 1945–1970* (Baltimore: Johns Hopkins Press, 1970), p. 36 n. 9.

95. Wolfe, *Soviet Power and Europe*, pp. 38–49.

96. Medvedev, *All Stalin's Men*, p. 45.

97. Isaac Deutscher, *Stalin*, 2d ed. (New York: Oxford University Press, 1949), p. 595.

98. Bader, *Austria between East and West*, pp. 198–99.

99. Alvin Z. Rubinstein, ed., *The Foreign Policy of the Soviet Union* (New York: Random, 1960), pp. 247, 249.

4. *Stalemate, November 1949–March 1953*

1. Telegram, Sir Harold Caccia, Vienna, to Foreign Office, 3 May 1950, F.O. 371/84903(C2985), Public Records Office, Kew (hereafter PRO).

2. John MacCormac, "Vienna May Bring Treaty before U.N.: Resort to the Hague Tribunal Also Considered If Soviet Persists in Delaying Pact," *New York Times*, 30 April 1950.

3. Telegram, Sir A. Cadogan, U.K. delegation to the United Nations, New York, to Foreign Office, 26 November 1949, F.O. 371/76453(C9091), PRO.

4. Telegram, Sir O. Harvey, Paris, to Foreign Office, 27 November 1949, F.O. 371/76453(C9092), PRO.

5. Telegram, Sir A. Cadogan, U.K. delegation to the United Nations, New York, to Foreign Office, 28 November 1949, F.O. 371/76453(9128), PRO.

6. Minute by I. F. Porter, 28 November 1949, F.O. 371/76454(C9228), PRO.

7. Telegram, Sir A. Cadogan, U.K. delegation to the United Nations, New York, to Foreign Office, 28 November 1949, F.O. 371/76453(9128), PRO.

8. Telegram, Sir O. Harvey, Paris, to Foreign Office, 25 November 1949, F.O. 371/76453(C9064), PRO.

9. Memorandum by the secretary of state for foreign affairs [E. Bevin] to the Cabinet, 11 April 1950, C.P. (50)66, Cabinet Office Papers 129/39, PRO.

10. Mallet, c/o the U.K. delegation to the United Nations, New York, to P. H. Dean, German Political Department, Foreign Office, F.O. 371/76452(C8709), PRO.

11. Foreign Office Minute, FP/BRIEF/6, Top Secret, "Four-Power Talks Preliminary Conference: Brief on the Austrian Treaty," 27 February 1951 (distributed in Foreign Office by E. J. W. Barnes), F.O. 371/93602(CA1071/15), PRO.

12. Foreign Office Minute by Mallet to Lord Henderson and Sir D. Gainer, 11 December 1950, F.O. 371/84911(C8022), PRO.

13. W. Hayter, U.K. Embassy, Paris, to Mr. P. Dean, German Political Department, Foreign Office, 21 December 1949, F.O. 371/76458(C9899), PRO.

14. Foreign Office Minute by Sir I. Kirkpatrick [concerning a meeting with the French ambassador], F.O. 371/84895(C58), PRO.

15. Sir H. Caccia to Sir Ivone Kirkpatrick, 19 December 1949, F.O. 371/76458(C9969), PRO.

16. Ibid. Years later, after they had achieved independence, the Austrians themselves implemented a similar plan, by building a huge complex on the outskirts of Vienna designed to supplement or even supersede New York and Geneva as the UN headquarters.

17. Foreign Office Minute by Sir I. Kirkpatrick, 4 January 1950, F.O. 371/84895(C58), PRO.

18. Memorandum given by French high commissioner [General Bethouart] to General Galloway, Vienna [October 1949], F.O. 371/76496(C8543), PRO.

19. Telegram from Sir D. Kelly, Moscow, to Foreign Office, 19 January 1950, F.O. 371/84896(C445), PRO.

20. Quoted in Lydia Kirk, *Postmarked Moscow* (London: Duckworth, 1953), p. 121.

21. "Soviet Position on Treaty Explained," *Christian Science Monitor*, 8 August 1950.

22. Cary Travers Grayson, Jr., "Austria's International Position, 1938–1953: The Reestablishment of an Independent Austria" (diss., Etudes d'Histoire Economique Politique et Sociale, Geneva, 1953), p. 149.

23. Minute for the secretary of state by Mr. Mallet, 23 May 1950, F.O. 371/84904-(C3578), PRO.

24. Gordon Shepherd, "Why Soviet Troops Are Still on Austrian Soil," *Daily Telegraph*, 22 May 1950. (Shepherd cites the argument in order to rebuff it.)

25. Telegram, minister in Austria (Erhardt) to acting secretary of state, no. 13, Vienna, 10 January 1949, in *Foreign Relations of the United States, 1949*, vol. 3: *Council of Foreign Ministers; Germany and Austria* (Washington, D.C., 1974), p. 1260.

26. Sven Allard, *Russia and the Austrian State Treaty: A Case Study of Soviet Policy in Europe* (University Park: Pennsylvania State University Press, 1970), pp. 91–93.

27. Memorandum from Dean Acheson, secretary of state, to Louis Johnson, secretary of defense, 19 June 1950, Secretary of Defense Files, NA, and "Summary Minutes of the Western Foreign Ministers' Discussions of Austrian Treaty Problems Held at Lancaster House," 12 May 1950 and 18 May 1950, The London Conferences, both in R.G. 330, Office of the Secretary of Defense, Subject File, 1949–52, Austria to Civil Affairs/Mil. Gov't., Fohey Report, Folder: Austria October 1949–May 8, 1952, Modern Military Records Division, NA.

28. See note from the Ministry of Foreign Affairs of the Soviet Union to the Embassy of the United States, no. 58, Moscow, 22 September 1950, in *Foreign Relations of the United States, 1950*, vol. 4: *Central and Eastern Europe; The Soviet Union* (Washington, D.C., 1980), p. 404.

29. Report to the president by the National Security Council on "U.S. Policy in the Event of a Blockade of Vienna," 16 February 1950, NSC 63/1, President's Secretary File, Truman Library.

30. Mark Clark, *Calculated Risk* (London: Hamilton, Panther ed., 1956), pp. 418–19 and 428–29.

31. Interview with Stephan Verosta, professor of international law (emeritus), University of Vienna, in Vienna, 6 December 1983. Professor Verosta was head of the International Law Section of the Foreign Office and the Austrian Government Delegation's legal adviser in Moscow, April 1955.

32. Sir H. Caccia (Vienna) to Mallet regarding paper drawn up by the Austrian Ministry of Foreign Affairs, containing suggestions as to the handling of the Austrian Treaty question at a meeting of the Council of Foreign Ministers, 28 February 1951, F.O. 371/93603(CA1071/19G), PRO.

33. George W. Hoffman, "Austria: Her Raw Materials and Industrial Potentialities," *Economic Geography* 24 (January 1948): 45–52.

34. "Austria and the Marshall Plan," a paper prepared in October 1947 by the British element of ACA [Allied Council Austria] with the assistance of the Austrian Federal Ministry of Economic Planning; passed to the U.S. State Department in talks in Washington on 27 October [1947], F.O. 371/64144(C14986), PRO.

35. Foreign Office minute, FP/BRIEF/6, Top Secret, "Four-Power talks Preliminary Conference: Brief on the Austrian Treaty," 27 February 1951, F.O. 371/93602-(CA1071/15), PRO.

36. Anne O'Hare McCormick, "Austria's Chancellor Faces a Great Test," *New York Times*, 19 August 1953.

37. K. W. Rothchild, *The Austrian Economy since 1945* (London: Royal Institute of International Affairs, 1950), pp. 70–71.

38. Telegram, Secretary Acheson to U.S. minister, Vienna, 13 October 1950, R.G. 330, Assistant Secretary of Defense (International Security Affairs), Office of Foreign Military Affairs, European Section, Subject File, 1949–52, Folder: Austria October 1949–May 8, 1952, Modern Military Records Branch, NA.

39. " 'Marshall Plan' Turns Austria into a Colony of Western Powers," *Pravda*, 28 June 1950, p. 4.

40. L. Bezymensky, "America's Plans for Austria," *New Times* no. 44 (31 October 1951), pp. 11–14.

41. "Conversation between the Secretary of State and the Austrian Chancellor," record sent by Anthony Eden to Mr. Adams, H.M. chargé d'affaires, Vienna, 8 May 1952, F.O. 371/CA10111/5(98045), PRO.

42. John MacCormac, "Austria to Charge Abuses by Soviet," *New York Times*, 1 March 1950, p. 16.

43. U.S. Department of State, Office of Intelligence Research, Report no. 6403, "Austria Attempts Independent Foreign Policy," 31 August 1953, Diplomatic Documents Division, NA.

44. See U.S. Central Intelligence Agency, "Review of the World Situation," 15 February 1950, President's Secretary File, Truman Library. The report speaks of a new Cold War offensive.

45. Minute from Mallet to Sir W. Strang and Sir D. Gainer, 3 July 1950, F.O. 371/84906(C4371), PRO.

46. "Soviet Tactics Again Stall Negotiations on Austrian Treaty," statement by Secretary Acheson released to the press 12 July 1950, published in *Department of State Bulletin* 23 (24 July 1950), pp. 131–32.

47. Sir Harold Caccia, Vienna, to W. D. Allen, German Political Department, Foreign Office, 1 August 1950, F.O. 371/84907(C509), PRO.

48. "Trouble in Vienna," *Time*, 9 October 1950, p. 36.

49. Telegram, U.S. chargé in Austria (Dowling) to the secretary of state, Vienna, 1 October 1950, *Foreign Relations of the United States, 1950*, vol. 4, p. 406.

50. Telegram, U.S. high commissioner for Austria, General Keyes, to the Department of the Army, Vienna, 26 September 1950; in *Foreign Relations of the United States, 1950*, vol. 4, pp. 404–5.

51. Ibid. The U.S. high commissioner was rotational chairman of the Allied Council for the month of September 1950.

52. Karl Gruber, *Between Liberation and Liberty: Austria in the Post-War World* (London: Deutsch, 1955), p. 179.

53. Ibid., p. 180, and Adolf Sturmthal, "The Strikes of 1950," in *The Austrian Solution: International Conflict and Cooperation*, ed. Robert A. Bauer (Charlottesville: University Press of Virginia, 1982), p. 70.

54. Gruber, *Between Liberation and Liberty*, pp. 180–83.

55. Ibid., p. 181, and U.S. high commissioner for Austria (Keyes), Vienna, to Department of the Army, 4 October 1950, *Foreign Relations of the United States, 1950*, vol. 4, pp. 407–9.

56. Chargé in Austria (Dowling) to secretary of state, Vienna, 1 October 1950, *Foreign Relations of the United States, 1950*, vol. 4, p. 406.

57. U.S. high commissioner for Austria (Keyes) to Department of the Army, Vienna, 4 October 1950, *Foreign Relations of the United States, 1950*, vol. 4, pp. 408–9.

58. William B. Bader, *Austria between East and West, 1945–1955* (Stanford: Stanford University Press, 1966), p. 177, and Gruber, *Between Liberation and Liberty*, p. 180.

59. Elisabeth Barker, *Austria, 1918–1972* (London: Macmillan, 1973), pp. 181–85.

60. Message dated 5 October 1950 to Secretary Acheson from Foreign Minister Gruber of Austria, published in *Department of State Bulletin* 23 (23 October 1950): 657.

61. Bader, *Austria between East and West*, p. 179.

62. After the "liberation" Austrian Communists had been relieved of their valuables as thoroughly as were members of any other party. See "Conditions in Styria during the Russian Occupation," U.S. Army OSS Report, 4 August 1945, R.G. 226, Report XL14014, Military Documents Division, NA.

Austrian officials today claim that without direct military Soviet intervention, the Austrian Communist party never really had a chance in Austria, and the Soviet Union did not consider Austria important enough to risk such an intervention. Federal President Dr. Kirchschläger explains the failure of the Austrian Communist party in the following way: "Once I said to Gromyko, when he said some negative words about the Austrian Communist party, 'Don't blame the Austrian Communist party. The Austrian Communist party is a good party. But *you* intervened in Hungary and *you* lost the seats in Parliament at the next election. . . . I think that it means that the [Austrian] people have good judgment." Interview with Bundespräsident Dr. Kirchschläger at the Hofburg Palace, Vienna, 5 December 1983.

63. U.S. Central Intelligence Agency, "The Current Situation in Austria," ORE 56-49, 31 August 1949, President's Secretary File, Truman Library, and Hoffman, "Austria: Her Raw Materials," p. 50.

64. Bader, *Austria between East and West*, pp. 190–91, and G. E. R. Geyde, "West Forcing Russia's Hand in Austria," *Observer* (London), 9 March 1952.

65. Grayson, "Austria's International Position, 1938–1953," p. 151.

66. "Moscow Seeks Big 4 Talks on Its German Unity Plans," *New York Times*, 4 November 1950, p. 1.

67. Charles E. Bohlen, *Witness to History, 1929–1969* (New York: Norton, 1973), p. 297.

68. Memorandum from J. H. Burns to secretary of defense, "Status of Four-Power Negotiations in Paris," 20 April 1951, R.G. 330, Records of the Office of the Secretary of Defense, Modern Military Records Division, NA.

69. Sir John Wheeler-Bennett and Anthony Nicholls, *The Semblance of Peace: The Political Settlement after the Second World War* (London: Macmillan, 1972), p. 476.

70. Telegram, Sir O. Franks, Washington, to Foreign Office [and for Foreign Office and Whitehall distribution], 4 October 1951, F.O. 371/93606(CA1071/92), PRO.

71. "1951 Military Assistance Program for Austria," undated in R.G. 330, Records of the Office of the Secretary of Defense, Subject File, 1949–1952, Austria to Civil Affairs/Mil. Gov't. Fohey Report, Folder: Austria October 1949–May 8, 1952, Modern Military Records Division, NA.

72. Memorandum for the secretary of defense from Archibald P. Alexander, acting secretary of the army, Subject: Future Courses of U.S. Action with Respect to Austria, [1] October 1950, R.G. 330, Subject File, 1949–52, Modern Military Records Division, NA.

73. "U.S. Replies to Soviet Charges of Remilitarization in Austria," statement by

Walter J. Donnelly, U.S. high commissioner for Austria, made in the Allied Council at Vienna, 12 October 1951, published in *Department of State Bulletin* 25 (29 October 1951): 691–93.

74. "Correspondence Relating to Soviet Attitude toward Austrian Treaty Negotiations," released to the press 25 January 1952, published in *Department of State Bulletin* 26 (3 March 1952): 326–27.

75. "The Austrian Treaty: A Proposal for Positive Action by the U.S." [paper prepared at the request of the secretary of state after the Rome meetings, approximately November 1951], R.G. 330, Subject File, 1949–52, Modern Military Records Division, NA.

76. Major General Almer J. Rogers, Jr., "Report to the Secretary of Defense and the Joint Chiefs of Staff" [Rogers was Department of Defense representative to the secretary of state for the September 1951 Washington foreign ministers' meetings], in R.G. 218, U.S. Joint Chiefs of Staff, Chairman's File, Admiral Leahy, 1942–1948, Military Records Division, NA, and telegram, Sir O. Franks, Washington, to Foreign Office, 14 September 1951, F.O. 371/93605(CA1071/82), PRO.

77. "Austrian Treaty," SECTO 68, attached to memorandum for Mr. Nash, Subject: Austrian Treaty, in R.G. 330, Subject File, 1949–52, Modern Military Records Division, NA.

78. Telegram, [Samuel] Reber, London, to secretary of state, 18 January 1952, in R.G. 330, Subject File, 1949–52, Modern Military Records Division, NA.

79. Foreign Office minute by G. W. Harrison, prepared at the request of the secretary of state, 20 November 1951, F.O. 371/93608(CA1071/137), PRO.

80. B. A. R. Burrows (Washington) to W. D. Allen, German Political Department, Foreign Office, London, 1 October 1951, F.O. 371/93605(CA1071/91), PRO.

81. Telegram, [Samuel] Reber, London, to secretary of state, Washington, D.C., 18 January 1952, in R.G. 330, Subject File, 1949–52, Modern Military Records Division, NA.

82. U.S. Department of State, Office of Public Affairs, Division of Publications, "The Austrian Treaty: A Case Study of Soviet Tactics," May 1953, European and British Commonwealth Series 43, no. 5012.

83. See, for example, Grayson, "Austria's International Position, 1938–1952," p. 153. Gerald Stourzh sees the abbreviated treaty as mainly an "instrument of protest and propaganda" (*Kleine Geschichte des Österreichischen Staatsvertrages* [Graz: Styria, 1975], p. 74). Manfried Rauchensteiner also argues that the Western powers did not consider the short treaty a serious basis for discussion but only wanted to take advantage of the propagandistic effects of the proposal (*Der Sonderfall: Die Besatzungzeit in Österreich 1945 bis 1955* [Graz: Styria, 1979], p. 311).

84. In the months following the introduction of the short draft treaty, Austrian federal chancellor Figl made a lengthy, extended visit to the United States, touring seven American cities. Shortly thereafter, Secretary of State Acheson returned the compliment by making a highly publicized visit to Vienna. See U.S. Department of State, "Program for the Visit to the United States of His Excellency, the Chancellor of Austria, and Mrs. Figl," press release dated 7 May 1952, in papers of Harry S Truman, President's Secretary File, Truman Library.

85. See, inter alia, "The Austrian Treaty: A Proposal for Positive Action by the U.S." [paper prepared at the request of the secretary of state after the Rome meetings, approximately November 1951], R.G. 330, Records of the Office of the Secretary of Defense, Subject File, 1949–52, Modern Military Records Division, NA.

86. Ibid., p. 3. The U.S. State Department thought that the short-draft treaty might

be accepted by the Russians, and U.S. representatives in Vienna began to make preliminary plans to extract "certain extra-treaty commitments" from the Austrians. These separate bilateral agreements would protect U.S. interests in the event of rapid signature of the abbreviated treaty. Telegram, [U.S. high commissioner] Donnelly, Vienna, to secretary of state, 24 January 1952, R.G. 330, Records of the Office of the Secretary of Defense, Subject File, 1949–1952, Modern Military Records Division, NA.

87. U.S. Defense Department officials seemed generally more skeptical of the negotiability of the short draft than U.S. State Department officials were. However, Defense officials joined State officials in being very much in favor of getting rid of, or at least substantially altering, the old draft treaty: "[The abbreviated treaty] is not expected to be any more acceptable to the Russians than the previous draft since they obviously do not want a treaty. However, at such time as they may again wish to negotiate, it places the burden upon them of restoring the validity of many articles of the previous treaty which were accepted by the western powers only in the hope of an early agreement and which have since become more undesirable than ever. The British and French do not favor closing the door on the possibility of an agreement along previous lines should the opportunity develop, but at the very least the new treaty would provide a strong trading point." Memorandum for Mr. Nash from H. P. Smith, Office of the Secretary of Defense, Subject: Austrian Treaty Negotiations, 6 February 1952, p. 2, Office of the Secretary of Defense, Subject File, 1949–52, Modern Military Records Division, NA.

88. Text of Soviet note of 14 August, published in *Department of State Bulletin* 27 (1 September 1952): 321–23.

89. Gruber, *Between Liberation and Liberty*, p. 203.

90. Memorandum of conversation, 5 December 1952, Papers of Dean Acheson, Truman Library.

5. *Signs of Change, 1953–1954*

1. Robert Griffith, *The Politics of Fear: Joseph R. McCarthy and the Senate* (New York: Hayden, 1970), pp. 132–33.

2. U.S. Joint Chiefs of Staff, "Report by the Director to the JCS on Further Action by NATO Deputies with a View to Immediate Strengthening of Defense Forces," 16 August 1950, R.G. 218, Records of the Joint Chiefs of Staff, Modern Military Records Division, National Archives, Washington, D.C. (herafter NA).

3. One issue of concern at the time was the status of U.S., French, and British troops in Austria with respect to the North Atlantic Treaty Organization. Declassified American documents indicate that French, British, and American defense planners agreed that in time of war the forces of all three Western nations stationed in Austria would pass to the operational control of the Supreme Allied Commander, Europe (SACEUR). It was, of course, only prudent that contingency plans for wartime operational control of these forces be made, to avoid stranding Western forces in Austria. However, because of the obvious political sensitivity of the issue in Austria and the possibility that the Soviet Union might misinterpret Western plans, the U.S. Defense Department asked the State Department to agree that ". . . any inquiries on this subject from non-NATO sources should be assured to the effect that no United States, United Kingdom, or French forces in Austria or Trieste are assigned to SACEUR." (This statement was correct, as long as the words "in peacetime" were understood.) J. H. Burns, Depart-

ment of Defense, to Mr. Perkins, assistant secretary of state for European affairs [mid-April 1951], R.G. 330, Subject File, 1949–52, Modern Military Records Division, NA.

4. Memorandum from Arthur Radford, chairman of the U.S. Joint Chiefs of Staff, to the secretary of defense, 9 October 1953, R.G. 330, Records of the Office of the Secretary of Defense, Modern Military Records Division, NA.

5. See memorandum from Vice Admiral A. C. Davis, deputy U.S. representative to the Standing Group of the North Atlantic Military Committee, to the chairman of the Joint Chiefs of Staff, 9 September 1953, and memorandum from the JCS to the secretary of defense, 11 September 1953; both in Records of the Office of the Secretary of Defense, Modern Military Records Division, NA.

6. William Lloyd Stearman, *The Soviet Union and the Occupation of Austria: An Analysis of Soviet Policy in Austria, 1945–1955* (Bonn: Siegler, 1962), pp. 131–34, and "On the Flanks," *Time*, 22 June 1953, p. 28.

7. U.S. Department of State, Office of Intelligence Research, Report no. 6278, "Pattern of Current Soviet Behavior," 21 April 1953, in R & A Reports File, Diplomatic Documents Division, NA.

8. "Memorandum of Discussion at the 141st Meeting of the National Security Council, 28 April 1953," Top Secret, Eyes Only, Washington, D.C., 29 April 1953 (from Eisenhower Library, Ann Whitman File), published in U.S. Department of State, Bureau of Public Affairs, *Foreign Relations of the United States, 1952–1954*, vol. 5 *Western European Security*, pts. I and II, (Washington, D.C., 1983), pp. 397–99.

9. Ibid.

10. Livingston T. Merchant [U.S. assistant secretary of state] to Llewellyn E. Thompson, Jr., U.S. high commissioner for Austria [for passage to Dowling], Vienna, 6 May 1953, R.G. 84 (Post Records of Vienna, Austria), Declassification Review Project NND 842433, Box 3, 320 Austria-US, Diplomatic Documents Division, NA.

11. Gordon Shepherd, *The Austrian Odyssey* (London: Macmillan, 1957).

12. TASS reports of 30 July 1953 and 4 August 1953, cited in Stearman, *Soviet Union and the Occupation of Austria*, p. 144.

13. U.S. Department of State, Office of Intelligence Research, Intelligence Reports nos. 5990 and 6403, "Possible Austrian Reactions to a Genuine Soviet Treaty Offer," 19 August 1952, and "Austria Attempts Independent Foreign Policy," 31 August 1953, Diplomatic Documents Division, NA.

14. U.S. Department of State, Office of Intelligence Research, Report no. 6403, "Austria Attempts Independent Foreign Policy," 31 August 1953, Diplomatic Documents Division, NA.

15. Foreign Service dispatch from American Embassy, Vienna, to Department of State, Washington, 30 September 1953, R.G. 59, 763.00/9-3053, Diplomatic Documents Division, NA.

16. State Department memorandum (from R. B. Knight to Mr. Merchant and Mr. MacArthur), 9 July 1953, R.G. 59, 763.00/6-953, Diplomatic Documents Division, NA.

17. U.S. Department of State, Office of Intelligence Research, Report no. 6403, "Austria Attempts Independent Foreign Policy," 31 August 1953, Diplomatic Documents Division, NA.

18. Ibid., pp. 5–6.

19. Sven Allard, *Russia and the Austrian State Treaty: A Case Study of Soviet Policy in Europe* (University Park: Pennsylvania State University Press, 1970), p. 113.

20. "Note from the American Ambassador at Moscow [Bohlen] to the Soviet Minister of Foreign Affairs [Molotov], December 8, 1953," published in *American Foreign Policy*

1950–1955: Basic Documents, vol. 2, Department of State, Publication 6446, General Foreign Policy Series 117 (Washington, D.C., 1957), pp. 1849–50.

21. Richard Goold-Adams, *The Time of Power: A Reappraisal of John Foster Dulles* (London: Weidenfeld & Nicolson, 1962), pp. 113–19.

22. Ibid., pp. 111–12.

23. John Foster Dulles, "Memorandum of Breakfast Conference with the President," 20 January 1954, Papers of John Foster Dulles, 1951–1959, White House Memoranda Series, meetings with the president 1953, Dwight D. Eisenhower Library, Abilene, Kansas.

24. C. D. Jackson (at Berlin Conference) to Marie McCrum, The White House, 1 February 1954, papers of C. D. Jackson, Eisenhower Library.

25. V. M. Molotov, *Statements at Berlin Conference of Foreign Ministers of U.S.S.R., France, Great Britain and U.S.A. (January 25–February 18, 1954)* (Moscow: Foreign Languages Publishing, 1954), pp. 112–13.

26. "Statement by the Secretary of State, February 13, 1954," published in *American Foreign Policy 1950–1955: Basic Documents,* vol. 2, Department of State Publication 6446, General Foreign Policy Series 117 (Washington, D.C., 1957), pp. 1858–61 (quotation from p. 1859).

27. Interview with Stephan Verosta, professor of international law (emeritus), University of Vienna, in Vienna, 6 December 1983.

28. Ambassador Ludwig Steiner, MP [formerly secretary to Federal Chancellor Julius Raab], "Was It a Miracle?" *Austria Today* 6 (Spring 1980): 10.

29. Interview with former chancellor Dr. Bruno Kreisky, Vienna, 2 December 1983.

30. *Foreign Ministers Meeting, Berlin Discussions, January 25–February 18, 1954,* Department of State Publication 5399 (Washington, D.C., 1954), pp. 233–34, cited in Stearman, *Soviet Union and the Occupation of Austria,* p. 145.

31. "Statement by the Secretary of State, February 13, 1954," published in *American Foreign Policy, 1950–1955: Basic Documents,* vol. 2, Department of State Publication 6446, General Foreign Series 117 (Washington, D.C., 1957), p. 1860.

32. Interview with former chancellor Dr. Bruno Kreisky, Vienna, 2 December 1983.

33. Telegram, Dulles to Eisenhower, 13 February 1954, Dwight D. Eisenhower Papers as President, Dulles-Herter Series, Dulles, February 1954 (1) Folder, Eisenhower Library.

34. Bruno Kreisky, *Die Herausforderung* (Dusseldorf, 1963), p. 63, cited by Kurt Waldheim, *The Austrian Example,* trans. Ewald Osers (London: Weidenfeld & Nicolson, 1973), p. 59, and Stearman, *Soviet Union and the Occupation of Austria,* p. 146.

35. U.S. Department of State, "Austrian Tactical Considerations," Draft 1 undated, in C. D. Jackson Papers, 1934–67, Time Inc. File, Berlin-Austrian Negotiations Folder, Eisenhower Library.

36. Waldheim, *The Austrian Example,* p. 76.

37. See inter alia, U.S. Department of State, "Points on Austria for Tripartite Ministerial Discussion," 9 February 1954, and "Austrian Tactical Considerations," undated, in the C.D. Jackson Papers 1934–67, Time Inc. File, Berlin-Austrian Negotiations Folder, Eisenhower Library.

38. U.S. Department of State, "Austrian Tactical Considerations," Draft 1, by Rutter, undated, and "Points on Austria for Tripartite Ministerial Discussion (First Draft)," 9 February 1954, Eisenhower Library.

39. See "Tripartite Preparations in Paris, December 1953," paper prepared by the Department of State, 12 December 1953, R.G. 84 (Post Records of Vienna, Austria),

Declass. Review Project NND 842433, Box 4, Diplomatic Documents Division, NA. This paper calls for the acceptance by the Western powers of an Austrian declaration of neutrality as a fallback position in the negotiations. The proposal was disputed by U.S. Department of State, Top Secret Telegram from Paris to Vienna, 17 December 1953, R.G. 84 (Post Records of Vienna, Austria) Declass. Review Project NND 842433, Box 4, Diplomatic Documents Division, NA. This document argues that altering the U.S. opposition to Austrian neutrality would demoralize the British and the French, who had been showing "commendable firmness on this point."

40. "Memorandum of Breakfast Conference with the President," 20 January 1954, Papers of John Foster Dulles, 1951–1959, White House Memoranda Series, Meetings with the President 1953 Folder, Eisenhower Library.

41. C. D. Jackson (at the Berlin Conference) to General Robert Cutler, special assistant to the president, 9 February 1954, in C. D. Jackson Papers, 1934–67, Time Inc. File, Berlin—Basics and Working Papers Folder, Eisenhower Library.

42. Sir Anthony Eden, *The Memoirs of Sir Anthony Eden: Full Circle* (London: Cassell, 1960), p. 290.

43. Quoted by Goold-Adams, *The Time of Power*, p. 127.

44. Ibid., pp. 90ff.

45. Karl Gruber, *Between Liberation and Liberty: Austria in the Post-War World* (London: Deutsch, 1955), pp. 12–14.

46. Foreign Service dispatch from American Embassy Vienna to U.S. Department of State, 21 July 1954, Subject: "Study of Possible Soviet Moves in Austria Aiming at Partition and Western Countermeasures Thereto," R.G. 59, 763.00/7-2154, Diplomatic Documents Division, NA.

47. Stearman, *Soviet Union and the Occupation of Austria*, p. 146n.

48. Telegram, Yost, Vienna, to secretary of state, 17 May 1954, R.G. 59, 763.00/5-1754, Diplomatic Documents Division, NA.

49. See, for example, "The Work of the Revanchists Becomes More Active in Western Austria," *Pravda*, 20 May 1954, p. 4, and "Austrian Ruling Circles Protect War Criminals," *Pravda*, 27 May 1954, p. 4.

50. "Occupation of Austria: New Appeal to the Four Powers," *Times*, 23 July 1954.

51. Allard, *Russia and the Austrian State Treaty*, pp. 123–26. Allard, a close friend of Kreisky, was the Swedish ambassador to Vienna from 1954 to 1964. His personal anecdotes, observations, and recollections of the years 1954 and 1955 are a unique source of information about the incidents leading up to the treaty.

52. Top Secret Foreign Service dispatch, American Embassy, Vienna, to Department of State, Subject: "U.S. Policy in Austria," 23 July 1954, R.G. 59, 611.63/7-2354, Diplomatic Documents Division, NA.

53. Allard, *Russia and the Austrian State Treaty*, pp. 127–30.

54. See Soviet notes of 24 July 1954 and 4 August 1954, published in *Department of State Bulletin* 31 (20 September 1954), pp. 398, 402.

55. See Soviet note of 23 October 1954, published in *Department of State Bulletin* 31 (13 December 1954), pp. 902–5.

56. See Soviet note of 13 November 1954, published in *ibid.*, pp. 905ff.

57. Department of State, Memorandum of Conversation, Subject: The Secretary's Meeting with the Austrian Chancellor, Participants: Dr. Julius Raab, Chancellor of Austria, Dr. Karl Gruber, Ambassador of Austria (2 others); The Secretary, Ambassador Llewellyn E. Thompson, Mr. Livingston T. Merchant, EUR (3 others), 22 November 1954, R.G. 59, 611.63/11-2254, Diplomatic Documents Division, NA.

58. U.S. note of November 29, published in *Department of State Bulletin* 31 (13 December 1954): 901.

59. Ibid., p. 902.

60. Thomas W. Wolfe, *Soviet Power and Europe, 1945–1970* (Baltimore: Johns Hopkins Press, 1970), p. 76.

61. U.S. Department of State, *The Austrian State Treaty: An Account of the Postwar Negotiations Together with the Text of the Treaty and Related Documents,* European and British Commonwealth Series 49, Publication 6437, April 1957.

62. "The Hard Road to an Austrian Treaty," *World Today* 11 (May 1955): 190–201.

63. Allard, *Russia and the Austrian State Treaty,* pp. 140–42.

64. Adam B. Ulam, *Expansion and Coexistence: Soviet Foreign Policy, 1917–1973,* 2d ed. (New York: Holt, Rinehart & Winston, 1974), pp. 558–59, and Wolfe, *Soviet Power and Europe,* p. 76.

65. Allard, *Russia and the Austria State Treaty,* pp. 134–35.

6. The Soviet Reversal, 1955

1. "Austria and the Berlin Conference," *World Today* 10 (April 1954): 149–58.

2. Ulam, *Expansion and Coexistence: Soviet Foreign Policy, 1917–1973,* 2d ed. (New York: Holt, Rinehart & Winston, 1974), pp. 545–47.

3. Nikita Khrushchev, *Khrushchev Remembers: The Last Testament,* ed. and trans. Strobe Talbott (New York: Bantam, 1974), pp. 250 and 562.

4. Ulam, *Expansion and Coexistence,* p. 556.

5. Carl A. Linden, *Khrushchev and the Soviet Leadership, 1957–1964* (Baltimore: Johns Hopkins University Press, 1966), pp. 30–32.

6. Sven Allard, *Russia and the Austrian State Treaty: A Case Study of Soviet Foreign Policy in Europe* (University Park: Pennsylvania State University Press, 1970), pp. 144–50. These arguments are largely based upon a conversation between Allard and a senior Soviet diplomat Allard calls "K." in Vienna. Allard discloses at the end of his account: "It was only some years later when Khrushchev and Mikoyan during their visits to Vienna had revealed to Kreisky the background of their conflict with Molotov about Austria that I fully understood to what extent K. had told the truth. The arguments he had advanced during the conversation with me in December 1954 reflected as a matter of fact the reasons which had prompted Molotov to oppose the evacuation of Austria. The conversation consequently proves that as late as the end of the year, he still exercised a considerable influence in Soviet foreign policy" (p. 150).

7. Vojtech Mastny, "Kremlin Politics and the Austrian Settlement," *Problems of Communism* 31 (July–August 1982): 37–51.

8. Linden, *Khrushchev and the Soviet Leadership,* p. 31.

9. Allard, *Russia and the Austrian State Treaty,* pp. 156–63.

10. Gordon Shepherd, *The Austrian Odyssey,* (London: Macmillan, 1957), p. 260.

11. See, for example, the record of the following meeting: Department of State, Memorandum of Conversation, Subject: The Secretary's Meeting with the Austrian Chancellor, Participants: Dr. Julius Raab, Chancellor of Austria, Dr. Karl Gruber, Ambassador of Austria (2 others); The Secretary, Ambassador Llewellyn E. Thompson, Mr. Livingston R. Merchant, EUR (3 others), 22 November 1954, Record Group 59, 611.63/11-2254, Diplomatic Documents Division, National Archives, Washington, D.C. (hereafter NA).

12. Shepherd, *The Austrian Odyssey*, p. 260.

13. Foreign Service dispatch, American Embassy, Vienna, to U.S. Department of State, 3 February 1954, Subject: "Views of a People's Party Functionary on Current Issues," R.G. 59, 763.00/2-354, Diplomatic Documents Division, NA.

14. Interview with former chancellor Bruno Kreisky, Vienna, 2 December 1983.

15. See, inter alia, William Lloyd Stearman, *The Soviet Union and the Occupation of Austria: An Analysis of Soviet Policy in Austria, 1945–1955* (Bonn: Siegler, 1962); Karl R. Stadler, *Austria* (London: Benn, 1971); Thomas O. Schlesinger, *Austrian Neutrality in Postwar Europe* (Vienna: Braumüller, 1972); and Mastny, "Kremlin Politics and the Austrian Settlement."

16. See *Pravda*, 10 March 1955, pointed out by Robert Conquest, *Power and Policy in the USSR: The Struggle for Stalin's Succession, 1945–1960* (1961; New York: Harper & Row, 1967), p. 265.

17. Khrushchev's memoirs do not specifically describe the decision to withdraw from Austria. However, in discussing generally the reasons for trimming the Warsaw Pact and withdrawing Soviet forces from Finland, Austria, and Romania, Khrushchev explains the rationale in the following way: "Even if we couldn't convince [the Western powers] to disarm themselves and give up the idea of war as a means of political pressure, at least we could demonstrate our own peaceful intentions and at the same time free some of our resources for the development of our industry, the production of consumer goods, and the improvement of living standards" (*Khrushchev Remembers: The Last Testament*, p. 251).

18. Allard, *Russia and the Austrian State Treaty*, pp. 187–89.

19. The terms included ten million tons of petroleum over ten years and $150 million in goods for the USIA concerns; "Austrian-Soviet Communiqué of April 15," *Department of State Bulletin* 32 (2 May 1955): 734–35.

20. Interview with former chancellor Bruno Kreisky, Vienna, 2 December 1983.

21. Ibid.

22. "Austrian-Soviet Communiqué of April 15," *Department of State Bulletin* 32 (2 May 1955): 734–35.

23. Kurt Waldheim, *The Austrian Example*, trans. Ewald Osers (London: Weidenfeld & Nicolson, 1973), pp. 66–67. The quotation was recalled by Walter Kindermann, the Austrian delegation's interpreter.

24. Former chancellor Bruno Kreisky, although widely considered to be responsible for the neutrality formula devised by the Austrians, insists that neither the Austrians nor the Western powers can claim credit for persuading the Russians to sign the treaty in the first place. The *nature* of the treaty was to their credit; the actual *achievement* of a treaty was the result of a change of Soviet foreign policy. Interview with Kreisky, Vienna, 2 December 1983.

25. Harold Macmillan, *Tides of Fortune, 1945–1955* (London: Macmillan, 1969), p. 596.

26. "The Birth of the State Treaty: Interview with Chancellor Kreisky and Professor Verosta," *Austria Today* 6 (Spring 1980): 8, and Michael L. Hoffman, "Neutral Austria Doubted by Swiss," *New York Times*, 14 May 1955.

27. William B. Bader, *Austria between East and West, 1945–1955* (Stanford: Stanford University Press, 1966), pp. 206–7, and Gerald Stourzh, "The Austrian State Treaty and the Origins of Austrian Neutrality," pt. 1 of *Austria and Its Permanent Neutrality* (Vienna: Austrian Federal Ministry for Foreign Affairs, n.d.).

28. Robert L. Ferring, "The Austrian State Treaty of 1955 and the Cold War," *Western Political Quarterly* 21 (December 1968): 651–67.

29. Ibid., p. 665.

30. Blair Gordon Ewing, *Peace through Negotiation: The Austrian Experience* (Washington, D.C.: Public Affairs, 1966), p. 70.

31. Ibid., pp. 70 and 76.

32. Imre Horvath, Hungarian foreign minister, made the following statement on Budapest Radio, 3 June 1957: "The neutrality of a socialist country must be assessed not only from the point of view of peace but also from that of the cause of socialism. While a true neutrality on the part of a capitalist country [i.e., Austria] means standing apart from the conquerors and those ready to go to war, the neutrality of a socialist country represents an underhanded attack on the cause of peace and socialism and its betrayal." Quoted by R. W. Pethybridge, *A History of Postwar Russia* (London: Allen & Unwin, 1966), p. 207.

33. Bader, *Austria between East and West*, p. 200.

34. Stearman, *Soviet Union and the Occupation of Austria*, p. 163.

35. Bader, *Austria between East and West*, p. 204.

36. Khrushchev, *Khrushchev Remembers: The Last Testament*, p. 204. The entire quotation is: ". . . Stalin had created bad feeling in Czechoslovakia, the German Democratic Republic, Rumania, Hungary, China and Austria as well as Poland by setting up international organizations to exploit our allies' natural resources. We had been meaning to terminate these organizations ever since Stalin's death. But liquidating them wasn't enough. We had to change the whole picture of our economic relations with our allies. We had to give our comrades the benefit of all reasonable doubt. This meant scrupulously analyzing all past treaties and contracts, then rectifying all the mistakes. . . ."

37. U.S. Department of State, Bureau of Public Affairs, *Foreign Relations of the United States, 1948*, vol. 2: *Germany and Austria* (Washington, D.C., 1973), p. 1462.

38. Shepherd, *The Austrian Odyssey*, pp. 208–10.

39. Ibid., p. 207.

40. Bader, *Austria between East and West*, pp. 204–5.

41. U.S. Department of State, "Policy Statement on Austria," Washington, 20 September 1948, in *Foreign Relations of the United States, 1948*, vol. 2: *Germany and Austria*, pp. 1341–51.

42. Karl Gutkas et al., *Österreich, 1945–1970* (Vienna: Österreichischer Bundesverlag, 1970), p. 67, cited in Elisabeth Barker, *Austria, 1918–1972* (London: Macmillan, 1973), pp. 197–98.

43. Barker, *Austria, 1918–1972*, pp. 197–98.

44. Khrushchev's personal coup was complete when Molotov was later forced to admit publicly that he had erroneously obstructed the Soviet-Yugoslav rapprochement. Through Khrushchev's accusations, Molotov's guilt was extended to include hindering Soviet efforts for an Austrian treaty, even though available sources imply that Molotov bore the major responsibility for the success of the actual Soviet démarche. Khrushchev was a clever opportunist, protecting himself to the last. At the close of the negotiations in Moscow, Khrushchev said of the Soviet-Austrian agreement, "We shall examine it, and if it has been done wrong we shall take comrades Molotov and Mikoyan to task." But in his memoirs Khrushchev wrote, "The Austrians gave me credit for having played a leading role in the decision to pull out of Austria, and they were quite right. They didn't have any idea what sort of internal struggle had taken place before we signed the peace treaty, and I don't deny it was on my initiative that the correct decision was finally made." Only in retrospect, long after the treaty had been signed, did Khrushchev boast of his personal pursuit of Austrian independence. See Vojtech Mastny, "Kremlin Politics and the Austrian Settlement," *Problems of Communism* 31

(July–August 1982), pp. 43–49, and Khrushchev, *Khrushchev Remembers: The Last Testament*, p. 562.

45. Charles E. Bohlen, *Witness to History, 1929–1969*, (New York: Norton, 1973), p. 375.

46. U.S. Congress, Senate, Committee on Foreign Relations, Hearing on the Austrian State Treaty, Statement of the Honorable John Foster Dulles, Secretary of State, Executive G, 84th Cong., 1st sess., 10 June 1955.

47. M. S. Handler, "Bonn Disavows Aim to Be Neutral State," *New York Times*, 30 April 1955, p. 1.

48. "Germany Not Tempted by Austrian Neutrality: Dr. Adenauer's Assurance," *Daily Telegraph*, 26 April 1955.

49. U.S. Department of State, "U.S. Policy on Neutrality," 24 May 1955, Press Release 290, published in *Department of State Bulletin* 32 (6 June 1955): 932.

50. U.S. Congress, Senate, Committee on Foreign Relations, Executive Sessions of the Senate Foreign Relations Committee, Historical Series vol. 7, 84th Cong., 1st sess., 1955. Printed for the use of the Committee on Foreign Relations and made public April 1978.

51. Interview with former chancellor Bruno Kreisky, Vienna, 2 December 1983.

52. U.S. Department of State, "U.S. Policy on Neutrality," 24 May 1955, Press Release 290, published in *Department of State Bulletin* 32 (6 June 1955): 932.

53. Statement by Dulles in U.S. Congress, Senate, Committee on Foreign Relations, Hearing on the Austrian State Treaty, Executive G, 84th Cong., 1st sess., 10 June 1955.

54. U.S. Congress, Senate, "Austrian State Treaty: Message from the President of the United States Transmitting the State Treaty for the Reestablishment of an Independent and Democratic Austria," 84th Cong., 1st sess., 1 June 1955.

55. According to Bundespräsident Dr. Kirchschläger, who was a junior member of the Austrian negotiating team, the Austrians ended up paying for the same assets several times over—sometimes for the benefit of both the Russians and the Western companies who held a legal claim (interview with Bundespräsident Dr. Kirchschläger at the Hofburg Palace, Vienna, 5 December 1983).

56. Stearman, *Soviet Union and the Occupation of Austria*, pp. 151–52.

57. Telegram, Dulles to Eisenhower, 12 May 1955, Eisenhower Library. According to a U.S. publication, Dulles decided that "he would not sign a treaty under which the Soviet Union would have the legal right to undertake an economic reoccupation of Austria." U.S. Department of State, *The Austrian State Treaty: An Account of the Postwar Negotiations Together with the Text of the Treaty and Related Documents*, European and British Commonwealth Series 49, Publication 6437, April 1957.

58. The eliminated articles were Article 6: "Naturalization and Residence of Germans in Austria"; Article 11: "War Criminals"; Article 13: "Liquidation of League of Nations"; Article 14: "Bilateral Treaties"; Article 15: "Restoration of Archives"; Article 16: "Displaced Persons"; Article 17: "Limitation of Austrian Armed Forces"; Article 19: "Prohibition of Military Training"; Article 25: "Prohibition of Excess War Material"; Article 36: "Restitution by Austria"; and Article 48-bis, which was the so-called "Dried Pea Debt" clause.

The three articles modifed were Article 18: "Prohibition of Service in the Austrian Armed Forces of Former Members of Nazi and Other Organizations" (became Article 12 in final treaty); Article 42: "United Nations Property in Austria" (became Article 25 in final treaty); and Article 48: "Debts" (became Article 28 in final treaty).

The three annexes eliminated were Annex I: "Definition of Military and Military Air

Training"; Annex VIII: "Special Provisions Relating to Certain Kinds of Property"; and Annex IX: "Contracts, Prescriptions and Negotiable Instruments."

59. Mastny, "Kremlin Politics and the Austrian Settlement," p. 48.

60. Livingston T. Merchant, "Recollections of the Summit Conference, Geneva, 1955," an account written for circulation to members of the U.S. delegation, November 1957, now held in the Seeley Mudd Library, Princeton University, Princeton, New Jersey.

Conclusion

1. Peter Holt, "Some Problems of Permanent Neutrality as a Security Policy in Europe: Austria and Switzerland" (diss., University of Sussex, 1978), pp. 7–8.

2. F. H. Hinsley, *Power and the Pursuit of Peace* (Cambridge: Cambridge University Press, 1963), p. 226.

Selected Bibliography

ARCHIVES AND MANUSCRIPT COLLECTIONS

Dwight D. Eisenhower Library, Abilene, Kansas
  John Foster Dulles Papers
  Dwight D. Eisenhower Papers as President
  C. D. Jackson Papers, 1934–1967
  Carl W. McCardle Papers, 1953–1957
Harry S Truman Library, Independence, Missouri
  Dean Acheson Papers
  Harry S Truman Papers. President's Secretary File
  ——. White House Confidential File
  Naval Aide Files of Harry S Truman
National Archives, Washington, D.C.
  Diplomatic Documents Division. Research and Analysis Division Files. U.S. Department of State
  ——. Record Group 59. U.S. Department of State
  Modern Military Records Division. National Security Council Files
  ——. Record Group 218. U.S. Department of Defense. Records of the U.S. Joint Chiefs of Staff
  ——. Record Group 218. U.S. Department of Defense. U.S. Joint Chiefs of Staff Chairman's File
  ——. Record Group 330. U.S. Department of Defense. Records of the Office of the Secretary of Defense
Public Records Office, Kew, Surrey
  Cabinet Office Papers (1945–1953)
  Foreign Office Files, F.O. 371 (1945–1953)
Seeley Mudd Library, Princeton University, Princeton, New Jersey
  Livingston T. Merchant Papers

PUBLISHED DOCUMENTS

Austria

Red-White-Red Book: Descriptions, Documents and Proofs to the Antecedents and History of the Occupation of Austria (from Official Sources). Vienna: Austrian State Printing House, 1947.

Selected Bibliography

Soviet Union

Molotov, V. M. *Problems of Foreign Policy: Speeches and Statements, April 1945–November 1948.* Moscow: Foreign Languages Publishing House, 1949.
_____. *Statements at Berlin Conference of Foreign Ministers of U.S.S.R., France, Great Britain and U.S.A. (January 25–February 18, 1954).* Moscow: Foreign Languages Publishing House, 1954.

United Kingdom

Royal Institute of International Affairs. *Documents on International Affairs, 1949–1950.* Selected and edited by Margaret Carlyle. London: Oxford University Press, 1953.
_____. *Documents on International Affairs, 1951.* Selected and edited by Denise Folliot. London: Oxford University Press, 1954.
_____. *Documents on International Affairs, 1952.* Selected and edited by Denise Folliot. London: Oxford University Press, 1955.
_____. *Documents on International Affairs, 1953.* Selected and edited by Denise Folliot. London: Oxford University Press, 1956.
_____. *Documents on International Affairs, 1954.* Selected and edited by Denise Folliot. London: Oxford University Press, 1957.

United States

"Text of Austrian State Treaty." *U.S. Department of State Bulletin* 32 (6 June 1955): 916–32.
U.S. Congress. Senate. *Austrian State Treaty: Message from the President of the United States Transmitting the State Treaty for the Reestablishment of an Independent and Democratic Austria.* 84th Cong., 1st sess. Washington, D.C., 1955.
U.S. Congress. Senate, Committee on Foreign Relations. *A Decade of American Foreign Policy, Basic Documents, 1941–49.* 81st Cong., 1st sess. Washington, D.C., 1950.
_____. *Hearing on the State Treaty for the Reestablishment of an Independent and Democratic Austria.* 84th Cong., 1st sess. Washington, D.C., 1955.
U.S. Congress. Senate. Committee on Government Operations. Subcommittee on National Security and International Operations. *International Negotiations: Some Operational Principles of Soviet Foreign Policy,* by Richard Pipes. Committee Print. Washington, D.C., 1952.
U.S. Department of State. *American Foreign Policy, 1950–1955: Basic Documents, Volume II.* General Foreign Policy ser. 117, pub. 6446. Washington, D.C., 1957.
_____. *The Austrian State Treaty: An Account of the Postwar Negotiations Together with the Text of the Treaty and Related Documents.* European and British Commonwealth ser. 49, pub. 6437. Washington, D.C., 1957.
_____. *The Austrian Treaty: A Case Study of Soviet Tactics.* European and British Commonwealth ser. 43, pub. 5012. Washington, D.C., 1953.
_____. Bureau of Public Affairs. *Foreign Relations of the United States, 1946.* Vol. 2: *Council of Foreign Ministers;* vol. V: *The British Commonwealth; Western and Central Europe.* Washington, D.C., 1970.
_____. *Foreign Relations of the United States, 1947.* Vol. 2: *Council of Foreign Ministers: Germany and Austria.* Washington, D.C., 1972.
_____. *Foreign Relations of the United States, 1948.* Vol. 2: *Germany and Austria.* Washington, D.C., 1973.

———. *Foreign Relations of the United States, 1949.* Vol. 3: *Council of Foreign Ministers: Germany and Austria.* Washington, D.C., 1974.

U.S. Department of State. Bureau of Public Affairs. *Foreign Relations of the United States, 1950.* Vol. 4: *Central and Eastern Europe; The Soviet Union.* Washington, D.C., 1980.

———. *Foreign Relations of the United States, 1951.* Vol. 3: *European Security and the German Question.* Pts. 1 and 2. Washington, D.C., 1981.

———. *Foreign Relations of the United States, 1952–1954.* Vol. 5: *Western European Security.* Pts. 1 and 2. Washington, D.C., 1983.

———. *Department of State Bulletin* (1945–1955).

———. *The United States and Germany, 1945–1955.* European and British Commonwealth ser. 47, pub. 5827 (1955).

INTERVIEWS

Khol, Andreas. Director, Austrian Foreign Policy Academy. Vienna, 30 November 1983.

Kirchschläger, Rudolph. Federal President of Austria. Hofburg Palace, Vienna, 5 December 1983.

Kreisky, Bruno. Former Chancellor of Austria. Vienna, 2 December 1983.

Neuhold, Hanspeter. Professor, Institut für Völkerrecht und Internationale Beziehungen. Telephone interview, Vienna, 7 December 1983.

Rauchensteiner, Manfried. Historian, Institute for Military History, Austria. Vienna, 7 December 1983.

Stourzh, Gerald. Professor of Modern History, University of Vienna. Vienna, 29 November 1983.

Verosta, Stephan. Professor of International Law (Emeritus), University of Vienna. Formerly Head of the International Law Section of the Foreign Office and the Austrian Delegation's Legal Adviser on trip to Moscow (April 1955). Vienna, 6 December 1983.

MEMOIRS

Acheson, Dean. *Present at the Creation.* New York: Norton, 1969.

Bohlen, Charles E. *Witness to History, 1929–1969.* New York: Norton, 1973.

Byrnes, James F. *Speaking Frankly.* London: Heinemann, 1947.

Campbell, Thomas, and George C. Herring, eds. *The Diaries of Edward R. Stettinius, Jr., 1943–1946.* New York: Watts, 1975.

Churchill, Winston S. *The Second World War.* Vol. 6: *Triumph and Tragedy.* London: Cassell, 1954.

Clark, Mark. *Calculated Risk.* London: Hamilton, Panther ed., 1956.

Clay, Lucius D. *Decision in Germany.* London: Heinemann, 1950.

Eden, Sir Anthony. *The Memoirs of Sir Anthony Eden: Full Circle.* London: Cassell, 1960.

Eisenhower, Dwight D. *Crusade in Europe.* London: Heinemann, 1948.

———. *The White House Years: Mandate for Change, 1953–1956.* London: Heinemann, 1963.

Gruber, Karl. *Between Liberation and Liberty: Austria in the Post-War World.* London: Deutsch, 1955.

Hull, Cordell. *The Memoirs of Cordell Hull.* 2 vols. London: Hodder & Stoughton, 1948.

Kennan, George F. *Memoirs, 1950–1963.* London: Hutchinson, 1973.

Selected Bibliography

Khrushchev, Nikita S. *Khrushchev Remembers*. Trans. and ed. Strobe Talbott. Boston: Little, Brown, 1970.

———. *Khrushchev Remembers: The Last Testament*. Trans. and ed. Strobe Talbott. Boston: Little, Brown, 1970.

Kirk, Lydia. *Postmarked Moscow*. London: Duckworth, 1953.

Lane, Arthur Bliss. *I Saw Poland Betrayed*. New York: Bobbs-Merrill, 1948.

Macmillan, Harold. *Tides of Fortune, 1945–1955*. London: Macmillan, 1969.

Micunovic, Veljko. *Moscow Diary*. London: Chatto & Windus, 1980.

Nagy, Ferenc. *The Struggle behind the Iron Curtain*. New York: Macmillan, 1948.

Polevoy, Boris. *A Russian Looks at Reborn Europe*. Illustrated Soviet Shilling Booklet. London: Soviet News, 1946.

Smith, Walter Bedell. *Moscow Mission, 1946–1949*. London: Heinemann, 1950.

Truman, Harry S. *The Memoirs of Harry S Truman*. Vol. 1: *Year of Decisions*. London: Hodder & Stoughton, 1955.

BOOKS

Acheson, Dean. *Sketches from Life of Men I have Known*. London: Hamilton, 1961.

Adenauer, Konrad. *Erinnerungen, 1953–1955*. Stuttgart: Fischer Bucherei, 1968.

Alexander, Charles C. *Holding the Line: The Eisenhower Era, 1952–1961*. Bloomington: Indiana University Press, 1975.

Allard, Sven. *Russia and the Austrian State Treaty: A Case Study of Soviet Policy in Europe*. University Park: Pennsylvania State University Press, 1970.

Ambrose, Stephen E. *Rise to Globalism: American Foreign Policy, 1938–1976*. Harmondsworth: Penguin, 1976.

Bader, William B. *Austria between East and West, 1945–1955*. Stanford: Stanford University Press, 1966.

Barker, Elisabeth. *Austria, 1918–1972*. London: Macmillan, 1973.

Barraclough, Geoffrey, and Rachel F. Wall. *Survey of International Affairs, 1955–56*. Issued under the auspices of the Royal Institute of International Affairs. London: Oxford University Press, 1960.

Bell, Coral. *Negotiation from Strength*. London: Chatto & Windus, 1962.

———. *Survey of International Affairs, 1954*. Ed. F. C. Benham. Issued under the auspices of the Royal Institute of International Affairs. London: Oxford University Press, 1957.

Bellush, Bernard. *He Walked Alone: A Biography of John Gilbert Winant*. The Hague: Mouton, 1958.

Blum, John Morton. *From the Morgenthau Diaries*. Vol. 3: *Years of War, 1941–1945*. Boston: Houghton Mifflin, 1967.

Blumenson, Martin. *Mark Clark*. New York: Congdon & Weed, 1984.

Bullock, Alan. *The Life and Times of Ernest Bevin*. Vol. 3: *Ernest Bevin: Foreign Secretary (1945–1951)*. London: Heinemann, 1983.

Calvocoressi, Peter. *Survey of International Affairs, 1949–1950; 1951; 1953*. Issued under the auspices of the Royal Institute of International Affairs. London: Oxford University Press, 1953–56.

———. *World Politics since 1945*. London: Longmans, 1968.

Clute, Robert E. *The International Legal Status of Austria, 1938–1955*. The Hague: Nijhoff, 1962.

Conquest, Robert. *Power and Policy in the U.S.S.R.: The Struggle for Stalin's Succession, 1945–1960*. Rpt. New York: Harper & Row, Harper Torchbooks, 1967.

Dallin, David J. *Soviet Foreign Policy after Stalin*. London: Methuen, 1960.

Davis, Lynn Etheridge. *The Cold War Begins: Soviet-American Conflict over Eastern Europe*. Princeton: Princeton University Press, 1974.

Deutscher, Isaac. *Stalin*. 2d ed. London: Oxford University Press, 1966.

Donovan, John C. *The Cold Warriors: A Policy-Making Elite*. Lexington, Mass.: Heath, 1974.

Donovan, Robert. *Conflict and Crisis: The Presidency of Harry S Truman, 1945–1948*. New York: Norton, 1977.

_____. *Tumultuous Years: The Presidency of Harry S Truman, 1949–1953*. New York: Norton, 1982.

Douglas, Roy. *From War to Cold War, 1942–48*. London: Macmillan, 1981.

Drummond, Roscoe, and Gaston Coblentz. *Duel at the Brink: John Foster Dulles' Command of American Power*. London: Weidenfeld & Nicolson, 1961.

Eatwell, Roger. *The 1945–1951 Labour Governments*. London: Batsford, 1979.

Eggleston, Patricia Blythe. "The Marshall Plan in Austria: A Study in American Containment of the Soviet Union in the Cold War." Diss., University of Alabama, 1980.

Ewing, Blair Gordon. *Peace through Negotiation: The Austrian Experience*. Washington, D.C.: Public Affairs Press, 1966.

Fanning, Leonard M. *American Oil Operations Abroad*. New York: McGraw-Hill, 1947.

_____. *Foreign Oil and the Free World*. New York: McGraw-Hill, 1954.

Feis, Herbert. *Churchill-Roosevelt-Stalin: The War They Waged and the Peace They Sought*. Princeton: Princeton University Press, 1957.

Fontaine, André. *History of the Cold War from the Korean War to the Present*. Trans. Renaud Bruce. New York: Random, 1969.

Fox, Annette Baker. *The Power of Small States*. Chicago: University of Chicago Press, 1959.

Gaddis, John Lewis. *Strategies of Containment: A Critical Appraisal of Postwar American National Security Policy*. New York: Oxford University Press, 1982.

Goold-Adams, Richard. *The Time of Power: A Reappraisal of John Foster Dulles*. London: Weidenfeld & Nicolson, 1962.

Grayson, Cary Travers, Jr. "Austria's International Position, 1938–1953: The Reestablishment of an Independent Austria." Diss., Etudes d'Histoire Economique Politique et Sociale, Geneva, 1953.

Guhin, Michael A. *John Foster Dulles: A Statesman and His Times*. New York: Columbia University Press, 1972.

Hinsley, F. H. *Power and the Pursuit of Peace: Theory and Practice in the History of Relations between States*. Cambridge: Cambridge University Press, 1963.

Hiscocks, Richard. *The Rebirth of Austria*. London: Oxford University Press, 1953.

Holt, Peter. "Some Problems of Permanent Neutrality as a Security Policy in Europe: Austria and Switzerland." Diss., University of Sussex, 1978.

Hoopes, Townsend. *The Devil and John Foster Dulles*. London: Deutsch, 1974.

Hough, Jerry F., and Merle Fainsod. *How the Soviet Union Is Governed*. 4th ed. Cambridge: Harvard University Press, 1979.

Howard, Michael. *Disengagement in Europe*. Harmondsworth: Penguin, 1958.

Jervis, Robert. *Perception and Misperception in International Politics*. Princeton: Princeton University Press, 1976.

Kissinger, Henry A. *The Troubled Partnership: A Re-appraisal of the Atlantic Alliance*. New York: McGraw-Hill, 1965.

Kohn, Hans. *The Future of Austria.* Headline Series no. 112. New York: Foreign Policy Association, 1955.

LaFeber, Walter. *America, Russia and the Cold War, 1945–1975.* New York: Wiley, 1967.

Laqueur, Walter. *Europe since Hitler.* London: Weidenfeld & Nicolson, 1970.

Linden, Carl A. *Khrushchev and the Soviet Leadership, 1957–1964.* Baltimore: Johns Hopkins University Press, 1966.

Lukacs, John A. *The Great Powers and Eastern Europe.* New York: American Book, 1953.

Luza, Radomir. *Austro-German Relations in the Anschluss Era.* Princeton: Princeton University Press, 1975.

McCauley, Martin, ed. *Communist Power in Europe, 1944–1949.* London: Macmillan, 1977.

Mastny, Vojtech. *Russia's Road to the Cold War: Diplomacy, Warfare, and the Politics of Communism, 1941–1945.* New York: Columbia University Press, 1979.

Medvedev, Roy. *All Stalin's Men.* Trans. Harold Shukman. Oxford: Blackwell, 1983.

———. *Khrushchev.* Trans. Brian Pearce. Oxford: Blackwell, 1982.

Medvedev, Roy A., and Zhores A. Medvedev. *Khrushchev: The Years in Power.* London: Oxford University Press, 1977.

Mee, Charles L., Jr. *Meeting at Potsdam.* New York: Evans, 1975.

Opie, Redvers, et al. *The Search for Peace Settlements.* Washington, D.C.: Brookings, 1951.

Passant, E. J. "The Problem of Austria." *Oxford Pamphlets on World Affairs* no. 72. London: Oxford University Press, 1945.

Paterson, Thomas G., ed. *The Origins of the Cold War.* Lexington, Mass.: Heath, 1974.

Pethybridge, R. W. *A History of Postwar Russia.* London: Allen & Unwin, 1966.

Pick, F. W. *Peacemaking in Perspective.* Oxford: Pen-in-Hand, 1950.

Prados, John. *The Soviet Estimate: U.S. Intelligence and Russian Military Strength.* New York: Dial, 1982.

Rauchensteiner, Manfried. *Der Sonderfall: Die Besatzungszeit in Österreich, 1945 bis 1955.* Graz: Styria, 1980.

Rees, Mark Stephen. "Anglo-American Relations, 1953–1955." Diss., London School of Economics and Political Science, 1976.

Rothschild, K. W. *The Austrian Economy since 1945.* London: Royal Institute of International Affairs, 1950.

———. *Austria's Economic Development between the Two Wars.* London: Muller, 1947.

Rothwell, Victor. *Britain and the Cold War, 1941–1947.* London: Cape, 1982.

Rubinstein, Alvin Z., ed. *The Foreign Policy of the Soviet Union.* New York: Random, 1960.

Rush, Myron. *The Rise of Khrushchev.* Washington, D.C.: Public Affairs Press, 1958.

Schlesinger, Thomas O. *Austrian Neutrality in Postwar Europe.* Vienna: Braumüller, 1972.

Shepherd, Gordon. *The Austrian Odyssey.* London: Macmillan, 1957.

———. *Russia's Danubian Empire.* London: Heinemann, 1954.

Siegler, Heinrich. *Austria: Problems and Achievements since 1945.* Bonn: Siegler, n.d.

Stadler, Karl R. *Austria.* London: Benn, 1971.

Stanley, Guy David Douglas. "British Policy and the Austrian Question, 1938–1945." Diss., University of London, 1974.

Stearman, William Lloyd. *The Soviet Union and the Occupation of Austria: An Analysis of Soviet Policy in Austria, 1945–1955.* Bonn: Siegler, 1962.

Stourzh, Gerald. "The Austrian State Treaty and the Origins of Austrian Neutrality."

Part 1 of *Austria and Its Permanent Neutrality*. Vienna: Austrian Federal Ministry for Foreign Affairs, n.d.

Stourzh, Gerald. *Geschichte des Staatsvertrages, 1945–1955. Österreichs Weg zur Neutralität.* Graz: Styria, 1980.

Stourzh, Gerald. *Kleine Geschichte des Österreichischen Staatsvertrages.* Graz: Styria, 1975.

Titarenko, S. *The Peaceful Co-existence of the Capitalist and Socialist Systems.* London: Soviet News, 1950.

" '. . . To defend with all the means at her disposal!' " Part 3 of *Austria and Its Permanent Neutrality.* Vienna: Austrian Federal Ministry for Foreign Affairs, n.d.

Ulam, Adam B. *Expansion and Coexistence: Soviet Foreign Policy, 1917–73.* 2d ed. New York: Holt, Rinehart & Winston, 1974.

———. The Rivals: America and Russia since World War II. New York: Viking, 1971.

Verdross, Alfred. *The Permanent Neutrality of Austria.* Vienna: Geschichte und Politik, 1978.

Vital, David. *The Inequality of States: A Study of the Small Power in International Relations.* Oxford: Clarendon, 1967.

Waldheim, Kurt. *The Austrian Example.* Trans. Ewald Osers. London: Weidenfeld & Nicolson, 1973.

Watt, D. C. *Britain Looks to Germany.* London: Wolff, 1965.

Welles, Sumner. *Where Are We Heading?* London: Hamilton, 1947.

Werth, Alexander. *Russia: The Post-War Years.* London: Hale, 1971.

Wheeler-Bennett, Sir John, and Anthony Nicholls. *The Semblance of Peace: The Political Settlement after the Second World War.* London: Macmillan, 1972.

Wolfe, Thomas W. *Soviet Power and Europe, 1945–1970.* Baltimore: Johns Hopkins University Press, 1970.

Yergin, Daniel. *Shattered Peace: The Origins of the Cold War and the National Security State.* London: Deutsch, 1978.

Zemanek, Karl. "Austria's Permanent Neutrality: 6 Questions—6 Answers." Part 2 of *Austria and Its Permanent Neutrality.* Vienna: Austrian Federal Ministry for Foreign Affairs, n.d.

ARTICLES

Adams, Ware. "The Negative Veto—A Breakthrough." In *The Austrian Solution: International Conflict and Cooperation,* ed. Robert A. Bauer. Charlottesville: University Press of Virginia, 1982.

Akhtamzyan, Abdulkhan. "Mutual Understanding Paves the Way for Good-Neighbourly Relations." *Austria Today* 6 (Spring 1980): 20–21.

"The Allied Commission for Austria: A Preliminary Account of Its Organization and Work." *The World Today* 1 (November 1945): 204–13.

"Austria and the Berlin Conference." *World Today* 10 (April 1954): 149–58.

"Austria, East or West?" *World Today* 4 (August 1948): 346–54.

"Austria: The End of a Chapter." *World Today* 11 (June 1955): 231–33.

"L'Autriche est libre." *Le Monde,* 14 May 1955. Trans. in *Austria Today* 6 (Spring 1980): 12.

Bader, William B. "Austria, The United States, and the Path to Neutrality." In *The Austrian Solution: International Conflict and Cooperation,* ed. Robert A. Bauer. Charlottesville: University Press of Virginia, 1982.

"The Birth of the State Treaty: Interview with Chancellor Kreisky and Professor Verosta." *Austria Today* 6 (Spring 1980): 7–9.

Selected Bibliography

Bock, Fritz. "Austrian Neutrality." In *The Austrian Solution: International Conflict and Cooperation*, ed. Robert A. Bauer. Charlottesville: University Press of Virginia, 1982.

Bromley-Gardner, R. "Russia—and the Austrian State Treaty." *Army Quarterly* 65 (October 1952): 56–60.

Cameron, Juan. " 'We Are Now Fighting on Two Fronts: In Vienna McCarthy and the Russians Attack Our Information Service.' " *New Republic* 128 (4 May 1953): 15–17.

Colvin, Milton. "Principal Issues in the U.S. Occupation of Austria, 1945–1948." In *U.S. Occupation in Europe after World War II: Papers and Reminiscences from the April 23–24, 1976 Conference Held at the George C. Marshall Research Foundation*, Lexington, Virginia, ed. Hans A. Schmitt. Lawrence: Regents Press of Kansas, 1978.

Cullis, Michael. "Preliminaries, 1947–1950." *Austria Today* 6 (Spring 1980): 15.

Dadiani, L. "Austria's New Path." *International Affairs* (Moscow) 2 (May 1956): 90–96.

Danspeckgruber, Wolfgang. "The Defense of Austria." *International Defense Review* 6 (1984): 721–31.

Ekern, Halvor O. "The Allied Commission for Austria." In *The Austrian Solution: International Conflict and Cooperation*, ed. Robert A. Bauer. Charlottesville: University Press of Virginia, 1982.

Erikson, Edgard L. "The Zoning of Austria." *Annals of the American Academy of Political and Social Sciences* 267 (January 1950): 106–13.

Ferring, Robert L. "The Austrian State Treaty of 1955 and the Cold War." *Western Political Quarterly* 21 (December 1968): 651–67.

"The Four Powers: Ambassador Peter Jankowitsch Talks to General Antoine Bethouart, Former French High Commissioner in Occupied Austria." *Austria Today* 6 (Spring 1980): 16–17.

"The Four Powers: Gen. (ret.) Mark Clark, First U.S. High Commissioner (1945–1947)." *Austria Today* 6 (Spring 1980): 18.

"The Four Powers: The Right Hon. the Lord Caccia, G.C.M.G., G.C.V.O., British High Commissioner (1945–1947)." *Austria Today* 6 (Spring 1980): 14–15.

Freymond, Jacques. "The European Neutrals and the Atlantic Community." In *The Atlantic Community*, ed. Francis O. Wilcox and H. Field Haviland, Jr. New York: Praeger, 1963.

Gruber, Karl. "Austria Holds On." *Foreign Affairs* 26 (April 1948): 478–85.

——. "Austria Infelix." *Foreign Affairs* 25 (January 1947): 229–38.

Hale, William Harlan. "Political Reunion in the Vienna Woods." *Reporter* 12 (5 May 1955): 22–24.

"The Hard Road to an Austrian Treaty." *World Today* 11 (May 1955): 190–201.

Herz, Martin F. "Allied Occupation of Austria: The Early Years." In *The Austrian Solution: International Conflict and Cooperation*, ed. Robert A. Bauer. Charlottesville: University Press of Virginia, 1982.

Hoffman, George W. "Austria: Her Raw Materials and Industrial Potentialities." *Economic Geography* 24 (January 1948): 45–52.

Keating, Frank A., and L. C. Manners-Smith. "The Soviet Army's Behaviour in Victory and Occupation." In *The Soviet Army*. Edited by B. H. Liddell Hart. London: Weidenfeld & Nicolson, 1956.

Kind, Christian. "Problematical Austrian Defense." *Swiss Review of World Affairs* 14 (August 1964): 10–11.

Kreisberg, Louis. "Noncoercive Inducements in U.S.-Soviet Conflicts: Ending the Occupation of Austria and Nuclear Weapons Tests." *Journal of Political and Military Sociology* 9 (Spring 1981): 1–16.

[209]

Kunz, Josef L. "Austria's Permanent Neutrality." *American Journal of International Law* 50 (April 1956): 419–25.

———. "Infelix Austria." *American Journal of International Law* 48 (July 1954): 453–58.

———. "The State Treaty with Austria." *American Journal of International Law* 49 (October 1955): 535–42.

"Letter from Vienna." *New Yorker* 26 (November 1955): 189–210.

Mair, John. "Four-Power Control in Austria, 1945–46." In *Survey of International Affairs*, ed. Arnold Toynbee. London: Oxford University Press, 1956.

Mastny, Vojtech. "Kremlin Politics and the Austrian Settlement." *Problems of Communism* 31 (July–August 1982): 37–51.

Mosely, Philip. "The Occupation of Germany: New Light on How the Zones Were Drawn." *Foreign Affairs* 28 (July 1950): 580–604.

———. "The Treaty with Austria." *International Organization* 4 (May 1950): 219–35.

Musulin, Janko. "Austria between East and West." *International Affairs* 30 (October 1954): 425–33.

Neuhold, Hanspeter. "Permanent Neutrality and Nonalignment: Similarities and Differences." In *The Austrian Solution: International Conflict and Cooperation*, ed. Robert A. Bauer. Charlottesville: University Press of Virginia, 1982.

Neumann, Robert G. "Austrian Neutrality—Precursor of Detente? Model for the Future?" In *The Austrian Solution: International Conflict and Cooperation*, ed. Robert A. Bauer. Charlottesville: University Press of Virginia, 1982.

Pahr, Willibald. "Austria between the Block-Systems." *Studia Diplomatica* 36 (1983): 327–36.

Rauchensteiner, Manfried. "Austria under Allied Occupation between 1945 and 1955." In *The Austrian Solution: International Conflict and Cooperation*, ed. Robert A. Bauer. Charlottesville: University Press of Virginia, 1982.

Renner, Karl. "Austria: Key for War and Peace." *Foreign Affairs* 26 (July 1948): 589–603.

Rosegger, Gerhard. "Austrian Neutrality and European Integration." *Orbis* 7 (Winter 1964): 849–60.

Seidl-Hohenveldern, Ignaz. "Relation of International Law to Internal Law in Austria." *American Journal of International Law* 49 (October 1955): 451–76.

Shepherd, Gordon. "Austria, the Reluctant Neutral." *Reporter* 23 (27 October 1960): 31–34.

Stearman, William L. "An Analysis of Soviet Objectives in Austria." In *The Austrian Solution: International Conflict and Cooperation*, ed. Robert A. Bauer. Charlottesville: University Press of Virginia, 1982.

Steiner, Ludwig. "Was It a Miracle?" *Austria Today* 6 (Spring 1980): 10.

Stourzh, Gerald. "Towards the Settlement of 1955: The Austrian State Treaty Negotiations and the Origins of Austrian Neutrality." *Austrian History Yearbook* (University of Minnesota) 17–18 (1981–1982): 174–87.

Sturmthal, Adolf. "The Stikes of 1950." In *The Austrian Solution: International Conflict and Cooperation*, ed. Robert A. Bauer. Charlottesville: University Press of Virginia, 1982.

"Summary of Activities: Council of Foreign Ministers." *International Organization* 6 (May 1952): 320–26.

"Summary of Activities: General Assembly: Appeal to the Powers, Signatories to the Moscow Declaration of 1 November 1943 for an Early Fulfillment of Their Pledges toward Austria." *International Organization* 7 (February 1953): 69–70.

"10 Years of Red 'Liberators.'" *U.S. News & World Report* 29 (16 September 1955): 42–44.

Selected Bibliography

"U.S. Policy on Neutrality." *U.S. Department of State Bulletin* 32 (6 June 1955): 932. (Press release 290 dated May 24.)

Verdross, Alfred. "Austria's Permanent Neutrality and the United Nations Organization." *American Journal of International Law* 50 (January 1956): 61–68.

Vishniak, Mark. "Forced Repatriation and the Austrian Treaty." *New Leader* 38 (9 May 1955): 13–14.

Zemanek, Karl. "Neutral Austria in the United Nations." *International Organization* 15 (Summer 1961): 408–22.

Index

Library of Congress Cataloging-in-Publication Data

Cronin, Audrey Kurth, 1958–
  Great power politics and the struggle over Austria, 1945–1955.

  (Cornell studies in security affairs)
  Bibliography: p.
  Includes index.
  1. World politics—1945–   . 2. Austria—Foreign relations—1945–
    . I. Title. II. Series.
D842·C67   1986   327'·09'04   85-24326
ISBN 0-8014-1854-2